The Changing Seasons

The Changing Seasons

Quilt Patterns from Japan

Jill Liddell
with
Patchwork Quilt Tsushin

Dutton Studio Books

**For my children
James, Joanna, and Charles
with love**

NOTE TO THE READER

The text and captions for this book were researched and written by Jill Liddell, and she takes full responsibility for the historical information and for the pattern symbolism contained in the book. As co-author, *Patchwork Quilt Tsushin* was happy to let Jill write the text and captions in view of her previous work on Japanese textiles.

Unless otherwise stated in the credit lines, all of the color plates in this book are reproduced by gracious permission of *Patchwork Quilt Tsushin* of Tokyo, Japan, and of their photographers, Susumu Tomita and Shoshi Ayabe.

DUTTON STUDIO BOOKS

Published by the Penguin Group
Penguin Books USA Inc., 375 Hudson Street,
New York, New York, 10014, U.S.A.

Penguin Books Ltd, 27 Wrights Lane,
London W8 5TZ, England

Penguin Books Australia Ltd, Ringwood,
Victoria, Australia

Penguin Books Canada Ltd, 2801 John Street,
Markham, Ontario, Canada L3R 1B4

Penguin Books (N.Z.) Ltd, 182-90 Wairau Road,
Auckland 10, New Zealand

Penguin Books Ltd, Registered Offices:
Harmondsworth, Middlesex, England

First published by Dutton Studio Books, an imprint of Penguin Books USA Inc.

First printing, October, 1992
10 9 8 7 6 5 4 3 2 1

Library of Congress
Catalog Card Number: 92-71071

Book designed by Marilyn Rey
Printed and bound by Dai Nippon Printing Co., Ltd., Tokyo, Japan

ISBN: 0-525-93438-3 (cloth); ISBN: 0-525-48601-1 (paperback)

Contents

Preface

Japanese design has inspired Western artists for centuries, but it is only recently that Western quilters have begun to appreciate the new patterns and ideas that are emerging from the Japanese quilt world today.

For a long time, Japanese quiltmakers borrowed heavily from the wonderful traditional American patterns, but now it is time to repay that debt. In this book, *Patchwork Quilt Tsushin* and I have put together a collection of unique quilts using traditional patterns that have developed over the centuries from the Japanese lyrical sensibility of the natural world. We show you how to make these patterns, and also some of the quilts.

We hope that it will be a voyage of discovery for you and that these patterns and design ideas will then become part of your own quiltmaking library, to be used however you like—and not just to make Japanese-style quilts.

As always, this book could not have been written without the help of a great many people. I would especially like to thank Yoshihiro Amano, president of Patchwork Tsushin Co., Ltd., for all his help and cooperation in getting the project started; Kumi Maekawa, editor, for going through my text so carefully; and Atsuko Ohta, for her kindness and patience in dealing with my many queries and acting as translator.

I owe everything to my husband, Andrew, not only for writing the introductory essay, "The Traditional Patterns of Japan," but also for his wonderful support and encouragement when the going got tough. Jenni Dobson too was a tower of strength. A big vote of thanks must go to her for all her hard work and advice in drawing up patterns, checking directions, drawing diagrams, and generally acting as a sounding board, not to mention the beautiful quilts that she made. I must also thank Gill Bryan and Barbara Holmes for managing to turn my incomprehensible scribbles into lucid patterns and diagrams, and for the sewing that Barbara and Violet Plume did for me.

In a way this book marks the end of a voyage of discovery for me that began in Tokyo in 1983, when Amanda Frew first drew up some Japanese family-crest patterns for my quilting classes. We have lost touch now, but I would like to thank her, wherever she may be. Finally, I must thank my editor, Cyril I. Nelson, who encouraged me to embark on my "Japanese" writing career over a cup of tea at the New Otani hotel in Tokyo in 1985, and who has been a good friend and mentor ever since.

The Traditional Patterns of Japan

Japanese designs have a distinctive character that arrests and then seduces the eye. There is nothing quite like them in the West, nor elsewhere in the East for that matter.

Some of the features that will strike you in the examples that follow are the simplification of form and codification of the elements of design, almost as if they were ideograms, like calligraphy. For instance, there are accepted ways of representing plum blossom, and the feathery umbrella shape used to denote a pine tree hardly ever varies.

These forms may have some connection with their respective symbolism, for plum blossom stands for winter fortitude, and the pine tree for stability and longevity—but it may also be the product of the discipline of the Japanese mind. Some of these features can be seen on the beautiful example of *washi* paper in figure 1, which in itself contains a treasury of designs representing the seasons of the year. Here you can see plum and cherry blossom, bamboo, wisteria, iris and peony, bush clover, gentian and autumn grasses, maple leaves, and even a hint of snow in the bottom right corner. Many of these motifs will appear, and their symbolism be clarified, in the quilts illustrated in this book. The progression of seasons is of special significance to the Japanese, and it is for this reason that we have divided the book into seasonal chapters.

The codification of design motifs does not lead to a boring or standardized effect. On the contrary, astonishment—even shock—is achieved through contrast, irregularity, asymmetry, broken patterns, and cropped images. In this way the Japanese create the effect of movement and liveliness, something that they see all around them in nature and try to copy.

An illustration of the Japanese love of contrast can be seen in the kimono illustrated in figure 2. Here the top half of the kimono is stencil-dyed with a geometric pattern of concentric semicircles, known as Blue Wave (*seigaiha*), and below it there is a scene of mandarin ducks and lilies with rippled water. Blue Wave is an ancient pattern, for there are traces of it going back to prehistoric times, and because it represents water, to the Japanese eye this combination of motifs is a natural one. An extra layer of meaning is supplied by the pairs of mandarin ducks that symbolize marital harmony. A quilt designed by Sanae Hattori in the Blue Wave pattern is illustrated in the Summer section (see fig. 38).

A striking example of movement, irregularity, and asymmetry is shown in figures 3 and 4. The magnificent design of knotted ribbons is found in all the decorative arts of Japan and is called a *noshi*. On the eighteenth-century kimono in figure 3, you can see the ribbons are gently stirring, as if the motif were about to move. On the modern lacquer screen in figure 4, the noshi has all but disappeared like the Cheshire Cat. There are two noshi quilts illustrated in figures 67 and 68. Take a look and guess which one was made by a Japanese!

Another Japanese custom is to scatter motifs randomly over the surface being decorated, overlapping some so that one impinges on another, such as you see on the *futon* cover illustrated in figure 5. Symmetrical circular forms originally came to Japan from China, but the Japanese artists twisted and softened their outlines, turning them into naturalistic floral wreaths. Jenni Dobson borrowed this idea for her quilt *Winter's Joy* (see fig. 61).

There is an enormous variety of elements in Japanese design. There are geometric patterns, both simple and complex, and designs with Buddhist themes. There are motifs taken from nature: birds, flowers, trees, plants, animals, and insects. There is heraldry, both feudal and aristocratic emblems, and down-to-earth, jocular variations. There are artifacts and utensils; there are scenic views and literary references. Let us look back and see where some of these designs came from.

Chinese Influence

Japan first appears on the world stage as a small country of "Eastern Barbarians" living on an isolated archipelago that was mentioned in a Chinese history book written in the third century A.D. It was an agricultural country divided into small kingdoms, or clans. The native religion, called *Shinto*, saw spirit in all things, inanimate as well as animate, including man-made utensils. This feeling for the spirit of things seems to have remained always with the Japanese, and with their quilters, to this day.

In those early times, China was the great power of the epoch, and of the region. Under the illustrious T'ang dynasty, which ruled China from A.D. 618-907, Chinese power, prestige, and technical abilities dominated Asia, and the echoes of this great civilization, together with its prized silk products, reached Europe along the Silk Road.

Inevitably, Japan, being on the periphery of China's great

1. All the traditional motifs of the changing seasons are featured on this piece of Japanese handmade *washi* paper. Winter, spring, and autumn are represented respectively by the stylized plum blossom on the left, cherry blossom in the middle, and maple leaves on the right, while peonies and iris, the flowers of early summer, bloom on the river bank together with small sprays of bamboo and chrysanthemum. Cranes are also a popular Japanese pattern, for they symbolize long life. Japanese quiltmakers have drawn upon most of these patterns for their quilts, and you will see them further on, classified under the various seasons. Full-size patterns for you to make are given in the PATTERN INDEX.

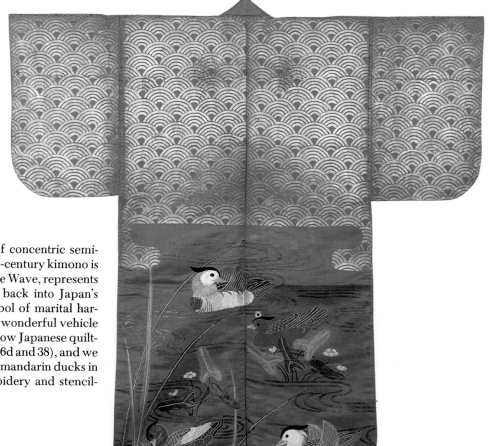

2. The contrast between the stylized pattern of concentric semicircles and the ducks on this beautiful eighteenth-century kimono is not so strange. The geometric pattern, called Blue Wave, represents water and is a treasured design that stretches back into Japan's prehistory. Pairs of mandarin ducks are a symbol of marital harmony, and their coloring has always provided a wonderful vehicle for skilled Japanese embroiderers. You will see how Japanese quiltmakers have interpreted these designs (see figs. 16d and 38), and we give the patterns for both the wave and a pair of mandarin ducks in the PATTERN INDEX. Eighteenth century; embroidery and stencil-dyeing on silk. (Tokyo National Museum)

3. In Japan's distant past, people pounded pieces of dried abalone (a type of shellfish) into long ribbons and tied them together to make a suitable offering for the gods. In time, the offering became a symbol of good fortune, and strips of abalone were wrapped in beautifully folded pieces of paper and were attached to gifts given on auspicious occasions. This talisman is called a *noshi*, which is an abbreviation of *noshiawabi*, meaning "flattened-out abalone." Nowadays, a strip of yellow paper acts as a substitute for the dried shellfish in this folded emblem, but the ancient origins of the motif also live on in another form. The original bunch of streamers became a vehicle for Japanese textile art, with each flattened strip embroidered or painted to represent a ribbon of rich fabric. You can see what a magnificent design it became on this resist-dyed eighteenth-century kimono, and at one time it was a fashionable motif for wedding kimono. There are two noshi quilts for you to look at in the Winter section (figs. 67 and 68), and you will also find a pattern for a noshi in the PATTERN INDEX. Eighteenth century; resist-dyeing on silk. Important Cultural Property. Photograph courtesy Kyoto National Museum. (Yuzen Historical Society)

4. On this contemporary lacquer table-screen, the noshi has all but vanished. We glimpse the end of the ribbons as the motif seems to fly away, perhaps never to return! The Japanese love to suggest the idea of continuous movement by cropping an image at the edge of a picture, thus leaving the viewer to imagine the rest. What a wonderful design for a Japanese wall-quilt this would make! Black lacquer and gold leaf. (Private collection)

5. A wonderful array of floating circular patterns decorates this nineteenth-century resist-dyed futon cover, and you can see how the Japanese achieve naturalness and movement by overlapping some of the patterns, so that one impinges on another. The Chinese introduced circular motifs to Japan, but these lovely free floral designs are a Japanese invention and were always popular for furnishing fabrics. An English quiltmaker has adapted some patterns from these resist-dyed fabrics (see fig. 61), and we give a selection of floral wreaths in the PATTERN INDEX. Nineteenth century; resist-dyed indigo cotton. (Courtesy the Board of Trustees of the Victoria & Albert Museum, London)

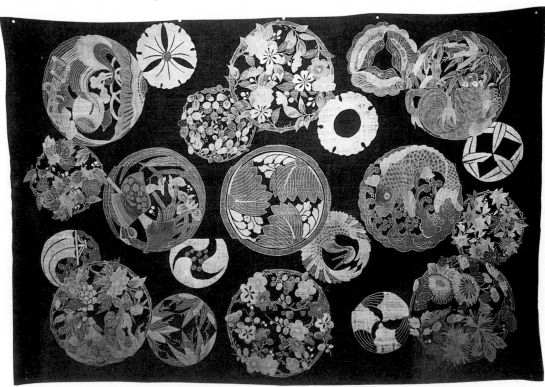

civilization, fell under its spell. The Japanese copied Chinese political institutions, adopted its writing system, borrowed its artistic forms, and the rulers took on the clothing, coloring, and customs of the Chinese court. Buddhism, which was imported from China sometime between A.D. 538-552, became the state religion, but it did not oust the native Shintoism, and the two religions learned to coexist happily.

The principles of Chinese design at that time reflected Confucian philosophy: hierarchical order, balance, and symmetry in primary colors. There were also geometric forms like triangles arranged in sawtooth sequence, diamonds, checkerboard, and the wave pattern that we have already seen.

Some of these patterns had occult significance, such as the hexagon which, representing a tortoise (and 10,000 years of life), was used in fortune telling. Astrological signs, the sun, moon and stars, and planets, were also used. These geometric patterns appear continuously in Japanese design—and are echoed in their decorative stitching called *sashiko*—as twill patterns on silks, as stencil-dyed or woven backgrounds on kimono (fig. 6) or, individually, as a means of framing other motifs. You can see a striking example of a diamond pattern being used as a frame in Sanae Hattori's remarkable seasonal quilts (see fig. 31, *Japanese Iris II*, fig. 51, *Red Maple Leaves III*, and fig. 62, *Dancing Pine Tree I*). The Chinese used designs of flowers, birds, and animals, but always symmetrically. It was in a later period that the Japanese gave them a twist of their own.

When Buddhism came to Japan from China it brought honeysuckle, peony, and mandala forms. A peony before a Buddhist temple can be seen in *Firewood* (fig. 16c) by Sachiko Gunji, and as a floral block made by Mary Herrold for a group quilt, *Japanese Flower Garden* (fig. 33a).

Chinese ideas and principles filtered to Japan through Korea, for it was Korean potters and weavers who brought the techniques to Japan and established guilds to teach the craft and protect the quality. Chinese artifacts were therefore transmitted with a Korean accent, having minor differences of color and form, but significant in the outcome. Chinese and Korean motifs were the raw materials with which the Japanese were to create their own style.

A *Japanese Style*

In the tenth century, the T'ang dynasty "lost the mandate of heaven" and came to an ignominious end. For more than one hundred years, China was in chaos and almost the whole of Asia felt the tremors. Only Japan remained unaffected. In the tenth and eleventh centuries, with Europe only just struggling out of the Dark Ages, Japan was probably the most civilized country on earth and left on its own, it set about discovering itself in conscious cultivated isolation.

It was during this period, known as *Heian*, meaning "peace and stability," that the Japanese elaborated their own treasury of designs, their own color schemes based on nature, and their own patterns of life.

Life in the capital city of Kyoto was a courtly society of aristocrats, but life lower down the scale was also tolerable. Buddhism exerted a humane influence, and there were no executions for three hundred years. The aristocrats whiled away their time with romantic intrigue, games, parties, and reading. Japan's great literary masterpiece, *The Tale of Genji*, reflecting the amorous life of Prince Genji of the title, was written in the early eleventh century by a lady-in-waiting at the Heian court, Lady Murasaki, and her example was followed by others.

Skilled Japanese artisans catered to this market and, indeed, it may have been they who ultimately determined Japanese taste. The court had turned away from Chinese influence and looked to nature for artistic inspiration. Artists evolved a new style of painting that differed from the Chinese style in that it depicted scenery and the daily lives of the people in detail. Japanese artisans seeking new inspiration focused their artistic attention on things near at hand, the world immediately around them, and items from their daily life.

They found inspiration in nature, in flowers and grasses, birds and insects, animals and fish, and above all in the changing seasons of the year. They took ideas from such artifacts as fans, straw hats, musical instruments, and carriage wheels. Of course, they retained the memory of forms received from China and Korea, but they subtly altered them. You will see many of these old Heian-period motifs reflected in the quilts in all sections of this book.

The Birth of Japanese Heraldry

Apart from their decorative function, patterns were also used to identify families and ranks. A particular geometrically patterned silk fabric or floral motif was adopted by high-ranking families as their personal insignia, a type of household uniform. The diamond pattern on the red and yellow robes of the courtly lady in figure 7 is a perfect illustration of such insignia.

But Japanese heraldry was born in the Heian period as the result of a phenomenon all too familiar to us today. Kyoto, the capital of Heian Japan, had broad streets, yet whenever there was an important reception in the city, there would be appalling traffic jams with the nobility's ox-drawn carriages and retinues of servants jockeying for position. In order to establish precedence, leading families took to having their personal insignia painted on the canopies of their carriages so that lesser mortals would know to get out of the way (fig. 8).

These "carriage crests," as they came to be called, were also used to identify other personal possessions. There is a beautiful example of a triple-fan design that served as a carriage crest, on the thirteenth-century lacquer cosmetic box in figure 9. Folding fans were a symbol of rank and were carried by both men and women. This circular fan motif appears on one of Sanae Hattori's *kamon* quilts (fig. 24b), and a single "courtly" fan can be seen on the group quilt, *Summer's Splendor* (fig. 34c).

In time these carriage crests became a form of heraldry.

6. Both the patterns on this eighteenth-century kimono came originally to Japan from China. A fragment of cloth woven with the same pattern that you see on the kimono silk was found in a Chinese tomb dating around 200 B.C., and the peony, of course, is well known from Chinese art. However, the way these two patterns have been combined is uniquely Japanese. They dislike symmetry, and will often find a way of breaking the regularity of a geometric pattern by over-laying it with floral motifs in the way you see here. The background pattern is called *ma-tsukawabishi* in Japanese, meaning "pine-bark diamond," and it is a favorite sashiko design. You will see it worked on quilts illustrated in the Summer and Winter sections (figs. 34 and 63), and a pattern for it, and another for a peony, are given in the PATTERN INDEX. Eighteenth century; woven silk. (Tokyo National Museum)

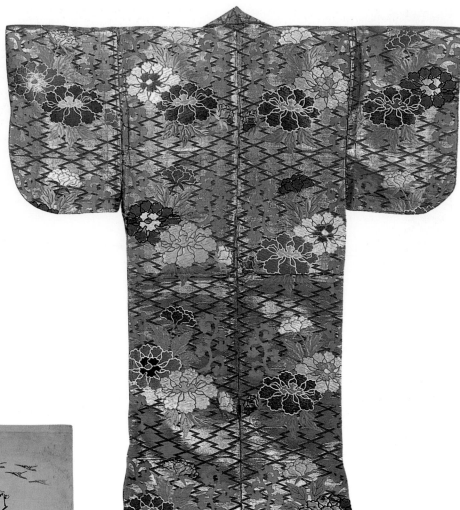

7. From the tenth to twelfth centuries, ladies at the Heian court wore several long flowing robes, one on top of another, over a red divided skirt. The outfit was called a *juni-hitoe*, meaning "twelve unlined robes," although it is known from the literature of the period that women wore as many as forty robes at one time! As clothing styles were fixed and the coloring of the robes depended upon the season, leading families began to have their clothing made in a particular patterned silk, like the diamond-lattice pattern you see on the red and yellow robes of the lady on the left. This then became the insignia of that family. The stylized floral emblems on her red robe are typical of Chinese design at that time, but the scrolling hollyhock leaves on the outer robe of her child attendant are much more in keeping with Japanese taste. Woodblock prints like this one were produced by the thousand during the sixteenth and seventeenth centuries, when nostalgia for the elegant courtly age of Heian times was at its height among the merchant classes in the cities. Seventeenth-century woodblock print; artist unknown. (Tokyo National Museum)

8. The Heian court was obsessed with rank and precedence, and because the traffic jams in the ancient city of Kyoto were so appalling, noble families painted their personal insignia on the canopies of their carriages so that lesser mortals would know to get out of the way. The motif on this carriage is a star symbol taken from Chinese fortune telling. Detail from a thirteenth-century handscroll, the *Heiji Monogatari Emaki*. (Tokyo National Museum)

9. The design of overlapping circular fans on the lid of this 600-year-old cosmetic box shows how Japanese artisans took items from everyday life and turned them into patterns. An emblem of circular fans is also to be found in Japanese heraldry. The Japanese are said to have invented the folding fan, which became an object of status carried by both men and women, and the number of slats varied according to rank. A Japanese quiltmaker has made a series of kamon wall-quilts (see figs. 24a–24d), and one of them features this circular fan design (fig. 24b). The pattern for it appears in the PATTERN INDEX. Thirteenth–fourteenth-century lacquered-wood cosmetic box. Important Cultural Property. (Tokyo National Museum)

Many emblems were taken originally from textiles, and as the fashion spread, motifs were drawn from the natural world, so that when Japan was wracked by inter-clan warfare in the thirteenth century, these graceful courtly emblems were adopted by the military and influenced the heraldic style for centuries to come. For example, the crest of a well-known warrior family was a butterfly.

It is perhaps in the design of family crests (*kamon*) that Japanese artisans achieved their most ingenious refinement. All the ingredients of nature are used; geometric and astrological designs are honed to a visual epigram, as you can see from the designs on the green silk wedding kimono in figure 10. The most prestigious kamon is the chrysanthemum, which was adopted by the imperial family; another is the peony, and a third is the triple hollyhock, the kamon of the famous line of military shoguns, the Tokugawas, who ruled Japan for two hundred and fifty years. You can see this crest on the magnificent porcelain jar in figure 11. Many of the patterns we give in the PATTERN INDEX are derived from kamon.

The Floating World

The period of clan warfare was brought to an end by the establishment of the Tokugawa shogunate in 1600. A long period of peace and isolation followed. The capital was moved from Kyoto to Tokyo, then known as Edo, and the period of the Tokugawa shogunate is called the Edo period. The merchant classes became rich and covertly influential, and pleasure flourished in the licensed quarters established for their entertainment on the outskirts of every major city in the country. This was the world of the woodblock print, where the graceful courtesans in their sinuous robes were the pin-ups of the period (fig. 12). Kabuki theatre expressed the witty, uninhibited and gaudy spirit of the age, and the actors became the tastemakers of the merchant classes.

It was a time when textile dyeing and printing techniques advanced rapidly, and it became possible to depict lavish and exaggerated designs. Kabuki actors and famous courtesans lived and dressed flamboyantly. The popularity of the checkerboard pattern stems from this period. See how Utako Fujiwara has used this pattern in true Japanese style in her quilt *Weeping Cherry Blossom* (fig. 21).

The nouveau riche adopted a mocking or jocular form of heraldry. The mother of a Tokugawa shogun, who was the daughter of a greengrocer (and achieved her position because of her beauty), did not forget her humble origins and took a radish as her personal kamon. A courtesan might choose a "clinging ivy," and a Kabuki actor some outrageous pattern from the costume of his most famous role.

Shopkeepers and businessmen adopted kamon as their company logo, such as the three diamonds of the Mitsubishi corporation (*mitsu* meaning three, *bishi* meaning diamond), or the stylized well-crib (the protective fencing placed around a well-head to prevent people from falling in) of the Sumitomo banking family, who made their first fortune in mining. These were old traditional patterns, but they were used with new vigor.

With the introduction of cotton during this period, sashiko, originally a form of running stitch used to strengthen and repair work clothing made from bast fibers, now became decorative. Freed from necessity, women adapted for their designs the lovely woven patterns on the figured silks worn by the nobility. We have chosen eight traditional sashiko patterns for you to try. You will find them in the PATTERN INDEX.

Textiles have always been important to the Japanese. In the past, servants and retainers were rewarded by a gift of clothing, or a length of silk. Rites of passage are observed by special clothing. When a girl comes of age, she receives a new kimono with bright, colorful patterns and long flowing sleeves. Although artists create contemporary designs for kimono, the department stores and kimono shops will tell you that it is the old traditional designs, the patterns of the Heian and Edo periods, that most people want.

And it is these traditional patterns that we feature in this book. The quilts that you will see in the pages that follow bear witness to the Japanese affection for their past and for the naturalistic patterns that are their heritage. We also hope that this will demonstrate another side of Japan that is often forgotten today as Japanese technological wizardry dominates the world.

ANDREW LIDDELL

8

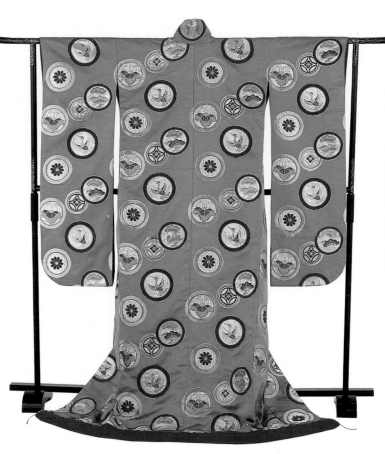

10. Heraldry was officially abolished after World War II, and although family crests are still used on kimono (the degree of formality of a kimono is determined by the number of crests it bears) these charming emblems have now entered the realm of general design. This is a modern wedding kimono and you can see a variety of kamon patterns that are woven into the fabric. Most family crests are enclosed within a circle of some sort, and we have borrowed the idea for many of the patterns in this book. This kimono would have been rented from a department store, as very few families could afford to buy such an elaborate robe today, and it would have been worn over thinner silk kimono. The padded hem dates from the seventeenth and eighteenth centuries, when it was the fashion to let the back of the robe flow out like a train. Photograph courtesy Kazuo Saito. (Author's collection)

11. Japan is a nation that is literally obsessed by textiles. The love of fabric is a thread that links all the decorative arts. This handsome storage jar is embellished with a simulated brocade cloth patterned with the well-known key-fret design (*sayagata*) that is such a favorite for sashiko today. The kamon on the brocade cloth is the triple-hollyhock emblem of the Tokugawa shoguns who ruled Japan for the best part of 250 years. A quiltmaker borrowed both these designs for a quilt that is illustrated in figure 61a, and we give the patterns for them in the PATTERN INDEX. Nineteenth-century Satsuma ware. (Trustees of the British Museum)

12. The Edo period in Japan (1600–1867) was the age of the woodblock print. Japanese artists delighted in depicting sinuous beauties dressed in beautifully patterned robes, which today provide historians with a wonderful source of information about the fashions of the period. These girls are on their way home from the bathhouse, and we can see the key-fret pattern once again on the bathrobe carried by the girl on the right. Woodblock print by Torii Kiyonaga (1752–1815). (Author's collection)

9

The Changing Seasons

The changing seasons hold a fascination for the Japanese. Their daily greetings will make mention of the state of the weather for the time of year. A formal business letter will always allude to the season and its beauties, or dangers (to one's health!) before getting down to prices, delivery dates, and contracts, the reason for writing the letter in the first place.

The Japanese are much more conscious of the changing rhythm of nature than are Westerners, perhaps because their ancestors in the distant past were so dependent upon nature for subsistence. Rice cultivation demands a regular pattern of weather, and was regarded as a religious act. Special rites known as *matsuri* were held for the various tasks to be performed, such as planting and harvest. These matsuri are still observed, not only in rural Japan (fig. 13), but each ward in a city like Tokyo will also hold an annual matsuri.

The ancient Shinto religion of Japan holds that all things possess a spirit: mountains, rocks, trees, flowers, artifacts, textiles, even household goods like sewing machines, needles, and television sets, and this feeling persists to this day. There is an annual ceremony called *Hari-Kuyo* that takes place at shrines all over Japan, for example, where women bury their worn-out needles in a bed of tofu, and thank them for all their noble work.

In a later age, more liberated from the bondage of agriculture, those feelings became etherealized and romanticized, and by the tenth century, flower and scenic-viewing had become important annual ceremonies among an aesthetically aware high society.

The Japanese still flock to famous scenic beauty spots to view mountains reflected in water, autumn colors enflaming a hillside, or the calm beauty of a temple seen by moonlight. Flower-viewing remains a regular part of the life of a Japanese family, and the year is punctuated by expeditions to visit flowering plum trees in February (the Japanese plum tree is a form of *prunus*), the iris gardens on a damp June day, peonies (fig. 14), and in the autumn, the glorious colors of the maples, and the magnificent, sometimes grotesque, displays of specially grown chrysanthemums in the public parks, shrines, and temples.

The Japanese will stand and admire, examine closely, view from a distance—or even upside-down, applaud and, of course, photograph these beautiful things. They take immense pleasure in the natural world, and since urbanization has all but destroyed nature in their cities, they will re-create it. Every shopping street is decorated with sprays of appropriate seasonal flowers made of plastic sprouting from the lampposts—cherry blossom in Spring, green leaves in Summer, maple leaves in Autumn, and snowflakes in Winter. Modern handmade *washi* papers are printed with the floral motifs of the changing seasons in the artistic style of the past (fig. 15).

Seasonal food, too, is still respected. The Japanese enjoy the changes, surprises, and rediscoveries of the annual cycle of vegetables and fruit. Old pleasures remain valid, even in a world where air-conditioning isolates us from the climate, and where air transport brings to the supermarkets a full range of delicacies simultaneously all the year round.

In her romantic novel, *The Tale of Genji*, written in the eleventh century, Lady Murasaki wrote "...it was the plum trees that gave the surest promise, for already their blossoms were uncurling, like lips parted in a faint smile." To this day, the Japanese see smiles, courage, romance, elegance, and gentle melancholy in the flowers, fruit, vegetables, utensils, and artifacts of the changing seasons, and Japanese quiltmakers have recorded all of this in a series of beautiful quilts for you to admire.

13. Festivals punctuate Japanese life, in the cities and in the countryside. This festival (*matsuri*) was photographed in a village near Hiroshima, and celebrates the planting of the rice seedlings. In the olden days planting was always done by women to bring fertility to the soil. Photograph courtesy JTB Photo, Tokyo.

14. In the days when women wore kimono every day, there were appropriate colors and motifs for each season. This elegant resist-dyed silk kimono with its delicate design of multicolored peonies would only have been worn for semiformal occasions during the early part of summer when peonies were in bloom. Today, because of the enormous cost of a hand-dyed silk robe like this, these rules of fashion are no longer strictly observed. A lovely peony decorates the quilt illustrated in figure 16c. Twentieth century; resist-dyeing on silk. Photograph courtesy Mitsukoshi Department Store, Tokyo.

15. Many of the seasonal flowers, birds, mountains, clouds, and stylized mist that appear on this piece of handmade washi paper, printed in the old painterly style of the premodern era, you will also see on quilts further on in the book. We also give the patterns for many of them.

16 a-f. *The 1990 Calendar for Narita Mountain Shinsho Temple* by Sachiko Gunji, Nara City, Nara Prefecture. 1989. Approximately 20″ x 20″ (50 x 50cm). Antique stencil-dyed fabrics, kimono silks, satin, lamé. Hand appliqué, quilting, and embroidery. We begin the journey through Japan's changing seasons with six enchanting calendar quilts made by Sachiko Gunji to celebrate Narita Mountain Shinsho Temple. "I was asked to make a calendar quilt by the temple," she tells us, "so when I was working on these quilts, I visited the temple many times during the year to see how it looked, and tried to capture the correct colors and forms. I had a collection of old indigo-dyed fabrics, but I mixed them with new fabric because I love the mysterious images created by the contrast of old and new. The beautiful color combinations and textures one can achieve have opened up a new world for me." The calendar quilts were very well received. The priests wrote a thank-you letter to Sachiko saying that they regarded her works as art. She was delighted by their reaction, because she considers quiltmaking to be a form of art. In the following pages, you can see how Sachiko divided her temple year into six seasons and worked into her quilts the traditional flora and fauna associated with those seasons. She is a quiltmaker of some note in Japan and took up quiltmaking in 1983. Now she runs a thriving quilt group. Photographs courtesy the artist.

16a. *The Sunrise on New Year's Day—January and February.* Sachiko begins the series with the New Year breaking over the main building of the temple. The brilliance of the early-morning sun illuminates the clouds, while below the building lies the sea. The shapes of the clouds are traditional, and she has set this picturesque scene against a backdrop of antique *aizome*, the kind of stencil-dyed fabrics the Japanese used for furnishings and bedding in the past. (Pattern 21 includes some traditional clouds.)

16b. *The Cherry Blossom Festival—March and April.* The essence of Spring, and the annual festival of cherry-blossom viewing, is captured by a glimpse of the temple roof silhouetted against a single petal. A few scattered blossoms and quilted bands of stylized mist complete this charming scene. (Pattern 4, Cherry Blossom; Pattern 21 includes an appliqué pattern for stylized mist that could also be used for quilting.)

16c. *Firewood—May and June.* During the summer months Noh plays are performed by the light of fires and lanterns in the grounds of shrines and temples throughout Japan, and Sachiko has honored this custom in her lovely quilt. This type of outdoor performance is called *Takigi-Noh*, which is the title she gave her quilt in Japanese. She has set her scene against a stylized leaf that is the temple's official crest, and see how beautifully she has worked the fire basket and flames. A peony, the symbol of early summer, completes the picture. (Pattern 23, Peony; Pattern 11 includes a small peony.)

16d. *Midsummer—July and August.* Sachiko captures the feeling of an early-summer's morning in this scene of perky mandarin ducks swimming in a lake near the temple. A pair of mandarin ducks is a familiar Japanese motif that symbolizes marital harmony. There are also many different traditional images for water. The classic shape of the lake that Sachiko has beautifully quilted with ripples is a larger version of the quilted mist pattern we saw on her cherry blossom quilt (fig. 16b). (Pattern 19, Sachiko's Mandarin Ducks)

16e. *Mid-Autumn Night—September and October.* Moon-viewing has always been a favorite festival in Japan. In ancient times, houses were built with special terraces where the moon could be viewed in ideal conditions, reflected in water. Even today, some Japanese enjoy moon-viewing, and a festival, when special rice-cakes are eaten, is held each September to celebrate the harvest moon. To celebrate this season, Sachiko has placed her temple roof against the deep blue of the harvest moon.

16f. *The End of the Year—November and December.* The first snow of the Winter season was always held to be lucky in ancient times, and it was the day on which court officials made their plans for the entire year. The white circle with crenelated edges symbolizes snow, while the roof of the temple peeks out above three stylized shapes, worked in antique indigo-cotton, that Japanese artists often use to represent pine trees. They, too, are frosted with snow. Sachiko's attractive little birds add a touch of life to this winter scene. (Pattern 25, Pine Wreath; Pattern 26, Pine Trees; Pattern 30, Snow-ring)

Spring

Spring begins with the Girl's Day festival on March 3 and is a time of pleasure and of renewal, when the land begins to quicken and the crops are planted. It is a time of high winds and sudden showers, of fresh green leaves that the Japanese call *shinryoku*, meaning "new green," and which, of course, they take time off to admire! And it is the season of the fabled cherry blossom.

Cherry blossom is Japan's national flower, and the trees grow wild in the hills around the ancient capital of Kyoto. While Japan was still under the spell of China, it was plum blossom that was admired, and plum blossom motifs decorated the clothing of the nobility. But in the tenth century, when Japan ceased to look to China for inspiration, the popularity of the plum waned and the native cherry became fashionable, although it never quite succeeded in supplanting plum blossom.

In the succeeding centuries, cherry blossom–viewing became a national pastime for rich and poor alike, and cherry blossom motifs appeared on everything from porcelain (fig. 17) to textiles (fig. 18). Cherry blossom brings revelry to Japan, worries are forgotten, and people picnic in the parks under the cherry trees, drinking sake and making merry.

But cherry blossom is not the only spring flower to be admired. Wisteria-viewing appears on the floral calendar for May, and crowds visit a famous temple in Tokyo where great canopies of wisteria are reflected in a carp-filled pond. Like the cherry, wisteria also became a favorite motif, and it can be found in various forms in all the decorative arts, including textiles (fig. 19). It was also one of the early family crests, and is especially associated with a noble family of the Heian period whose name was Fujiwara, meaning "field of wisteria," and who ruled as hereditary regents for three hundred years.

17. Cherry blossom (*sakura*) appears in many guises in Japanese decorative art. This eighteenth-century porcelain plate shows a venerable tree awash with these lovely springtime blossoms. Nabeshima porcelain. (Tokyo National Museum)

18. Drooping branches of cherry blossom are a favorite textile pattern and can be seen flowing from the shoulders of this elegant satin kimono. The same style of cherry blossom appears in figure 21. Eighteenth-century; dyeing and embroidery on white figured satin. (Tokyo National Museum)

19. The lovely drooping fronds of wisteria that are such a feature of the late spring in Japan have decorated many a kimono in the past, and have also inspired a Japanese quiltmaker, Sanae Hattori, a detail of whose beautiful quilt is featured on the cover of this book. The complete quilt is shown in figure 23. Note the familiar geometric pattern of interlocking circles in the background of this eighteenth-century robe. It is a traditional Japanese pattern called *shippo*, meaning "seven treasures." Dyeing and embroidery. (Tokyo National Museum)

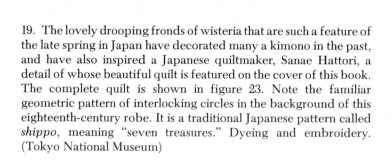

20. *Hina Dolls* by Chie Hodaiji, Miyako City, Iwate Prefecture. 1987. Approximately 58″ x 57″ (147 x 145 cm). Cottons and *obi* fabrics (the wide sash worn with kimono). Hand-appliqué and quilting. Early spring is highlighted by the festival for little girls held on March 3 each year, when a collection of dolls dressed in the traditional multilayered costume of the Heian period are displayed in every home and department store. The dolls are often heirlooms, passed down from mother to daughter. At the top of Chie's charming quilt sit the emperor and the empress; next come the ladies-in-waiting, and beneath them are the court musicians, gifts of food, and traditional flowers. Chie has seven grandchildren, and she made this quilt for her two granddaughters because it was a way of displaying the Hina dolls in a small space. Her family are in the clothing business, so she had access to fabric remnants from a friendly wholesaler. "It was very enjoyable, very nostalgic for me to collect traditional Japanese kimono and obi fabrics, because I am old enough to have lived during the time when more women wore kimono in everyday life." Chie says she took up quiltmaking about ten years ago and always sews by hand, as do so many Japanese quiltmakers.

21. *Weeping Cherry Blossom* designed by Utako Fujiwara and made by Hiromi Yamamoto, Hiroshima City, Hiroshima Prefecture. 1988. Approximately 99″ x 54″ (138 x 99 cm). Cottons. Hand-piecing, appliqué, and quilting. "The weeping cherry is very Japanese," Utako says, "and I am attracted by the gentle, fleeting appearance of this particular form of cherry. I live in a part of Hiroshima that suffered badly from the atomic bomb, and even though we were told that the ground would be useless, every April we can see the cherry trees blooming in great profusion with the atomic dome behind them. It is a very peaceful scene and cherry blossoms in April are a symbol of peace for me." The combination of a geometric pattern overlaid with floral motifs is also very Japanese (see figs. 6 and 57), and one that has been effectively adapted by several quiltmakers, including the well-known Japanese quilt artist, Setsuko Segawa, with whom Utako studied for seven years. The checkerboard pattern she has used for the background is known as *ichimatsu* in Japanese, which is actually the name of a famous eighteenth-century kabuki actor who made the pattern his stage trademark. Utako has been making quilts now for twelve years and is a member of an academy of quilt teachers in Hiroshima. The delicate beauty of this quilt reflects her love of traditional design. (Pattern 4, Cherry Blossom)

22. *Floating Flowers* by Toshiko Yamamoto, Kamo County, Hiroshima Prefecture. 1989. Approximately 75″ x 59″ (190 x 150 cm). Cottons. Hand-piecing, appliqué, and quilting. Toshiko has created a tapestry of seasonal flowers in this lovely scrap quilt, but as you can see, it is the traditional flower of spring, the weeping cherry, that holds pride of place in the center. The inspiration for the design came from kimono. "When I was window shopping, I noted that dress fashions change rapidly, but kimono designs and colors maintain their beauty and appeal no matter how old they are," she explains. "I am attracted by their timeless beauty, and even though I use a variety of quilting techniques that have come from America, I enjoy trying to use color and design that express the fact that I am Japanese." Her fabrics are all household scraps, pieces that she had saved—for example, fabric from her sister's old miniskirt. Toshiko has been making quilts for seven years and was taught originally by her sister. She feels that it is good training to look at beautiful things like kimono, handkerchiefs, scarves, and illustrated books in order to get ideas for quilt designs.

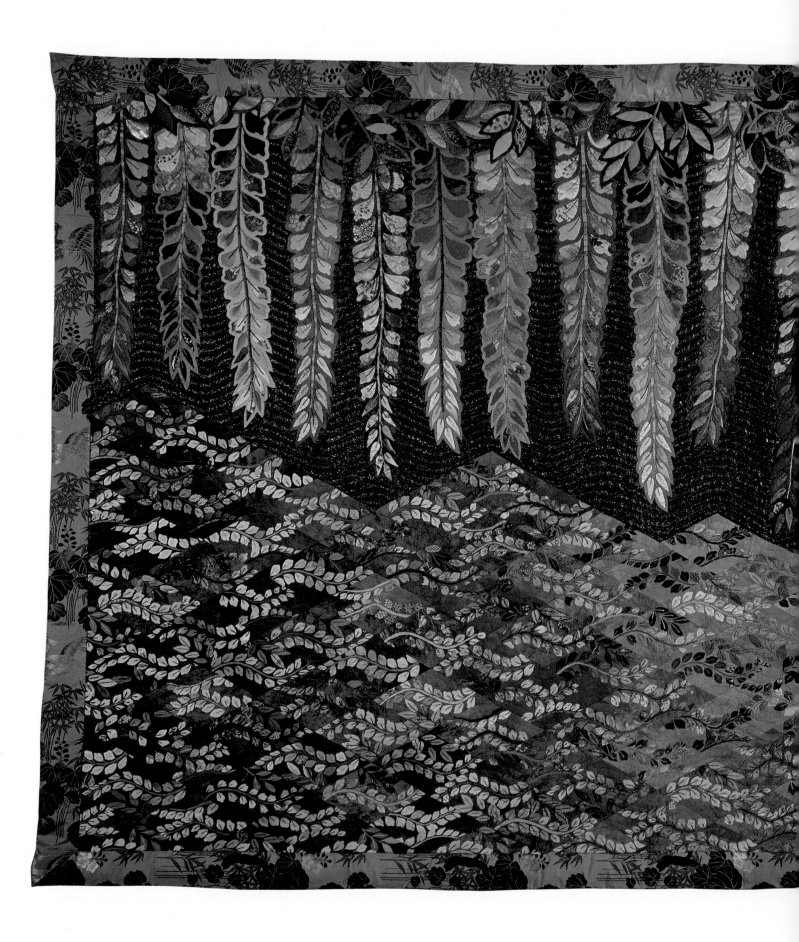

23. *Wisteria Like a Fall* designed and made by Sanae Hattori, Tokyo. 1990. Approximately 73″ x 106″ (185 x 270 cm). Cotton, silk, polyester, kimono, and obi fabric. Hand piecing, appliqué, embroidery, and quilting. It was fronds of wisteria hanging from a trellis in a Japanese garden that provided Sanae Hattori with the inspiration for this stunningly original quilt. "I spent a long time wondering how I could put the elegant wisteria pattern into a quilt and decided, finally, to make it in two contrasted sections. The upper part is vertical and shows the wisteria falling like a waterfall. The lower part is horizontal with the wisteria being blown about by the wind." Apart from these contrasted sections, the design has other interesting elements. The horizontal section is composed of diamond-shaped blocks that are typically Japanese. In Japanese art and heraldry, you often find decorative motifs framed in circles, hexagons, or diamonds, and Sanae has made a feature of using diamond-shaped blocks in her quilts (see figs. 31, 51, and 62). The zigzag formation dividing the two sections is also traditional as it echoes a design from a well-known sixteenth-century kimono that is said to have belonged to Tokugawa Ieyasu, Japan's most famous shogun. Her border of fine obi silk complements this beautiful work. This quilt appeared in Sanae's book, *Sanae Quilt Art*, published by Gakken, Tokyo, 1991. Photograph courtesy the artist.

a.

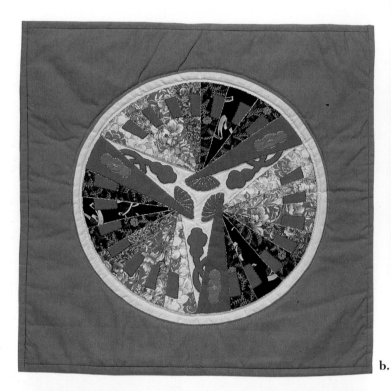

b.

c.

d.

24a, 24b, 24c, 24d. *Kamon (Family Crest) Quilts* by Sanae Hattori, Tokyo. 1985. Approximately 18″ x 18″ (45 x 45 cm). Cotton, silk, kimono fabric. Hand-appliqué, piecing, and embroidery. As you can see from one of this series of attractive wall quilts featuring Japanese family-crest motifs, Sanae Hattori was attracted by the wisteria pattern some five years before she made *Wisteria Like a Fall*. These quilts appeared originally in her book, *The Quilt Japan*, published by Gakken in 1985, and she was among the first of the Japanese quilters to use her country's distinctive heraldic emblems in her work. Illustrated are (a) the peony; (b) the same circular-fan pattern seen in figure 9; (c) stylized wisteria; and (d) plovers and waves. Photographs courtesy the artist. (Pattern 5, Circular Fans; Pattern 28, Wisteria)

a.

b.

25a, 25b. *Bird Mandalas* by Sachiko Gunji, Nara City, Nara Prefecture. 1988. 20½″ x 14½″ (52 x 37 cm). Antique stencil-dyed fabrics, kimono silk, satin lamé. Hand-appliqué, quilting, and embroidery. A year before she made the series of calendar quilts (figs. 16a–f), Sachiko tried her hand at six mandala quilts, two of which appear here and a third in figure 52. She wanted to feature the changes in the seasons as seen through a window frame, "...a symbolic impression of the seasons rather than a photo image." She perfected this technique in her calendar quilts, of course, but here we catch a glimpse of cherry blossom again in figure 25a, and the pattern of raindrops on water in 25b, is cleverly conveyed by broken lines of quilting. Photographs courtesy Nobutoshi Sato and Nobuo Takizawa. (Pattern 4, Cherry Blossom)

a.

26a, 26b. *March 28, 1986: Rain at Fushimi Inari* by Judi Warren, Maumee, Ohio. 1988. 72″ x 84″ (183 x 213 cm). Commercial and hand-dyed, hand-painted, silk-screen-printed cottons, and lamé. Machine-piecing, hand-appliqué and quilting, and embellished with beads. "To me, Japan is a place of great beauty," Judi says. "On March 28, 1986 a soft rain was falling at Fushimi Inari in Kyoto. The wet stone path reflected the red-orange of the shrine's *torii* gate, and the soft green of new leaves and the misty sky were gentle and delicate. I did not want to leave." This was Judi's first visit to Japan; she went with a group of American quilters on a teaching trip, and fell in love with the country. When the Japanese visit shrines, they buy fortune-telling papers called *omikuji* from a booth set up in the temple grounds, and then tie the paper strips to trees and bushes near the shrine itself. You can see Judi's omikuji scattered in the center of her striking quilt, framed by the torii gate. The detail photograph shows that on one of them she embroidered her own fortune-telling wish: *Nihon ni mata kaeritai*, which means "I want to return (come home) again to Japan." She tells us that she did return "...and each time I go it is more wonderful. I treasure my friendships with Japanese quiltmakers for their kindness and the wonderful memories we have together." Photograph courtesy the artist.

b.

Summer

Summer in Japan is a season with phases. It starts with "Golden Week," a series of public holidays when, in a fit of rare hedonism, the Japanese give up work and skip from holiday to holiday, like a child on stepping stones. The best known of these "stepping stones" is the Boy's Day festival on May 5th, a celebration going back to the days when a boy child (or, to be more precise, a future daughter-in-law) meant the assurance of descendants and an old-age pension.

The weather in May is lovely, but in June the monsoon arrives. For approximately six weeks it rains continuously; cold and gloomy for humans, but wonderfully nurturing for the plants. Apart from rice, one water lover is the Japanese iris which is strongly associated with this phase of summer (fig. 27).

The latter part of July is usually fine and hot; the cicadas start their grinding song that serves as background music for the rest of the season. Insects abound, and Japan is noted for its magnificent butterflies (fig. 28).

In August, the weather becomes humid and oppressive. In the subways and on the streets, men and women pull folding fans out of their pockets and fan themselves. In days past, on a hot summer's evening, couples would stroll along the banks of Tokyo's Sumida river, wearing their cotton kimono called a *yukata*. Even today, the yukata remains a popular garment. It is probably the only form of kimono still consistently worn by the Japanese, and much of the pretty indigo-blue-and-white patterned fabric is still dyed with the old traditional stencils. The beaches become crowded with holiday-makers, and the bays are filled with wind surfers—brightly colored sails on the blue water.

The summer is a period when the gardens of Japan produce a rich sequence of flowers, vegetables, and fruit. The Japanese love flowers; they buy them to decorate their homes, grow them on the balconies of their apartments, and enjoy the rich floral patterns of summer clothing (fig. 29). In the open-fronted shops, eggplants, green and red peppers, asparagus, cherries, plums, and huge, delicately flavored pears beckon the customer.

The summer comes to an abrupt halt in August when the Japanese abandon the beaches and return eagerly to work.

27. Irises occupy a special place in the hearts of the Japanese, and the annual pilgrimage to view the irises growing in the nation's parks and gardens takes place in June. This beautiful hand-dyed carrying cloth (*furoshiki*) was made in Okinawa from a traditional design by Anna McMahon, an English girl who went there to study the art and history of *bingata*. This is the Okinawan form of stencil-dyeing, noted for its bright coloring. There are two quilts in this section that use similar iris patterns (figs. 31 and 32). Photograph courtesy Anna McMahon and Noel Manchee.

28. Butterflies are a feature of the Japanese summer, and on this piece of Japanese washi paper, they are hovering above a river bed patterned with bamboo, cherry blossom, and grasses. The three clamshell patterns that you see in the top right-hand corner are a Japanese symbol for water. The pattern is called Blue Wave, and a quilt made in this pattern is illustrated in figure 38.

29. Flower-arranging only became fashionable in Japan in the fifteenth century, when it was encouraged by an aesthetic shogun. The Japanese associate wheels with good fortune, so a charming pattern of wheeled flower carts was devised that appeared soon thereafter on clothing and lacquer ware. It is now one of the most popular design motifs for traditional Japanese embroidery, and a group of British quiltmakers made an appliqué pattern from it that is illustrated in figure 34, and we give a pattern for it in the PATTERN INDEX. Eighteenth century; embroidery on silk. (Tokyo National Museum)

30. *Carp Banners* by Chieko Ouchi, Osaka City, Osaka Prefecture. 1983. Approximately 63″ x 57″ (160 x 144 cm). Cottons, antique kimono fabric, rope. Hand-appliqué and quilting. The Boy's Day festival is held each year on May 5th, which is the day on which giant carp-shaped windsocks (*koinobori*) flutter from flagpoles all over the country. According to Japanese mythology, the carp is tough and brave and can jump cataracts with ease, all virtues that are necessary for a small boy entering a masculine world. Chieko says that unsophisticated scenes of traditional Japanese events are disappearing, and as "I cannot display a koinobori outside, I decided to make a koinobori quilt instead. When my three children were small, they would lie on this quilt and say, 'This is our koinobori!' So this quilt became a bond between us." It took her six months to make, but she adds that seeing the children's enjoyment made it all worthwhile. Chieko has also featured irises in her charming piece, for once upon a time May 5th was the date of an iris festival when people decorated their houses with a type of wild iris to drive away evil spirits. Nowadays, the cultivated iris flowers in June and iris-viewing have become the highlight of that month. (Patterns 14 and 15, Irises)

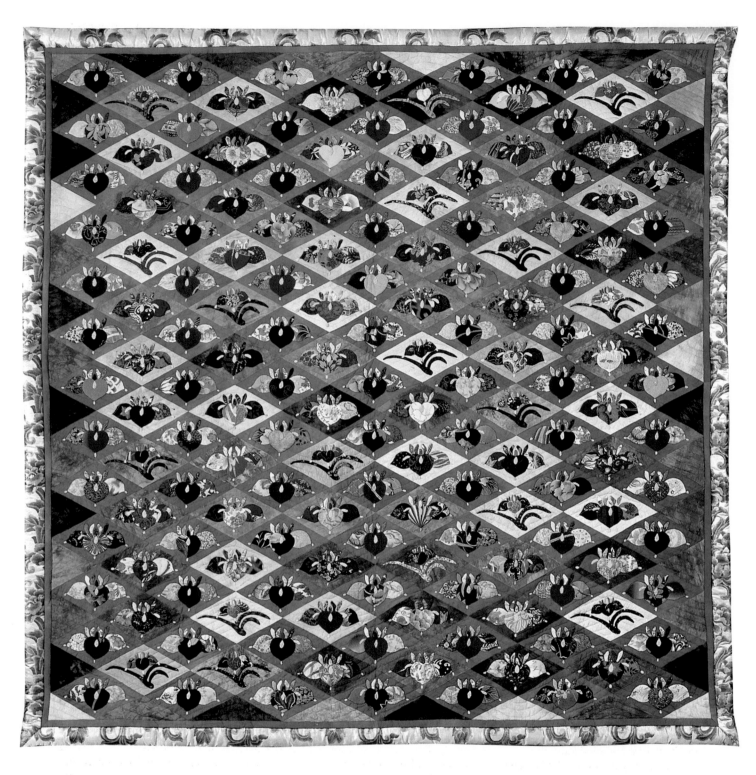

31. *Japanese Iris 11* designed by Sanae Hattori and made by Akiko Ninomiya, Tokyo. 1989. 75″ x 75″ (190 x 190 cm). Cotton, silk, polyester. Hand-piecing and appliqué. Sanae's bewitching quilt is redolent of early summer when the magnificent Japanese irises are in bloom and thousands of people flock each day to see them in the parks and gardens all over Japan. Japanese irises grow in water, and Sanae has tried to reflect this in the coloring of her diamond-shaped blocks. She has used two iris motifs, both of which were taken from kamon. Like so many of the floral emblems, irises were first introduced during the Heian period as a decorative device on the clothing and carriages of the Kyoto nobility. In the past, not only was the iris thought to be capable of driving away evil spirits (see fig. 30), but also rich and poor alike bathed in water steeped with iris leaves because they believed it would keep them free of disease for the rest of the year. Perhaps sleeping under a diamond-block iris quilt like Sanae's might have the same effect! With her permission, we give you instructions on how to make one in PATTERN PROJECTS. This quilt was illustrated in Sanae's book, *Sanae Quilt Art*, published by Gakken, Tokyo, 1991. Photograph courtesy the artist. (Pattern 14 and 15, Irises)

Between the iris-blossom and the water

She walks among the loveliness she made

She walks among the patterned pied brocade

Each flower her son and every leaf her daughter

32. *In the Garden* by Josephine Ratcliff, Preston, Lancashire, England. 1989. 90″ x 90″ (approximately 228 x 228 cm). Cotton sateen, glazed chintz. Machine appliqué, quilting, and hand-embroidery. Irises taken from family crests are featured on this lovely piece made by an English quiltmaker who says she has always been fascinated by Japanese design, and by kamon in particular. Josephine used two kamon, a circular iris in the center medallion, similar to the furoshiki in figure 27, and a spray in the four corners, which she then modified for the borders. She made the quilt specifically to sell at the British National Patchwork Championships that take place each year on the grounds of a stately home near London. The theme in 1989 was "A Gardener's Paradise," and so around the center Josephine hand-embroidered a verse from a poem by the English writer and poet Vita Sackville-West. "My daughter-in law was about to undergo surgery, and she wanted to choose her own anesthetist, having had a bad previous experience, which meant that she had to opt for private medicine, rather than have the operation free under the National Health scheme," Josephine explains. "I hoped to sell the quilt because I wanted to help her financially. It did not sell until the very last day of the show when, believe it or not, it was bought by an anesthetist!" The new owner, Dr. A. Triscott, loves her iris quilt and says she redecorated her bedroom to match it. Photograph courtesy the artist, Dr. A. Triscott, and Noel Manchee.

a.

b.

33a, 33b. *Japanese Flower Garden*, a group quilt with blocks made by Vicki Beauchamp, Isabelle Cunningham, Patricia Hercus, Lois Stewart, Carol Conomos, Rebecca Copeland, Helen Lawson, Catherine Felix, Mary Herrold, Adrienne R. Trythal, Lois Urquhart, Sylvia Fei and Jill Liddell, Tokyo. 1984. 90″ x 72″ (approximately 228 x 183 cm). Japanese sheeting. Hand-appliqué, quilt-as-you-go. We had already been making quilts from Japanese family-crest patterns in my classes, but during the long, hot summer of 1984, some of my kind students made this group quilt for a book that I was trying to write. The book never got off the ground, but this quilt did and making it remains one of the happiest memories of my Japanese life. Everyone chose her own pattern, and we tried out a key-fret sashiko design for the quilted blocks. Mary Herrold chose the peony, the flower of early summer that both the Chinese and Japanese call the "Queen of Flowers," and you can see her block in the detail photograph. We were a cosmopolitan group, and I have lost touch with nearly everybody. But if any of you should read this book in whatever part of the world you happen to be, I would just like to say a big thank you for all your hard work!—Jill Liddell. Photograph courtesy Ben Simmons, Tokyo. (Pattern 23, Peony; Sashiko Pattern 6, Key-fret)

a.

34a, 34b, 34c, 34d. *Summer's Splendor*, a group quilt designed by Gill Bryan, made by Violet Plume and Barbara Holmes, and quilted by Jenni Dobson, London, England. 1991. 52″ x 39″ (132 x 99 cm). Batik and cottons. Hand-appliqué and quilting. The flower-cart pattern (*hana garuma*) that you see in figure 34b is such a favorite in all the Japanese decorative arts that a book about Japanese patterns would not be complete without it. We therefore asked Gill Bryan to draw up the pattern and design a quilt for us. Nobody is quite sure when the pattern first appeared, but by the eighteenth century it was used in kimono design, as you can see in figure 29. Flower arranging in Japan was originally confined to votive flowers in temples, but toward the end of the fifteenth century, an aesthetic shogun made domestic flower arranging fashionable and so, inadvertently, gave birth to *ikebana*. Wheels are also a popular Japanese design motif. They imply good fortune, which may have something to do with the Buddhist prayer wheel, or the fact that in premodern Japan, only the aristocracy rode in carriages, while everybody else walked or were carried in palanquins. Fashion, good fortune, and prestige are therefore combined in Gill's charming design of flower-filled carts, courtly fans, and butterflies. Barbara Holmes and Violet Plume stitched the patterns, and Jenni Dobson did the quilting. She used four different sashiko patterns, all of which you will find in the Sashiko Pattern index. Photographs courtesy the artists and Noel Manchee. (Pattern 5, Courtly Fan; Pattern 10, Flying Butterflies; Pattern 11, Flower Cart; Sashiko Patterns 1, 4, 5, and 7)

b.

34b. The flower-cart pattern is an old one and appears in all the decorative arts even today. Gill Bryan took her design from the kimono in figure 29.

34c. The courtly fan is also traditional. In the olden days this slatted version was part of a courtier's official regalia. Barbara Holmes drew up the pattern from a kamon.

c.

d.

34d. Butterfly motifs have always been favored by courtiers and commoners alike. The pattern is Gill Bryan's own design.

35. *A Gift for My Mother* by Yasuko Sawai, Kasugai City, Aichi Prefecture. 1984. Approximately 32″ x 42″ (81 x 106 cm). Kimono silks and lining fabric. Hand-pieced and quilted. The wheel of fortune, associated with the flower-cart pattern in the previous quilt, appears here as the main motif on a colorful quilt made entirely from kimono silks. "I wanted to make use of fabrics given to me by mother," Yasuko explains. "Most of the fabric is from the 1920s, kimono that my mother brought with her as a bride. My father died eight years ago, so I included some pieces from the silk lining of his *haori* (a coat worn with a man's kimono), and also part of a kimono belonging to my sister that got burned, and bits from a traditional type of coat in which my brother was carried as a baby…the quilt is filled with memories of my family." She made the quilt as a gift for her mother, but she says that it has returned to her, "and I treasure it now." Yasuko took up quiltmaking eleven years ago when her youngest child no longer took up so much of her time.

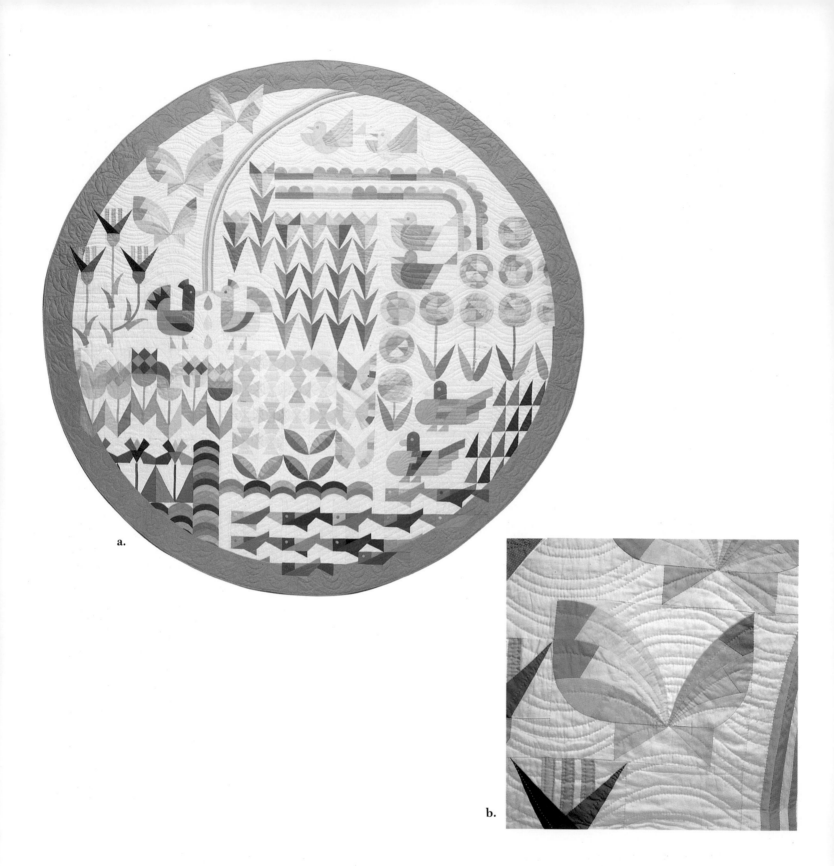

a.

b.

36a, 36b. *Happy Animals* by Hiroko Mayahara, Takatsuki City, Osaka Prefecture. 1989. Approximately 100″ (255 cm) in diameter. Cottons and cotton sateen. Hand-piecing, appliqué, and quilting. An unusual asymmetrical butterfly pattern (see detail illustration) joins a riot of pieced bird and flower designs in this wonderful contemporary quilt. Here we see irises, tulips, mandarin ducks, waves, birds, fish, and roosters—a perfect evocation of a childhood summer. Hiroko tells us that she is interested in creating original patterns. She made this quilt for a group exhibition and because most of her group seemed to favor quiet colors, she decided to make hers as bright as possible. "I looked at photographs of animals and selected popular ones. I designed this quilt with the hope that all the animals on this earth will live happily in nature, and that we will stop destroying our environment and pass on a beautiful world to the next generation." Hiroko has made other quilts from her own animal patterns and intends to continue until she has enough for her own show. She learned the craft seventeen years ago, when she lived in Texas, and then attended a well-known quilting school on her return to her native country.

37. *Dogwood and Butterflies* by Yukiko Maeda, Chofu City, Tokyo. 1986. Approximately 69″ x 69″ (175 x 175 cm). Cottons. Hand-piecing, appliqué, and quilting. Scattered butterflies appear on this delicately colored quilt, a memorial to the early days of summer when the beautiful blossoms of the dogwood tree delight the eye all over Japan. Yukiko took the design for her quilt from the dogwood blossoms in her own garden. "I designed the quilt when our dogwood tree was in bloom," she explains, "and exactly one year later, when I had finished my quilt and took it into the garden to photograph, the dogwood was flowering again!" She lived in Los Angeles some ten years ago and learned quiltmaking there, although she continued going to classes on her return to Japan. Now, she says, quiltmaking has become an important part of her life. (Pattern 10, Flying Butterflies)

38. *Thousand Waves* designed by Sanae Hattori and made by Akiko Shirakawa, Tokyo. 1991. Approximately 83″ x 79″ (210 x 200 cm). Cottons, polyester, and obi fabrics. Hand-piecing, appliqué, and quilting. The wave pattern seen on this striking quilt is an ancient one, common to many countries in the Orient. It seems to have first appeared in Japan decorating the clothing on a terra-cotta figurine excavated from a fifth-century tomb, and has remained a perennial favorite ever since. Its Japanese name, *seigaiha*, means Blue Wave, and the varied shades of blue, frosted with pink and violet, that Sanae chose for the quilt conjure up a vision of the seaside on a summer's day. An earlier version of this quilt was featured on the cover of Sanae's first book, *Patchwork & Quilt*, published by Fujinseikatsusha, Tokyo, 1987. There are three versions of the pattern in popular use in Japan today, the two you see here that are based on the clamshell, and a geometric version that is normally used for sashiko, but which appears as a quilting design in figure 67 and as a piecework pattern in figure 73. Because it is such a popular Japanese design, we feature three versions in the PATTERN INDEX. Photograph courtesy the artist. (Pattern 2a, Blue Wave piecework version; Pattern 2b, Blue Wave appliqué version; Sashiko Pattern 2)

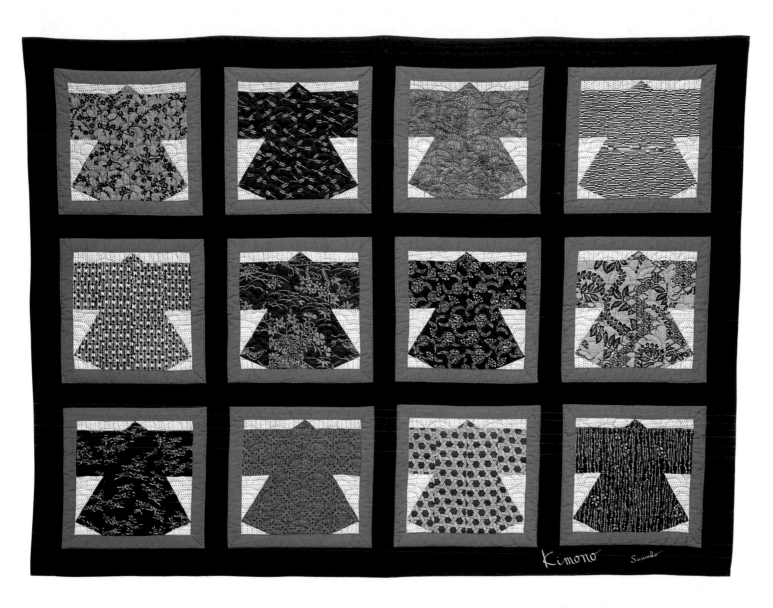

39. *Kimono* by Sawako Tsurugiji, Kanazawa City, Ishikawa Prefecture. 1980. Approximately 43″ x 56″ (110 x 143 cm). Yukata cottons. Hand-piecing and quilting. A feature of the Japanese summer is the yukata, the fresh blue-and-white cotton kimono that is probably the only kimono still universally worn by the Japanese today. It serves as a bathrobe, and as a light, comfortable garment to wear during the hot, humid evenings. Sawako loves Japanese indigo-dyed fabrics, and for a long time she made all her quilts with these fabrics. This appealing quilt is from the beginning of her "blue" period. "I was surprised to find that antique kimono fabrics were so modern and daring in their design," she says. "Endeavoring to show off the beauty of the fabric by using a simple pattern is interesting, and I designed my pattern to look like a kimono spread out and hung on a stand." (You can see a real kimono on a traditional stand in figure 14.) In the old days, traveling salesmen used to make sample books of yukata patterns to show their customers. Sawako's quilt is done in similar style, and she has quilted each block with the Blue Wave pattern featured in figure 38. She has kindly allowed us to reproduce her kimono pattern in the PATTERN INDEX. (Pattern 17, Sawako's kimono; Sashiko Pattern 2, Blue Wave)

40. *Scattered Fans II* designed by Sanae Hattori and made by Keiko Sumi, Tokyo. 1987. Approximately 93″ x 93″ (235 x 235 cm). Cotton, polyester, kimono fabric. Hand-piecing, appliqué, and quilting. This marvelous design of fluttering fans captures the dog days of summer, when the heat and the humidity make life almost unbearable in the cities of Japan, and any whisper of air is a relief. Sanae has designed two scattered-fan quilts that are illustrated in her most recent book, *Sanae Quilt Art*, published by Gakken, Tokyo, 1991. The second quilt was created in shades of pink and yellow. In this quilt each fan was first pieced together and then scattered over the background at different angles to create a wonderful sense of swirling color and movement, like a flock of butterflies. The Japanese love to bring a sense of movement and irregularity into their art, for this is what they see and appreciate in nature. Sanae specializes in traditional designs and the Japanese custom of scattering and overlapping patterns is something Western quiltmakers might like to copy. (Pattern 5, Courtly Fans)

41. *Fan-ta-see* by Chizuko Hana Hill, Cadiz, Kentucky. 1989. 90″ x 65″ (approximately 229 x 165 cm). Cottons. Hand-appliqué and quilting. Scattered fans are also a feature of this striking stained-glass appliqué quilt made by a Japanese who, although she now lives permanently in the United States with her American husband, takes her inspiration from her native culture. Chizuko took the design for the background from an old Japanese candy box, but when she came to the big center fan, she wanted a particular shade of golden yellow, but could not find anything appropriate. "I then decided to embroider around the fan with gold thread," she tells us. "It took me over two months, and there were many occasions when I was tempted to give up, but I stuck at it, and the quilt won the *Better Homes and Gardens* blue-ribbon award at the Kentucky State Fair Quilt Show in 1990. I often find that I come up against unforeseen difficulties when I make original designs and sometimes I fail, but when I'm successful it gives me great satisfaction." Chizuko is noted for her fine quilting, and if you look carefully, you can see that she has used a variety of patterns on the fans that illustrate the two cultural influences in her life—everything from the classic American Princess Feather to miniature sprigs of bamboo.

42a, 42b, 42c, 42d, 42e, 42f. *Vegetable Mandala* by Sachiko Gunji, Nara City, Nara Prefecture. 1988. Each quilt is approximately 22″ x 20″ (55 x 50 cm). Antique Japanese batik (*sarasa*), kimono silk, vegetable-dyed fabrics, synthetic crepe, satin. Hand-appliqué, piecing, and quilting. Fresh vegetables are one of the delights of living in Japan, and nowadays all the vegetables that you see in this series of six ravishing wall quilts are available throughout the year. Sachiko has worked old and new fabrics with effective simplicity to create her delectable plates. She says, "In the kitchen, vegetables are always the supporting actors, but when I look at them carefully, I find they have strange shapes and beautiful colors. These quilts star them in leading roles." She set each plate against a background of white crepe and quilted it with strong geometric patterns done in colored thread. "By using this technique, I was able to create shadows and show greater dimension." The vegetables are (a) turnips, (b) carrots, (c) eggplants, (d) leeks (the Japanese call them Welsh onions), (e) peppers, and (f) pumpkin. You will find all these patterns in pattern 27. Photographs courtesy Nobutoshi Sato and Nobuo Takizawa. (Pattern 27, Sachiko's Vegetables)

a.

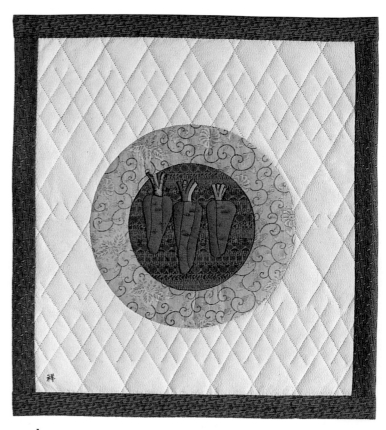

b.

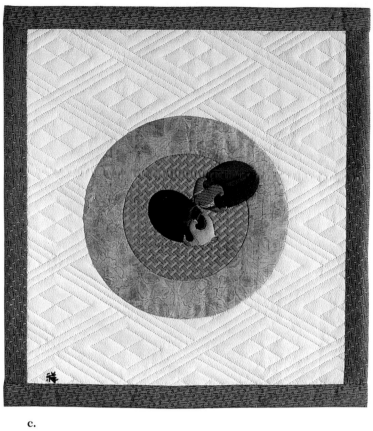

c.

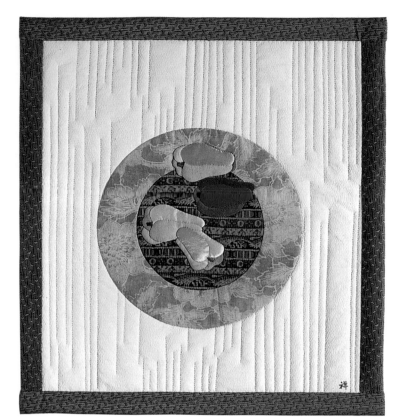

e.

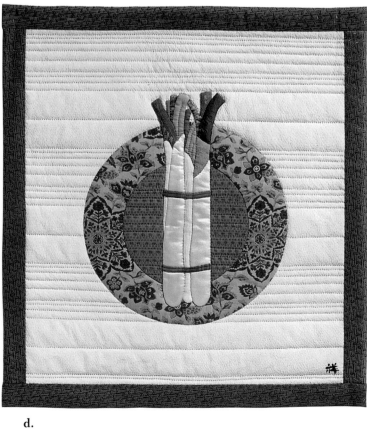

d.

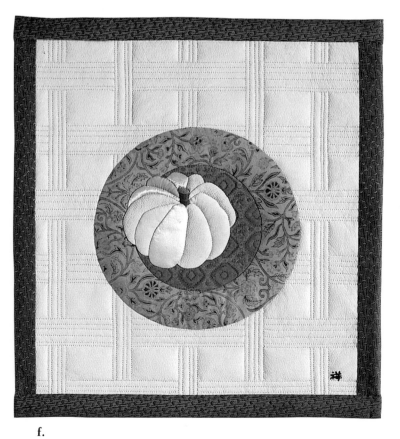

f.

Autumn

Tinged with gentle melancholy as the summer foliage dies away in a defiant blaze of color, autumn is a favorite season of the Japanese. Autumn grasses, foliage, and coloring are depicted more often by Japanese artists than the flowers and tints of any other season. The traditional patterns associated with this season are chrysanthemums and water (fig. 43), maple leaves (fig. 44), and a decorative combination known as the "seven grasses of autumn," which is often seen in art, but which does not seem to have attracted many quiltmakers as yet.

The season starts with the ceremony of the harvest moon on the thirteenth night of September when special offerings are made to the gods, and people enjoy a feast of rice cakes. September is also the season when Mount Fuji settles down for the winter. During the summer season, tens of thousands of people climb Mount Fuji before the climbing season officially ends on August 26. To climb Mount Fuji is a pilgrimage for the Japanese.

Autumn is the season of foliage-viewing, when another kind of pilgrimage is made to see the magnificent fiery red of the maple trees illuminating the countryside, and it is the season when the long-necked cranes arrive from Siberia to winter in Japan.

Cranes are auspicious birds. They are symbols of longevity because once upon a time they were believed to live for a thousand years. The Japanese also use an expression, "the voice of the crane," when a prominent official makes an important decision. Crane patterns abound in Japanese textile art (fig. 45).

43. This detail taken from an antique embroidered kimono, shows chrysanthemums in full bloom being carried along on a flowing stream. This form of chrysanthemum, so similar to the Dresden Plate pattern, appears frequently in Japanese art. Chrysanthemums are often associated with water patterns because it was believed that if you drank the water in which chrysanthemum petals had fallen, you would live forever. This combination of patterns is used on quilts 49 and 50. Eighteenth century; woven silk. (Suntory Museum of Art, Tokyo)

44. This wonderfully colorful fragment of cloth comes from Okinawa, which was an independent kingdom that paid tribute to Japan in the eighteenth century, when this piece was made. Now Okinawa is part of mainland Japan, and this particular form of dyeing, known as *bingata*, was in danger of being lost until efforts were made to revive it as a craft after World War II. Here we see maple leaves scattered across a background patterned with the traditional key-fret design, one of the most popular geometric sashiko patterns. You will find an interesting diamond-block maple-leaf quilt (fig. 51) in this section, but the design on this piece of dyed cloth would also make a lovely quilt. There are patterns for maple leaves and a sashiko key-fret design in the PATTERN INDEX. Eighteenth century; resist-dyeing on silk. (Courtesy the Trustees of the Victoria & Albert Museum, London)

45. Crane patterns were a feature of the stencil-dyed indigo fabrics that were used for furnishings and are so popular with collectors today. Here are pairs of facing cranes set amid scrolling vines, and a stylized version of this pattern is shown in figure 61e. Crane patterns have proved popular with quiltmakers, and there is a crane quilt and two more crane patterns for you to admire in figures 54, 55, and 56c. Twentieth century; stencil-dyed cotton. (Private collection)

46. *Fascinated by Hokusai* by Masako Yamamoto, Beppu City, Oita Prefecture. 1988. Approximately 46″ x 65″ (116 x 164 cm). Old kimono fabrics, cotton, obi fabrics. Hand-pieced and hand-quilted. Katsushika Hokusai was a famous woodblock artist of the nineteenth century, who created a series of pictures featuring Mount Fuji known as the *Thirty-six Views of Mount Fuji*. This one shows the early autumn face of the mountain before the veil of snow arrives. Masako makes an original quilt each year for her group's annual exhibition, and over the years her choice of subject has become more traditionally Japanese. "In 1988, I decided I wanted the challenge of piecework rather than appliqué and so I decided to try and recreate this woodblock print in fabric," she tells us. "I wanted the color to be as close as possible to the original picture, so I spent a great deal of effort looking for old fabrics, and I had the fabric for the clouds especially dyed by a master dyer." She says making this quilt taught her the importance of balance. Notice how she has cleverly changed the scale of her patches to simulate the surface and height of the mountain.

47. *Mount Fuji in the Wind I* by Shizue Kuribayashi, Shizuoka City, Shizuoka Prefecture. 1988. Approximately 67″ x 47″ (170 x 120 cm). Silk kimono fabrics. Hand-piecing and quilting. Shizue is fascinated by Mount Fuji, and this dramatic piece is the first in a series of seven quilts that she has made of the mountain in its various moods. The third in the series was exhibited at the Houston Quilt Festival in 1990. "This one was made from old and new fabrics, including silk kimono pieces given to me by my sister-in-law. The kimono belonged to her husband's mother when she was alive and I thought it was a waste to throw them away," Shizue explains. She is the only quiltmaker to be a member of the Craftmaker's Association of her home prefecture, and she was nominated for membership as a result of the recognition she received for her pictorial quilts made with kimono silk. "And the quilt that started me off was this one, *Mount Fuji in the Wind I*."

48a. *Mount Fuji and Mist* and 48b. *Moon over Water* by Catherine Felix, Ridgewood, New Jersey. 1984. 36″ x 36″ (91 x 91 cm). Cotton, kimono and obi silks, satin. Hand-appliqué, embroidered, and quilted. Catherine made these two attractive floor cushions when she was living in Japan during the early 1980s. For *Mount Fuji and Mist* she selected a well-known kamon that shows the mountain with the same stylized rendering of mist, or water, that we saw on Sachiko Gunji's quilts (figs. 16b and 16d). Catherine is skilled at embroidery, and she has embellished her stylized mist with lines of couched gold thread.

Catherine made *Moon over Water* to celebrate the festival of the harvest moon, the official beginning of the autumn season. Here, she has made the best possible use of her fabric by making the woven patterns reflect her theme. The graceful markings on the moon could be a tree growing beside the flowing stream. She couched with silver thread this time, and the effect of water is created by the woven pattern on the border fabric. The Japanese sit on these large cushions, called *zabuton*, on their tatami mats, so we had them photographed in a traditional setting. Photographs courtesy Ben Simmons. (Pattern 21, Mount Fuji and Mist)

49. *Chrysanthemum* designed by Sanae Hattori and made by Masako Teshima, Tokyo. 1989. Approximately 45″ x 39″ (115 x 100 cm). Cotton, silk, kimono and obi fabrics. Hand-appliqué and quilting. Quilted water patterns make the handsome background in this lovely quilt designed by Sanae Hattori to celebrate the chrysanthemum, the flower of autumn, and which she has worked in a variety of traditional silks. Chrysanthemums and water are usually associated in Japan because of an old Chinese legend that says if you drink the water into which chrysanthemum petals have fallen, you will achieve immortality. Sanae has designed her piece so that it looks like a three-fold screen. The pine-needle pattern on the beautiful obi fabric used for the border is another traditional motif. This quilt appears in Sanae's book, *Sanae Quilt Art*, published by Gakken, Tokyo, 1991. Photograph courtesy the artist. (Pattern 6, Chrysanthemum)

50. *Chrysanthemums and Water* designed by Akio Kawamoto, made by Sachiko Maruyama, Tokyo. 1989. 27″ x 21″ (68 x 53 cm). Hand-dyed cotton. Hand-piecing, appliqué, and quilting. The classic pattern for a chrysanthemum in Japan is the one that quilters everywhere know as Dresden Plate. It forms the crest of the imperial family because of its similarity to the sun; indeed, the alternative names for chrysanthemums in Japanese are "sun splendor" (*nikka*) and "sun spirit" (*nissei*). The imperial family are traditionally said to be descended from the sun goddess. Akio says that he was struck by the fact that this pattern exists in both Japan and America, but it seems likely that the Dresden Plate pattern was inspired by Japanese porcelain in the first place. When the Dresden factory opened in Germany in the eighteenth century, it copied many of its designs from Japanese porcelain, and this particular form of chrysanthemum pattern was often seen on Japanese Imari plates, with each "petal" painted in a different color and with a different geometric pattern. Dresden designs were subsequently copied by the Chelsea and Worcester factories in England, both of which also exported to the United States, so perhaps some enterprising quiltmaker recognized the pattern's potential and thus made quilting history! Akio's intriguing design shows an interesting way of using this old favorite, and he also includes water patterns.

51. *Red Maple Leaves III* designed by Sanae Hattori and made by Masako Kobayashi, Tokyo. 1989. Approximately 79″ x 79″ (200 x 200 cm). Cotton, silk, polyester, kimono fabric. Hand-appliqué, reverse appliqué, piecing, embroidery, and quilting. Here is another of Sanae's spectacular diamond-block quilts, this time made with maple leaves and worked in beautiful autumn colors. Note how she has subtly changed the coloring of the blocks so that they echo maple trees in nature, where each leaf seems to be a different shade. Sanae has used two maple-leaf kamon patterns and worked the veins on one in reverse appliqué, while the other shows the leaf floating on stylized water. Maple leaves and water are another favorite theme in Japanese art. The strong central diamond illuminates the entire quilt like a sudden ray of autumn sunshine. This quilt was featured in Sanae's book, *Sanae Quilt Art*, published by Gakken, Tokyo, 1991. If you would like to make a diamond-block quilt like Sanae's, she has kindly given us permission to include instructions in the PATTERN PROJECTS. Photograph courtesy the artist. (Pattern 20, Maple Leaf)

52. *Bird Mandala—Grapes* by Sachiko Gunji, Nara City, Nara Prefecture. 1988. 20½″ x 14½″ (52 x 37 cm). Antique stencil-dyed fabrics, kimono silk, satin, lamé. Hand-appliqué, quilting, and embroidery. This is another quilt from the series made by Sachiko to celebrate the changing of the seasons as seen through an exotic window. Two others (figs. 25a and 25b) are illustrated in the Spring section. This mandala honors the autumn grape harvest. Although wine drinking is relatively new in Japan, grapes have always been a delicacy and have been grown as much for their beauty as for their flavor. Sachiko's grapes have a wonderfully graphic quality achieved by the clever way she has worked solid and patterned fabrics in different colors. Photograph courtesy Nobutoshi Sato and Nobuo Takizawa.

53. *The Vintage* by Jill Liddell, London, England. 1989. 57″ x 42″ (145 x 107 cm). Furnishing cottons, jacquard weaves, and hessian. Machine-piecing, hand appliqué. I was bored with printed calicoes and wanted to try and make a quilt from furnishing fabrics, so I bought some remnants from a local shop, and as my husband and I had just returned from France where the grape harvest had been in full swing, I chose grapes as my subject. I have long been fascinated by the way the Japanese break up geometric patterns, either by overlaying them with floral motifs, or by dissolving parts of the pattern as if it was shrouded in mist. So much of the habitable land in Japan is composed of narrow mountain valleys where mist often lingers and one's vision is fragmented, so this type of design actually reflects Japan's landscape. The broken check pattern was taken from an eighteenth-century kimono in the Tokyo National Museum collection, and the circular pattern of grapes and leaves is a family crest. I scattered extra leaves, reversing them to add interest. (Pattern 12, Grapes)

54. *Autumn Nostalgia* by Chizuko Hana Hill, Cadiz, Kentucky. 1989. 90″ x 67″ (229 x 170 cm). Cottons. Hand-and machine-piecing, hand-quilting. Chizuko is a Japanese, married to an American, and came to live in Kentucky in 1984. A neighbor introduced her to the local quilting guild, and since then she has made thirteen quilts, three of which have been accepted by the American Quilter's Society for their annual show at Paducah, Kentucky. This fascinating quilt won first prize for "innovative pieced quilts" in the 1991 show. The design is a happy mixture of East and West, for Chizuko has taken an American pieced pattern of maple leaves but has scattered the leaves randomly in the Japanese manner. She says that the arrangement was based on her knowledge of kimono design, and the coloring of the quilt and her positioning of the two *origami* cranes at bottom right reflect this. The Japanese have a special affection for cranes, which come each year from Siberia to winter in Japan. An old legend says that they live for a thousand years, so crane patterns are often used on wedding kimono and trousseaux. Another of Chizuko's award-winning quilts, *Fan-ta-see*, appears in the Summer section (fig. 41). (Pattern 9, Origami Crane)

55. *Thousand Cranes* by Kazuko Yoneyama, Chigasaki City, Kanagawa Prefecture. 1988. 51″ x 72″ (129 x 184 cm). Cotton, hand-appliqué, and quilting. This is Kazuko's first quilt. Hitherto she had done embroidery, but a friend invited her to join a quilting class in 1987, and she says that "by making this, I learned everything there is to know about quiltmaking. I designed the quilt as I worked, appliquéing the cranes one by one. I did not plan where to put each crane, so I had no idea of the overall design until it was finished. Then I saw a documentary on TV about the cranes in Kyushu (the southern island of Japan) flying back to Siberia at the end of the winter, and I was pleased to see that in flight they looked exactly the same as my quilt design!" Kazuko is interested in her country's history and often visits museums and art galleries. She likes to make up traditional Japanese patterns in Western fabrics, because, she says, "that way I can introduce classical Japanese patterns into modern life."

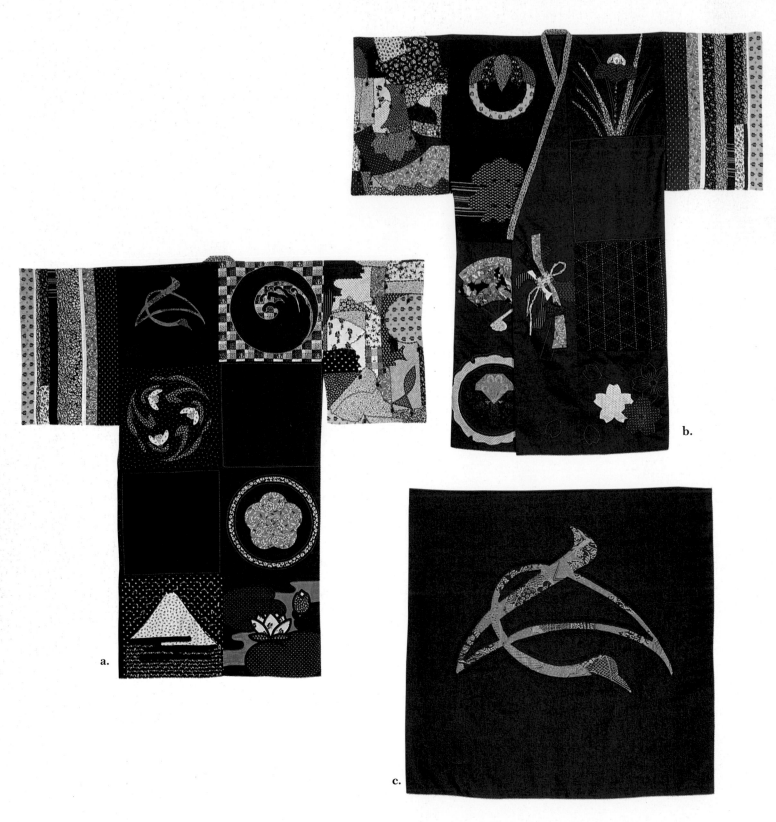

56a, 56b, 56c. *Japanese Kimono* by Jenni Dobson, Loughborough, England. 1990. Cottons, poly-cottons, crepe-de-chine, lace, beads, fusible interfacing. Hand-and-machine appliqué, machine-piecing, stained-glass window technique, sashiko stitching, and embroidery. "I really wanted to make something for myself for a change," Jenni says. "So many of my quilts have been given away, and as I love Japanese designs I decided to make myself a kimono in blue and white fabrics, but with the odd flash of color." Jenni's interest in Japanese design was sparked by the "Great Japan Exhibition" held in London in 1981–1982, and she thought she would design her kimono like a sampler quilt to illustrate various piecing and appliqué techniques, but using typical Japanese designs based on nature. "I was astonished to find that my kimono took more 14-inch blocks than you would need for a double quilt, but designing them was both an intellectual and a practical exercise." She strip-pieced one sleeve and crazy-quilted the other, which she then embellished with beads. She has given us permission to feature her design of a calligraphic crane (detail illustration), and you will find it in the PATTERN INDEX. Amazingly, considering all the work involved, Jenni wears this beautiful kimono as a bathrobe! (Pattern 7, Jenni's Calligraphic Crane)

60

Winter

Winter in parts of Japan means lovely, crisp, cold days, air like chilled champagne, no rain, and just a frosting of snow. On the west coast and in the mountains, snowfalls are heavy and villages can be cut off for weeks. But snow is auspicious; it fills the rivers and fertilizes the soil, and the Japanese honor it with a motif, a crenelated ring that is often used to frame flowers of all the seasons (fig. 57).

In the olden days, fires were a winter hazard. Charcoal burners kept people warm inside their traditional wooden houses, and watchmen patrolled the streets at night warning householders to extinguish all fires before they went to bed, but some did not listen, and their houses went up in smoke. Burning houses were known euphemistically as the "flowers of Edo," Edo being the old name for Tokyo.

The floral motifs associated with Winter are the pine, the bamboo, and the plum, a decorative combination known as "the three companions of the deep cold" to Chinese and Japanese artists of the past, and as *shochikubai* (pine, bamboo, and plum) to the Japanese today.

In the Confucian classics this attractive trio symbolized fidelity and fortitude because the pine and the bamboo withstand the worst weather with their leaves intact, while the plum (in reality a form of *prunus*) flowers in mid-winter, and the blossoms remain faithfully on the tree for several weeks, no matter what the weather brings.

When Confucian virtues became fashionable in Japan during the Edo period (1600–1867), the ideals of perseverance and fidelity associated with these three trees made this decorative combination a popular and an appropriate motif for brides! It was found on wedding kimono and on household furnishings—the lovely indigo-dyed furniture covers and bedding that used to form part of a bridal trousseau before American percale arrived on the scene (fig. 58).

Today, most young Japanese have forgotten the Confucian associations and merely regard pine, bamboo, and plum as an auspicious pattern. They do, however, remain a popular combination for wedding kimono.

As we discussed in the introduction, the Japanese are very fond of circular patterns. The majority of kamon are circular or are enclosed in a circle. This type of pattern derived originally from Chinese textile patterns, but in their inimitable way the Japanese have altered the symmetry of the old Chinese woven motifs and made them more naturalistic by introducing irregularity. These circular patterns are called *marumon*, and they are some of the loveliest of all the Japanese patterns (fig. 59). We shall see some on quilts in this section.

Mid-winter brings the New Year, and the New Year brings renewal. The Japanese housewife scrubs the house from top to bottom, debts are settled, and bills are paid. It is a family celebration that shuts the whole of the country down for three days, and when it is over, the Japanese see a promise of spring and the cycle of the changing seasons beginning once more.

57. Snow is lucky in Japan; it fills the rivers and waters the land. With their affection for incongruity, the Japanese designers of the eighteenth century often enclosed summer flowers such as wisteria and irises within a crenelated ring to represent snow, such as you see on this fine kimono. An English quiltmaker borrowed the snow-ring to enclose patterns on her quilt (fig. 61), and we liked the idea so much that you will find a pattern for it in the PATTERN INDEX. Eighteenth century; embroidery on silk. (Tokyo National Museum)

58. One of the most popular decorative combinations in Japanese art and design is a group of three floral patterns associated with winter. These are clusters of pine leaves, sprays of bamboo, and scattered plum blossoms. The Japanese generally call this combination *shochikubai*, which means "pine, bamboo, and plum," but in the past Chinese and Japanese artists gave them the romantic name of "the three companions of the deep cold," or "the three friends of winter." On this *futon* cover, the three trees are representational, but you will find them interpreted in pattern form on several quilts in this section. Late nineteenth century; stencil-dyed cotton. (Private collection)

59. Because the crane is a symbol of good luck and long life, crane patterns appear in all Japanese decorative arts. This fragment of seventeenth-century kimono fabric is woven with scattered medallions set against a background of diamonds. Here you can see the facing crane pattern and the triple hollyhock, both of which appear in figure 61. Seventeenth century; woven silk. (Tokyo National Museum)

60. *Firemen's Standards* by Tomiko Kikuchi, Toride City, Ibaragi Prefecture. 1989. Approximately 106″ x 102″ (270 x 260 cm). Cotton, aizome, and kimono fabrics. Hand-piecing, appliqué, and quilting. In the olden days fighting the fires that regularly ravaged the big cities was a vital task, particularly during the winter when an overturned charcoal heater could set a whole street of wooden houses alight. The big landlords provided their own fire-fighting teams, consisting mostly of samurai, and each neighborhood also had a private team who kept watch throughout the night. There was a hierarchy, of course, and different uniforms for different grades of firemen. The local teams were naturally less dressy and it was the sight of a happi coat in an antiques shop with a crest on the back, the sort of thing a local fireman would have worn, that inspired this interesting quilt. Firemen still carry special standards bearing crests and streamers on ceremonial occasions, so Tomiko placed her two standards against a pyramid of pieced flames. The strip-piecing in the background creates the effect of the city asleep under the night sky. Tomiko says she likes to work with her country's traditions: "I like to look for new ideas in old things."

61a, 61b, 61c, 61d, 61e, 61f, 61g, 61h. *Winter's Joy* by Jenni Dobson, Loughborough, England. 1991. 63″ x 44″ (160 x 111 cm). Cottons, cotton furnishing fabrics. Hand-appliqué and quilting. Knowing Jenni's interest in Japanese design, and having seen her lovely kimono made with kamon patterns (fig. 56), we asked her if she would like to make a scattered marumon quilt for us (marumon is the Japanese name for circular patterns). We gave her two patterns to start her off and she adapted the rest from antique stencil-dyed furnishing fabrics, or from kamon. She has given us permission to reproduce her patterns, so you will find all the ones shown in the detail illustrations in the PATTERN INDEX. "While I was making the quilt," she tells us, "I made a real effort to try and free myself from the Western obsession with symmetry and matched colors. Although I found it difficult to scatter the patterns in the natural way the Japanese do, after I had finished I felt I knew much more about Japanese design. The quilt was a marvelous learning exercise—and a joy to make!" We were delighted with the result. See how she has framed some of her patterns in the crenelated ring that represents snow, a nice touch for a winter quilt, and she has done some beautiful quilting with the key-fret pattern that you will also find in the PATTERN INDEX. If you would like to make a marumon quilt like Jenni's, directions are given in PATTERN PROJECTS. Photographs courtesy the artist and Noel Manchee.

61b. Bamboo Wreath (pattern 1). This pattern was drawn up by Gill Bryan from a resist-dyed futon cover, and we gave it to Jenni to try out.

61c. Pine Wreath (pattern 25). This was taken from a stenciled pattern on a piece of antique furnishing fabric.

61d. Chrysanthemum (pattern 6). Jenni gave the chrysanthemum pointed petals for a change.

61e. Facing Cranes (pattern 8). This is the pattern we saw on the fragment of brocade in figure 59.

61g. Hollyhock (pattern 13). This is the crest of the Tokugawas, the shogunal family that ruled Japan for the best part of 250 years. It also appears in figure 59, and on the storage jar in figure 11.

61h. Bush Clover (pattern 3) and Snow-ring (pattern 30). Jenni enclosed her bush-clover kamon pattern in a snow-ring. She also used one to enclose the character for "Joy" (top right corner of the quilt). "Joy" is Jenni's Oriental signature. You will find it embroidered on her kimono in the bottom left corner of the calligraphic crane block (fig. 56c), and it is also reflected in the title of this quilt.

62. *Dancing Pine Tree 1* designed by Sanae Hattori and made by Yoko Ogata, Tokyo. 1989. Approximately 69″ x 67″ (185 x 180 cm). Cotton, silk, kimono and obi fabrics. Hand-piecing, appliqué, and quilting. Here is another of Sanae's diamond-block quilts, this time depicting pine trees, which are always associated with winter. The coloring of this intriguing piece is faintly autumnal, as if Sanae was loath to say goodbye to the warmth and color of the final months of the year. The umbrella shape of the pine trees is typical of both Chinese and Japanese art, and it is used not only to represent the tree, as you see here, but also clusters of needles at the end of a branch. The pine is an auspicious pattern, for it symbolizes stability and resilience, and together with bamboo and plum blossom, it was called by Chinese and Japanese artists one of the "three companions of the deep cold." However, the pine tree is often used on its own to denote long life. This quilt is featured in Sanae's book, *Sanae Quilt Art*, published by Gakken, Tokyo, 1991. If you would like to try your hand at making a diamond-block quilt, Sanae has kindly given us permission to include instructions in PATTERN PROJECTS. Photograph courtesy the artist.

63. *The Three Companions of the Deep Cold* by Jenni Dobson, Loughborough, England. 1990. 32″ x 32″ (81 x 81 cm). Kimono cottons, hand-dyed cotton, and silk. Hand- and machine-piecing, hand-appliqué, and quilting. The theme of the Great Northern British Quilt Show in 1991 was "Influenced by Japan," and this was Jenni's entry. "I chose the patterns for several reasons," she says. "I like the idea of patterns having auspicious meanings. I liked the ancient title the Japanese gave to this particular combination of motifs, but I also chose them because I have a January birthday!" Jenni was given some samples of Japanese indigo-dyed cottons that she pieced for the background. The three pine trees, and the partially hidden plum blossom in the center, were adapted from kamon, and she continued her theme with a sashiko pattern known as "pine-bark diamond" (*matsukawabishi*), which she broke in places to create irregularity in true Japanese style. Jenni does her sashiko-stitching with normal quilting thread through all three layers, but just makes a larger stitch. She gave us permission to reproduce her pine-tree pattern, and you will find it in the PATTERN INDEX. Photograph courtesy the artist and Noel Manchee. (Pattern 26, Jenni's Pine Trees; Sashiko Pattern 7, Pine-bark Diamond)

64. *Snow on the Bamboo Leaves* by Sanae Hattori, Tokyo. 1988. Approximately 53″ x 57″ (135 x 145 cm). Kimono and obi fabric, cotton, silk, polyester. Hand-piecing, appliqué, quilting, and embroidery. Most of Sanae's quilts are gorgeous representations of traditional Japanese art, but in this instance, she has deliberately used subdued colors to create the subtlety of Japanese black-ink painting (*sumie*), which is reproduced in the central panel. This outstanding work is truly Japanese in other respects, for the inspiration for the design came from *Kyogen* costumes. Kyogen is a comic interlude that is always enacted during a production of a classical Noh drama, and Sanae's bamboo with its halo of snow is also traditional. Snow is often depicted as a crenelated ring (see figs. 16f and 61). Sanae likes to mix her fabrics. "The brightness of Western fabrics suits my quilts," she says, "but my subject matter is always Japanese. Ever since my childhood, I have been interested in my country's history and culture." This quilt won an American International Quilt Association's gold-ribbon award at Houston in 1989 and is also featured in Sanae's book, *Sanae Quilt Art*, published by Gakken, Tokyo, 1991. Photograph courtesy the artist.

65. *Souvenir of Japan* by Erica Main, Wellington, New Zealand. 1985. 68″ x 45″ (172 x 114 cm). Yukata cottons, Japanese sheeting. Hand-appliqué and quilting. Bamboo and plum blossoms appear on this charming quilt (top left and top right) made by Erica as a souvenir of her stay in Japan during the 1980s, but she has substituted an origami crane for the other traditional winter pattern, the pine tree. Cranes are a lucky pattern symbolizing long life and are often seen in conjunction with bamboo, plum blossom, or pine motifs. All Erica's designs were taken from kamon, and she liked the idea of using them in a traditional marumon form. She first worked each of the circular patterns on a square of fabric to avoid stretching the bias edges, and then cut them out and applied them to the background. She quilted two more circular kamon patterns at the top or bottom of each line of blocks, and used the traditional Blue Wave as a quilting pattern on the borders.

66. *God of Thunder* by Miwako Kimura, Tokyo, Japan. 1992. Approximately 68″ x 68″ (175 x 175 cm). Antique stencil-dyed cottons, *kasuri* (Japanese ikat), old kimono silk, new cottons. Hand-piecing, appliqué, reverse appliqué, quilting, and sashiko stitching. The marvelous depth and texture in this magnificent quilt depicts the storms of winter to perfection. Miwako likes to work with traditional images, building pattern upon pattern. Her theme represents *Raijin*, the god of thunder, one of a pair of gods that are frequently seen in Buddhist painting and sculpture. (The other god is *Fujin*, the god of wind.) "Raijin is the ruler of thunder and lightning," Miwako explains, "and usually carries a number of drums around with him, but my interpretation of this motif is the rhythm and music of the universe rather than ritual figures." You can see the drum in the top right corner, and under it Miwako has pieced what she calls "the drum's echoes" reverberating into a storm-tossed sea. The reverse-appliqué cloud shapes and sashiko-stitched diamonds in the sky are traditional patterns. The concentric design on the diamonds echoes the blinding streak of lightning in the center of the quilt. Miwako creates her masterpieces by making a full-scale drawing and then working each section using various quilting techniques. She loves to work with old fabrics.

67. *Noshi* by Jill Liddell, London, England. 1984. 67″ x 43″ (178 x 114 cm). Printed cottons. Hand-appliqué and quilting. The year's cycle is finished, and we end our journey through the changing seasons with the traditional Japanese talisman, the *noshi*, which is an emblem of good fortune associated with the New Year. I fell in love with the noshi the moment I first saw it on the beautiful eighteenth-century kimono that illustrated figure 3. The kimono was one of the centerpieces of an exhibition in Kyoto, and the emblem seemed to beckon to me. I thought it would make a marvelous quilt as it embodied all the elements of Japanese design—movement, irregularity, asymmetry. I made a full-scale drawing of the design and used this for my templates. Because the noshi was once connected with the sea, I set my noshi against a quilted background of water-based sashiko patterns (diamond, Blue Wave, and the net pattern). The cranes and the hexagons are there for luck, and the quilt has indeed proved lucky for me. It was chosen for a major exhibition of Japanese quilts in Tokyo and consequently gave me an *entrée* into the Japanese quilt world. I used the complete noshi, but see what a Japanese quiltmaker, Hiroko Oyama, does with the same emblem on the opposite page! This quilt was also reproduced in *Hands All Around*, published by E. P. Dutton, New York, 1987.

68. *Noshi* by Hiroko Oyama, Oita City, Oita Prefecture. 1987. Approximately 33½" x 22½" (85 x 57 cm). Old fabrics, aizome, kasuri. Hand-appliqué and quilting. In her version of the ancient noshi, Hiroko creates a wonderful sense of mystery. It is as if the old year is over so the emblem is beginning to slip away, set on some unknown course of its own. Hiroko says that she was attracted by the design after she had seen an entire wall in a hotel covered with noshi emblems, and she made her quilt with old fabrics because she loves the sense of calm that working with old fabric brings. "With a little ingenuity, even fabric with holes in it, or fabric that has become thin with wear, can be reborn and this gives me great pleasure." Hiroko silhouetted her noshi against a background of sashiko hexagons, another symbol of good fortune and long life. She has given us permission to reproduce her noshi in the PATTERN INDEX. (Pattern 22, Noshi)

Geometric Patterns

Japan is richly endowed with a number of beautiful geometric patterns that crop up in all aspects of Japanese life.

Many of these patterns are very ancient and resulted from improved weaving techniques in China. The Chinese developed relatively sophisticated looms capable of weaving complex structures at least a thousand years before the Christian era. The popular key-fret design (*sayagata*) that appears on the ceramic storage jar in figure 11 and resist-dyed on the fragment of cloth from Okinawa in figure 45 is one of these woven patterns.

Chinese geometric patterns were transmitted to Japan by Korean weavers, who were brought to the country in the sixth century to teach the local craftsmen. The patterns then became part of the Japanese design treasury, and they were used by craftsmen working in all branches of the decorative arts. For example, the old Chinese design of interlocking squares that you see on the lovely tie-dyed kimono in figure 69, is also used in architecture, on porcelain, as a marquetry pattern, or in a simplified form of two interlocking squares as a family crest. It has now become a piecework pattern, as you will see below.

The Japanese added patterns to the treasury, of course, and usually gave them names associated with nature, or with tangible objects. The well-known pattern that you see worked in sashiko on the coat sleeves in figure 70 began life as a woven pattern, but some artisan noticed that it bore a resemblance to a hemp leaf, so renamed it *asanoha*. You will find other examples with names taken from rush mats, the bark of a pine tree, and flying plovers in the SASHIKO PATTERN INDEX.

These ancient geometric patterns are, of course, tailor-made for sashiko (fig. 71). Originally, sashiko was merely a running stitch, a form of flat-quilting that was used to repair or strengthen the coarse cloth made from woven fibers such as hemp and mulberry, with which peasant clothing was made before cotton became widely available. Women used to stitch layers of these bast-fiber fabrics together for warmth (there was no wool in those days), and the coldness of a winter would be judged by the number of layers needed to keep warm. "It's been a winter of three layers," farmers would say.

Sashiko ceased to be necessary once cheap cotton clothing became available, and the craft then became decorative, much as quilting did in Europe. Nowadays, sashiko is international. Needlewomen everywhere are borrowing this attractive craft to embellish vests, placemats, or to add an Oriental sparkle to their quilts.

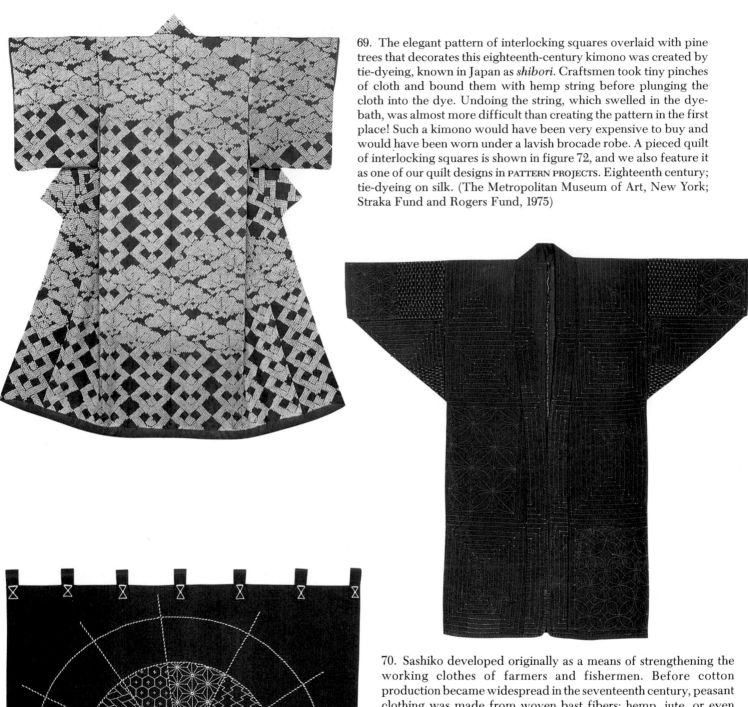

69. The elegant pattern of interlocking squares overlaid with pine trees that decorates this eighteenth-century kimono was created by tie-dyeing, known in Japan as *shibori*. Craftsmen took tiny pinches of cloth and bound them with hemp string before plunging the cloth into the dye. Undoing the string, which swelled in the dye-bath, was almost more difficult than creating the pattern in the first place! Such a kimono would have been very expensive to buy and would have been worn under a lavish brocade robe. A pieced quilt of interlocking squares is shown in figure 72, and we also feature it as one of our quilt designs in PATTERN PROJECTS. Eighteenth century; tie-dyeing on silk. (The Metropolitan Museum of Art, New York; Straka Fund and Rogers Fund, 1975)

70. Sashiko developed originally as a means of strengthening the working clothes of farmers and fishermen. Before cotton production became widespread in the seventeenth century, peasant clothing was made from woven bast fibers: hemp, jute, or even mulberry. Several layers of this loosely woven cloth were also stitched together for warmth. Originally, sashiko was no more than a running stitch that followed the weft of the fabric, but in time it became decorative, and borrowed heavily from the library of traditional geometric patterns, as can be seen in this handsome nineteenth-century cotton work coat. (Collection of Takako Onoyama, Tokyo; photograph courtesy the owner)

71. Sashiko is a popular hobby for many Japanese women, and kits can be bought at any department store. Traditionally, sashiko is done in white stranded cotton on indigo-dyed fabric, such as you see here in this attractive sampler of traditional patterns, which was designed and made by Kazuko Yoshiura. Photograph courtesy Noel Manchee.

72. *Interlocking Squares* by Yukiko Endo, Minami–Ashigara City, Kanagawa Prefecture. 1988. Approximately 91″ x 83″ (232 x 210 cm). Cotton and kimono fabric. Machine-piecing and hand-quilting. The pattern of interlocking squares seen on the kimono in figure 69 is often used by the makers of the popular marquetry that comes from Hakone near Mount Fuji. Yukiko was born and raised near Hakone and says that just as people long ago found patterns in things around them, so she also finds her quilt designs from things around her. "There are many beautiful and simple Japanese designs," she says, "which I enjoy interpreting in a fabric medium." In this lovely, tranquil quilt she used some kimono fabric that was left to her by an aunt. "I have no children, so after I am gone, I feel that my quilts may serve as a proof of my existence. My aunt was also childless and among her possessions was a kimono that was given to her by her mother (my grandmother) as a keepsake. I used this kimono fabric in my quilt to keep her memory alive too." Yukiko has kindly agreed to let us adapt her quilt design as a project for you to make. You will find the directions in PATTERN PROJECTS. We also give another pattern of interlocking squares taken from a kamon that has a different construction in the PATTERN INDEX. (Pattern 16, Interlocking Squares)

73. *Sounds of the Sea* by Emiko Toda Loeb, New York. 1991. 65″ x 86″ (165 x 218 cm). Antique Japanese cottons. Machine-pieced, hand-sashiko stitching. Emiko is Japanese, and married to an American, and although she makes stunning quilts based on American patterns, she says that working with traditional Japanese patterns and fabrics seems more natural to her. "I grew up with these patterns; they were all around me, although not necessarily in fabric." The piecework pattern she has used on this outstanding quilt is the diamond version of the ancient Blue Wave pattern. (Sanae Hattori used a clamshell version of this pattern in her quilt, *Thousand Waves*, figure 38.) Emiko has created a wonderful sense of movement by varying the size of her diamond blocks, the largest measure 20″ (50.8 cm) across and the smallest 4″ (10.2 cm), and one can sense the surge of the waves. Being a true Japanese, she chose to break the geometry of the design, by overlaying it with a curvaceous sashiko pattern based on flying birds called Linked Plovers *(Chidori-tsunagi)*, which she did by hand; no mean feat considering the thickness of her antique fabrics and the number of seams in each block! Emiko held a one-woman show in New York in 1991, where this quilt was a centerpiece. She has kindly allowed us to adapt her design as one of our PATTERN PROJECTS. Photograph courtesy the artist. (Pattern 2, Diamond Blue Wave; Sashiko Pattern 8, Linked Plovers)

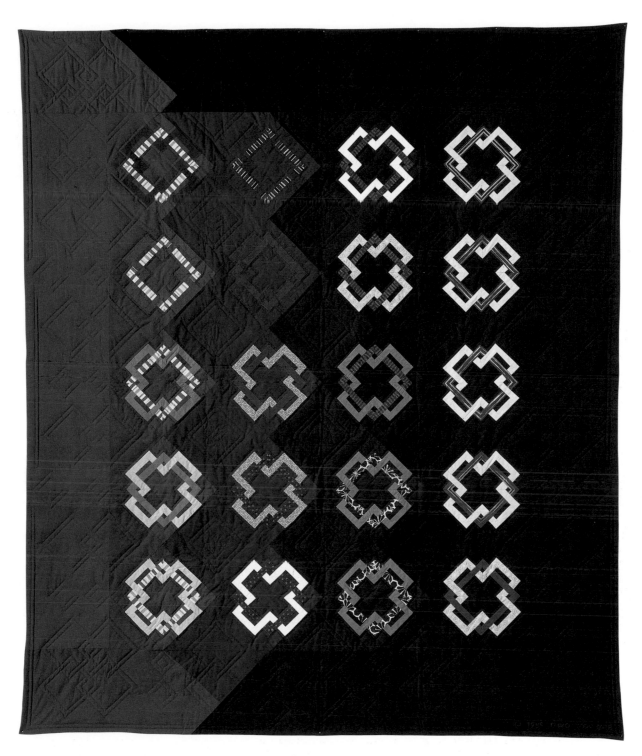

74. *Knotted Square* by Emiko Toda Loeb, New York. 1985. 80″ x 67″ (200 x 167.5 cm). Japanese and American cottons. Machine-pieced, hand-quilted with silk thread. "This was the first time I had tried making the background of a quilt in different shades of one color," Emiko told us. "At the time, this was exciting, but it is less so today because I have done it frequently since then." She adapted the pattern for this interesting quilt from a kamon and shares the pattern with us in the PATTERN INDEX. Notice how some of the alternate blocks are quilted with a design of two interlocking squares that is similar to Yukiko Endo's pattern in figure 72. Emiko has enjoyed sewing from childhood, although she never thought of it other than as a hobby until she took up quiltmaking seriously in 1981. She majored in music at Kyoto University of Education and taught the piano until 1977, when she came to the United States to marry an American composer. Ironically, it was then that she decided that music was not the right profession for her! Since 1981, Emiko has made a name for herself with a series of fabulous reversible Log Cabin quilts and systematic Crazy quilts, and has a growing collection of prize-winning ribbons to show for it. She teaches in New York and every summer returns to her native Kyoto, to teach there also. Photograph courtesy the artist. (Pattern 18, Knotted Square)

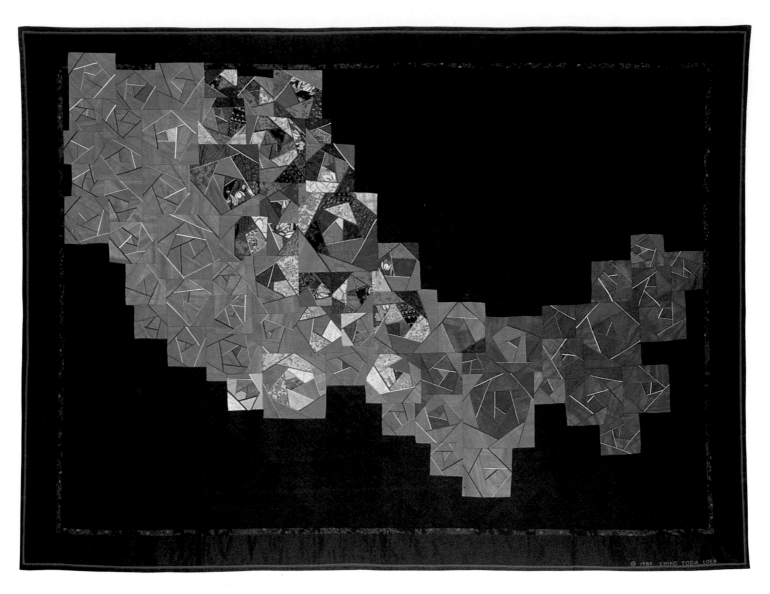

75. *Flower Poem* by Emiko Toda Loeb, New York. 1989. 67″ x 91″ (139 x 232 cm). Silk, hand-dyed cotton, commercial cottons, some rayon. Machine-piecing and hand appliqué. Emiko's design for this outstanding quilt is quintessentially Japanese. Quite apart from the asymmetric placement of the flower blocks, the coloring and pattern of the background could very well be that of a kimono. We have already seen from the introductions to the other sections how the Japanese enjoy the contrast of a strong geometric pattern overlaid with floral motifs; the antique kimono shown in figure 6 is a good example. Emiko has taken this traditional artistic concept and given it a contemporary twist. For the black background, she has pieced a geometric pattern known as *higaki*, meaning "cypress fence," and contrasted it with a spray of pieced flowers. Even the way the flower petals fold is reminiscent of a kimono. Emiko says she took the idea from the way women fold their kimono collars at the neck, one on top of another. This quilt was hung in the Fabric Gardens exhibition at Expo '90 in Osaka, Japan, and a photograph of it was made into a postcard to be sold at the exhibition. Photograph courtesy the artist. (Sashiko Pattern 4, Cypress Fence)

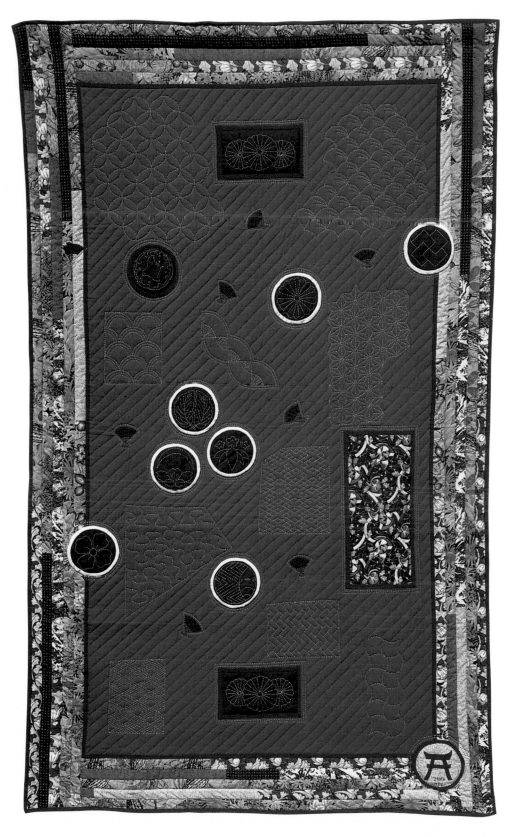

76. *Sashiko Fantasy* by Irma Chelsworth, Via Lismore, N.S.W., Australia. 1989. 94″ x 54″ (240 x 142 cm). Cotton fabrics. Sashiko stitching in traditional sashiko thread, hand-appliqué and quilting. Many elements of Japanese design are combined in this handsome sashiko quilt made by an Australian. "Three trips to Japan, and an interest in Japanese history gave me the idea of a quilt embodying traditional sashiko patterns with floating symbols and family crests," Irma tells us. "The scattered fans represent the elegance of Japanese culture (notice how one fan is escaping into the left border), and the various sashiko designs and emblems helped me to demonstrate to my students the versatility of sashiko in a contemporary quilt." Irma has a Japanese daughter-in-law who helped her translate books on sashiko as there is very little on the subject written in English. She says, "The simplicity of sashiko stitching appeals to my sense of order, and the interesting story behind each crest and symbol added so much to my enjoyment." Irma is a self-taught quilter and has exhibited her work in three capital cities in Australia where one of her quilts won a major award and Viewer's Choice. Photograph courtesy Hugh Nicholson.

77. *Foggy Day Leaves* by Roberta Horton, Berkeley, California. 1984. 34″ x 43″ (86 x 109 cm). Japanese yukata cottons. Machine-pieced, hand and sashiko-quilted by Roberta and Mary Mashuta. This quilt combines a pleasing blend of East and West; classic American piecework patterns, Japanese fabrics, and panels of fine geometric sashiko stitching. "I was attracted to Japanese fabrics because they were so unlike the American textiles available to us in the early 1980s," Roberta tells us. "San Francisco has a very strong Asian influence—Japanese food and Japanese architecture—so it was logical to get interested in Japanese textiles. Of course, having a store that imported yukata fabrics right here in Berkeley was a big factor too." Roberta had seen sashiko stitching on garments in local museums and immediately recognized its potential. She actually taught sashiko before she started working with Japanese fabrics. Even though she has moved on now to other fabrics, she says that her work still has a Japanese influence. She has published several books: *Stained Glass Quilting Techniques, An Amish Adventure, Calico and Beyond,* and *Plaids and Stripes*, published by C & T Publishing, Lafayette, California. Photograph courtesy Sharon Risedorph and Lynn Keller.

78. *Tama (Jewel)* by Janet Shore, Berkeley, California. 1984. 32½″ x 24″ (82 x 61 cm). Japanese yukata fabrics. Machine-pieced, hand and sashiko-quilted (through the top only). Janet joined one of Roberta Horton's classes and designed this attractive quilt of a jewel suspended against a quilted background, which she intersected by a panel of sashiko done in the hemp-leaf pattern. Since making this quilt, she has visited Japan and she, too, says that her work still reflects a Japanese influence. Photograph courtesy Sharon Risedorph and Lynn Keller. (Sashiko Pattern 5, Hemp Leaf)

79. *My Grandmother* by Tetsu Wakamatsu, Sapporo City, Hokkaido. 1986. 29" x 17" (74 x 43 cm). Silk crepe and antique indigo-dyed cotton. Hand-piecing and sashiko-stitching. The pieced blocks made in multi-colored silk crepe in this attractive quilt were put together some seventy years ago by the grandmother of a quilter named Toyoko Fujisaki. This particular pattern was fashionable at that time and many women made ornamental patchwork from scraps of kimono fabric. When her aunt gave Toyoko these blocks, she decided to combine them with traditional sashiko. She has used a number of patterns that you will find in our PATTERN INDEX, either as appliqué patterns that could be adapted for sashiko, or as sashiko patterns. Toyoko exhibited the quilt in 1986 under her grandmother's name, Tetsu Wakamatsu, and was delighted when the quilt was featured in *Patchwork Quilt Tsushin*. She says that she feels her grandmother "would also be very happy to know that her quilt was going to appear in a book published in America." (Pattern 9, Origami Crane; Pattern 28, Wisteria; Sashiko Pattern 4, Cypress Fence; Sashiko Pattern 8, Linked Plovers)

80. *The Tale of Genji Picture Scroll* by Chizuko Tatsuyama, Beppu City, Oita Prefecture. 1989. 71″ x 71″ (180 x 180 cm). Old kimono silk, crepe, old indigo-dyed fabrics, obi silk. Hand-piecing and quilting. This stunning quilt captures the essence of old and new Japan, and it is a splendid piece with which to end this section of our book, for it combines traditional Japanese and American designs and thus pays homage to both cultures. The title is reflected in the fabric the artist used for the border. It was cut from an old obi that was painted with scenes from the eleventh-century Japanese literary masterpiece, *The Tale of Genji*, which is discussed in the introduction. Genji illustrations have formed one of the main themes for Japanese scroll-paintings since the novel was written, and Chizuko explains that her striking composition of circles is also suggestive of a rolled-up picture scroll. "I feel nostalgia for the colors and patterns of old fabrics, and I think it is important to hand down our traditions by reviving them in a contemporary form," she tells us. "So I wondered how it would look if I made Nine Patch blocks from all these old fabrics that I had been given, or had bought myself. That is the way my design started, and then it developed into something quite different." She feels that her "Genji" theme is also evident in the elegant coloring and the flower patterns on the silks she used.

Tips and Techniques

In the following section, you will find a description of all the various techniques that you will need to make a quilt with the patterns contained in the PATTERN INDEX. Each technique is listed under the appropriate heading and is given in chronological order. Thus we start with design, and then work through template-making, various sewing techniques, and finish with quilting and binding.

At the end of the book, following the PATTERN INDEX, you will find a section called PATTERN PROJECTS. This section contains construction diagrams for five quilt settings based on quilts that are featured in this book and includes yardages and directions. These settings are intended to be just a launching pad, and we hope that after having made one or two of them, you will then go on to use the patterns to make a quilt of your own design.

Good design knows no boundaries, and one of the great strengths of quiltmaking is that it has constantly absorbed influences from all over the world. Quilters today regularly mix traditional American patterns with designs that originated in China, Persia, India, or Europe, and the purpose of this book is to contribute a range of new patterns and design ideas to the standard quiltmaking library.

In the first section of TIPS AND TECHNIQUES, we give you five basic principles of Japanese design to play around with, and, of course, you will have absorbed other ideas from the wonderful quilts illustrated on the preceding pages. But please do not think that you have to make a "Japanese" quilt with Japanese fabrics and in Japanese colors unless that is what you *want* to do.

You could make an album quilt, for example. The 1850s witnessed the creation of the Baltimore Album quilts with their elaborate appliqué patterns, so the 1990s might see the start of a new fashion for Japanese album quilts!

You could include some of our patterns in your next sampler quilt, or one of the wreath patterns could be enlarged on a photocopier to form the centerpiece of a medallion quilt.

Make use of modern technology and enlarge or reduce the patterns on a photocopier to suit your fancy, but it is important to remember that you may only use such a photocopy for your own personal use, otherwise you infringe the law of copyright. For example, you may not make copies of a pattern for distribution to your friends or your students, without prior permission from the publisher.

You could play around with the patterns and extract individual elements such as a single sprig of bamboo, an individual plum blossom, or a pine tree and enlarge these on a photocopier to make yet more patterns.

The possibilities are endless and we hope you will enjoy working with these patterns.

1. DESIGN

Most quiltmakers shy away from designing an original quilt, for they prefer to stick to the tried and the trusted. But if you can find the courage to explore your own creativity, the reward for the extra effort is really so great.

Japanese design has so much to offer the contemporary quiltmaker. Unfortunately, we cannot cover it in detail, but here are five basic principles to help you on your way:

Simplicity. Together with the deep feeling of the Japanese for nature, runs an equally strong feeling for what they call "simplicity." This is a distillation, or working over, of the material until they arrive at its essence. Although some Japanese designs may appear quite complex, they will have been explored and refined by the artist until they express exactly what he or she wishes to say. When planning your quilt keep your design objective in mind—aim for clarity and quality. The ideal of perfect workmanship has been the guiding principle of all Japanese craftsmen for centuries. Japanese sword-makers work and temper their steel until it becomes a perfect product. Japanese quiltmakers do the same with their quilts.

Space. Space is, of course, linked to simplicity. The Japanese like using blank space to set off areas of pattern (hence the gold clouds so often used on Japanese screens). They call this space *ma*, which means "a pause," and one of the ways the Japanese interpret ma is that it is a place to rest the eye; thus it becomes an aesthetic pause.

So many quilts today are crowded with pattern. We seem to have forgotten the lessons of the early quiltmakers who liked the sense of repose created by simple patterns surrounded by space; so plan to include areas of space in your quilt.

Space has to be quilted of course, but this is where the geometric patterns devised for sashiko find a new role as background grids for quilting. (Examine the quilts illustrated in figs. 16d, 42, 49, 50, 61, 65, 67, 68.)

Asymmetry. The cornerstone of Japanese design is asymmetry, which sounds alarming until you realize that it is just irregularity masquerading under another name. The Japanese affection for placing patterns off-center is linked to their love of nature. Nature is varied and unpredictable, and they try to reproduce these qualities in their design. Changes of background coloring are one way of introducing irregularity, and unexpected flashes of color are another. Breaking up the geometry of pieced backgrounds by overlaying them with scattered appliqué floral patterns is a third.

Although it is not strictly asymmetrical, another trick the Japanese use to challenge the eye is using the diagonal division. In Western design the usual way of bisecting a square is to divide it in half either vertically or horizontally. The Japanese prefer to divide diagonally from corner to corner; therefore many of their designs lie on a diagonal axis. You might like to try changing the axis of your quilt. (Examine the quilts illustrated in figs. 16e, 23, 38, 41, 49, 53, 54, 61, 68, 73, 75, 77.)

Circular Forms. To the Oriental mind, the circle represents harmony and peace, and although circular motifs (*marumon*) came originally from China, they have been so thoroughly absorbed into Japanese design that they represent an important principle. Most of the patterns in this book are circular, or can be enclosed within a circle, but there is nothing to stop you from also turning traditional American patterns into circles.

The Japanese use other shapes as vehicles for decorative motifs: the diamond for which we give you a pattern, the hexagon, fan shapes, and the rectangle. With the exception of the fan, all of these can be used for repeating block quilts, or you can scatter them across a whole-cloth background—another important principle of Japanese design that is easily copied. (Examine the quilts illustrated in figs. 23, 24, 31, 33, 36, 51, 60, 61, 62, 63, 65, 76. There are instructions given for making a marumon quilt in PATTERN PROJECTS 2.)

Scattering. This is an extension of asymmetry. The Japanese love to scatter patterns in an apparently random fashion. However, the principle on which they work is to make sure that the space *between* the patterns is harmonious. In other words, they look at the voids rather than the patterns. If the voids look pleasing, then the relative weight and color of the patterns is considered to be less important. This concept is also used in Western art, but it is almost totally opposite to the usual approach in Western quiltmaking. However, you might be surprised at the spontaneity you achieve if you try it.

Cropping and overlapping patterns are an important element of scattering. The Japanese like to suggest continuous expansion by cropping patterns off at the edge. In Japanese art this often takes the form of a branch truncated at the edge of the picture, leaving the viewer to visualize the rest of the tree. You could crop patterns at the border of your quilt, or you could let some patterns run over onto the border. Both give the illusion of movement, of the design continuing to expand.

Overlapping patterns are also about movement and expansion. After all, the pattern underneath is only temporarily obscured; it will reappear at any minute!

Scattering, cropping, and overlapping can be wonderfully arresting if you have the courage to try them. (Examine the quilts illustrated in figs. 16b, 40, 41, 49, 50, 61, 67, 76, 80.)

2. COLOR

Japanese color is difficult for the Westerner to imitate and it is perhaps best not to try. Traditional Japanese color tends to have a gray tone, and a host of conventions governs the way in which colors are put together. Modern Japanese color is the same as Western color.

Probably your best bet is to look at Japanese art and porcelain and take inspiration from those sources. Popular traditional colors are indigo blue (*ai*), scarlet (*beni*), purple (*murasaki*), green (*midori*), and yellow (*yamabuki*), and these were put together in various combinations such as the indigo blue, lacquer red, jade green, blue-gray, and gold of Imari porcelain; the gold and green of screen paintings; the red and green paintwork found in temples and shrines; and of course, the ubiquitous blue-and-white palette that appears everywhere in Japan—from the shaded indigo hues of traditional stencil-dyed fabrics to the cheerful prints of yukata cottons.

Analogous harmonies, those colors that lie next to each other on the color wheel, or any color scheme that includes secondary or tertiary colors that derive from the basic color are considered harmonious. For example, if you take red as the basic color, the Japanese might put with it the full range of associated colors from pink, orange through to the deepest purple.

To Western eyes these colors may clash but of course they exist in nature. Look at a rose, and you will see that the highlights and shadows will scale from palest pink through orange-red to deep violet, and for a real clashing color harmony how about a bed of azaleas! The Japanese take nature's palette for their inspiration.

Graduated color is important even today, but the graduation is often tonal rather than confined to shades of one particular color. Therefore you can skip from one color to another—blue, green, yellow, brown—just as long as the tonal values are harmonious.

The full range of grays are widely used to set off color schemes, while black and red are both traditional background colors. Red and white is an auspicious combination and is consequently favored for bridal kimono.

3. FABRICS

As the majority of the patterns given in this book are appliqué patterns, 100% cotton is the best fabric to use. You will be working with small pieces, and in some cases narrow seam allowances, and 100% cotton finger-presses much more easily than a blend.

Traditional Japanese fabrics, namely yukata cottons and stencil-dyed or woven indigo-dyed cottons, are sold in the

United States, but such fabrics are only 14″ (35.6cm) wide and are expensive. One source is *Kasuri Dyeworks, 1959 Shattuck Avenue, Berkeley, California 94704. Tel: (415) 841-4509,* or you can write to a shop in Japan called *Blue & White, 2-9-2 Azabu Juban, Minato-Ku, Tokyo 106. Tel: (03) 3451-0537* and ask them for their price list. Also, a new source for Japanese fabrics has recently opened in New York City. It is *Susan B. Faeder, Quilter's Express to Japan, 80 East 11th Street, Suite 623, New York, N.Y. 10003; Tel: (212) 504-0480; FAX: (212) 505-0510.* By appointment only.

Prewash all fabrics before cutting, run them through a warm-water rinse, or soak them in a basin of warm water and spin dry. Watch out for "bleeding." You can test for this by cutting a swatch, wetting it in hot water, and laying it out on a piece of kitchen towel for ten minutes or so. Dark colors are the worst, and they should be washed by themselves on a full warm-wash cycle. If the bleeding is excessive, don't use the fabric.

Fold the fabrics selvedge to selvedge, right-side out and straighten the grain lines as best you can. Hang them over a bar or a line to dry. Unless they are very creased, they need not be ironed until you come to use them.

4. TEMPLATES AND MARKING

The templates that you will need to make are clearly marked on each pattern with lines that are darker than the rest of the pattern, and the relevant numbers are given in the directions.

Some templates are marked with an "r" after the number. This often occurs with leaf templates, for example, and means that you will need to flip them over when drawing around them in order to cut a reverse set of pattern pieces.

Permanent templates can be made from clear plastic or acetate, but if you are just making a single block, trace the templates on ordinary typing paper and glue them to firm cardboard or sandpaper before cutting out. Mark each template with its number, and the name of the pattern, and store them in envelopes.

For some types of appliqué you may prefer to bypass template-making and just trace the outline directly on your fabric. This method is described in section 7b.

Appliqué patterns are marked on the *right* side of the fabric so that you can see the turn-under seam allowance easily, and pieced patterns are marked on the *wrong* side of the fabric because you will be seaming them together from this side.

Generally, a number 2 or number 3 pencil works best except on dark fabrics where you may have to use a silver, white, or yellow pencil. Keep your pencil well sharpened in order to achieve a fine line, and *always remember to allow enough space for seam allowances when marking the fabric.* Cut the seam allowances by eye. Appliqué pattern pieces should be cut with a scant ¼-inch (7mm) or even 3/16-inch (5 mm) seam allowance; you do not need more. Piecing should have the full ¼-inch (7mm) seam allowance.

5. TRACING THE PATTERN

In some of the pattern directions, you will note we recommend that you trace the outline of the pattern on your

background fabric to help you place the pattern pieces correctly.

If your background fabric is a light color, this will not be a problem. Just trace the pattern on white paper and go over it with a black pen. Don't forget the center markings as you will be needing these. Fold your background fabric in half and then in quarters and finger-press the folds gently to give you a visible crease (diag. 1). Pin the fabric on top of the

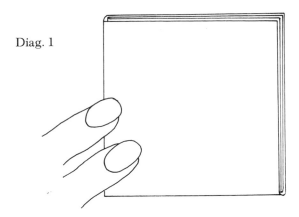

Diag. 1

tracing, matching the crease marks to the center lines on the pattern. *Pin through the center first* to anchor it—pin both vertically and then horizontally (diag. 2)—and lay it down on

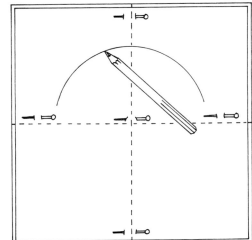

Diag. 2

a light-colored surface. You should be able to see the pattern quite clearly, particularly if you work under a lamp.

Use tailor's chalk, a sliver of soap, a water soluble pencil (available from art stores; pale blue is a useful color), or some other commercial marker, to trace the pattern on the fabric. Your appliqués may not quite fit when you come to sew them down, and you can sponge out, or erase, any uncovered lines afterward.

If your background fabric is dark, you will need to use a light source. There is always the window, of course (tape the pattern and the fabric to the glass), but this is an impractical method for anything other than a small pattern. See section 6 for alternative ideas.

6. LIGHT SOURCES

Light boxes can be bought at most good art stores, and are an invaluable investment for the dedicated quiltmaker, but it is easy to make your own. Buy a sheet of thick plastic approximately 24 inches x 28 inches (61 x 71 cm), or plate glass (remember to have the edges polished). Suspend this on two piles of books on your work table and place a low-watt bulb on a cord underneath (diag. 3). A 15-watt bulb is

Diag. 3

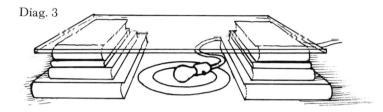

about right, and you can lay it on a plate or something to protect your table. Tape the pattern to the plastic and then tape your fabric over it, matching up center lines.

Alternately, if you don't mind kneeling on the floor, you could suspend the plastic on two chairs and use a small table lamp underneath without its shade, or you could use a glass-topped coffee table.

7. APPLIQUÉ TECHNIQUES

There are various methods of doing appliqué, and we do not have the space to cover them all. Here are the basic techniques that you will need for our patterns.

a. Conventional Basted Appliqué. Having marked your patches on the right side of the fabric, cut them out with a scant ¼-inch (7mm) or ³/₁₆-inch (5mm) seam allowance and turn this under, finger-pressing as you go. Clip seams at Vs or concave curves to make the patch lie flat, and baste with a contrasting-color thread (diag. 4). Leave the knot on the

surface so that you can remove the basting threads easily. Pin the patch in position and blindstitch in place (diag. 5). The advantage of this method is that it allows you to prepare all your appliqués peacefully, at odd moments.

b. Needle-turn Appliqué. If you do not want to bother with templates for some of the pattern pieces—circular stems for example—you can trace them directly on your fabric from the pattern. Cut them out with a scant ¼-inch (7mm) seam allowance and baste them to the block. Then turn under the seam allowance with the point of your needle as you sew (diag. 6). This is an ideal way of applying circular enclosures

Diag. 6

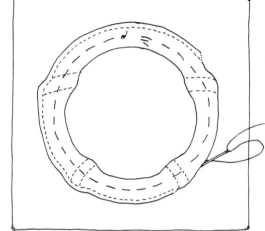

(see section 11); stylized mist patterns (see pattern 21), or any patch with lots of curves. Needle-turn appliqué is also useful for sharp points, or those places where you have to pare away the seam allowance (if fraying is a problem, use one of the specialist sprays such as No-Fray or Fray-check).

c. Freezer-paper Appliqué. This method has many converts because it makes for accuracy. It differs from conventional appliqué in that you iron the seam allowances over paper instead of basting them. Cut out freezer-paper templates and lay them with the waxy side down on the wrong side of your fabric. Press them gently with a hot iron to hold them in place, and then cut the fabric leaving ¼-inch (7mm) seam allowances. Press the seam allowances over the paper (diag. 7) and blindstitch the patch to your block. You can either pull

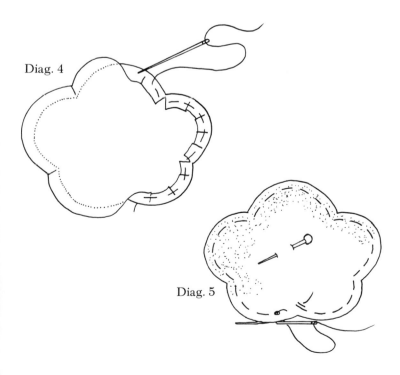

Diag. 4

Diag. 5

Diag. 7

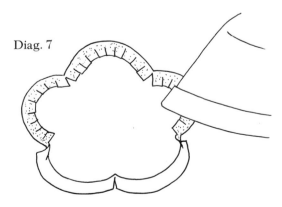

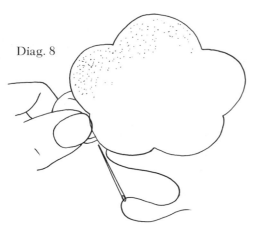

Diag. 8

the paper out before you complete the stitching (diag. 8) or you can remove it when you cut away the background fabric prior to quilting (see section 14). You can, of course, make your templates from ordinary paper such as old magazines or typing paper, but instead of ironing the seam allowances, you must baste them down in the conventional way. Freezer-paper or ordinary-paper appliqué is the ideal way to make small center circles and odd-shaped leaves, where you need to keep the shape accurate (diag. 9).

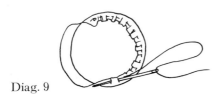

Diag. 9

d. Machine Appliqué. With machine appliqué you do not need to leave a seam allowance as you will be covering the raw edges of your patch with zig-zag stitching. To stabilize the patches iron a light-weight fusible interfacing such as PELLON™ to the back of your fabric. Cut out the patches and pin or stick these to your block. Run around the edges of the patches with a straight stitch just to hold them in place (diag. 10). Then go over the edges again with a close zig-zag (satin) stitch, approximately ⅛ inch (3mm) wide (diag. 11). Your stitching should just cover the edges of the patch and not

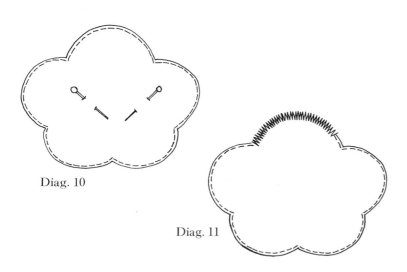

Diag. 10

Diag. 11

extend too far into the background fabric. If you are a novice, experiment first because you may have to adjust the tension of your machine. The important thing to remember when navigating a curve, or turning a corner, is to leave your needle in the work *on the longer edge,* then pivot the work and start machining again over the last bit of your previous stitching (diags. 12a, b, c, d). This not only prevents gaps

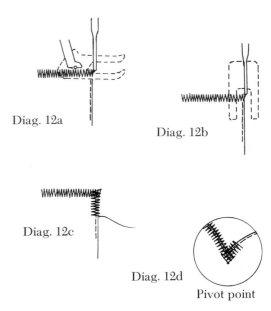

Diag. 12a

Diag. 12b

Diag. 12c

Diag. 12d

Pivot point

from appearing but also gives a smooth appearance to the satin stitch. You can also use a suitable machine-embroidery stitch instead of satin stitch for an extra decorative finish.

e. Reverse Appliqué. We recommend this type of appliqué for the decoration on the pine trees in patterns 25 and 26, but you could also use it for an entire pattern such as the Wisteria Wreath (pattern 28). The principle here is different from that applied to the other forms of appliqué. Instead of placing your patches on your background fabric and sewing them down, you layer two or more fabrics together, and then cut away the layers to reveal the design.

If you are working with two layers, you start by drawing

Diag. 13

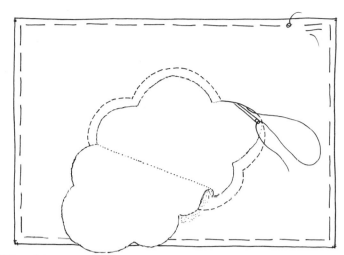

Diag. 14

with a small running stitch, starting at one corner and ending at the next. Do not sew to the edge of the fabric. Finger-press both seam allowances to one side (toward the darker fabric if possible).

When you sew lines of patches such as squares together, you need to be careful to match the vertical seams. To do this, make sure that you have the seam allowances lying opposite one another, one to the left and the other to the right (diag. 16). Then match up the vertical seams and pin securely

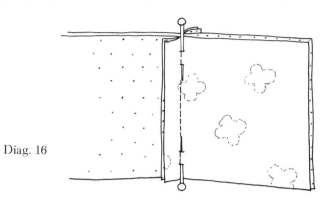

Diag. 16

through the stitching. Sloppy piecing, where the corners don't meet, occurs because the seams were not pinned securely and the seam allowances did not lie in the opposite directions.

b. *Machine Piecing.* For machine-piecing, you add the seam allowance to your template and cut out the patches *on the marked line.* With this method you can cut out several layers of patches at one time. However, pin them together before cutting out, otherwise the layers may shift.

Pair up your patches with the right sides together and match up the outer edge with the right side of your pressure foot. When you start stitching, this will automatically give you your ¼-inch (7mm) seam allowance (diag. 17). Some

your pattern on the top fabric (see section 5). Then iron the two fabrics together right-side uppermost and baste well (diag. 13). Lay the block down on a table and with a pair of sharp scissors snip away the top layer to reveal the design. You must leave a ³/₁₆-inch (5mm) seam allowance which you then roll under with your needle as you stitch (diag. 14). If you are working with several layers, you snip each one away until you reach the color you want (see the tip about using a pin in section 14). Because the design is underneath, rather than on top, this technique creates a marvelous sense of depth.

8. PIECEWORK

Although we do not feature many pieced patterns, you will have seen from the illustrations of antique kimono in the first part of this book that the Japanese are very partial to overlaying geometric backgrounds with floral motifs, and many Japanese quiltmakers have used this device most effectively in their quilts. The quilts illustrated in figures 21 and 63 are good examples. If you want to try this idea, you could make a pieced background of squares, triangles, or strip-piecing and then appliqué floral patterns on top of it.

a. *Hand-Piecing.* For hand-piecing place the templates on the wrong side of the fabric and cut out the pieces leaving a ¼-inch (7mm) seam allowance. Each patch has to be cut separately because you will sew along the marked line.

Place your patches with the right sides together and pin through the corners carefully matching your drawn lines. Pin again in the middle (diag. 15). Then sew along the drawn line

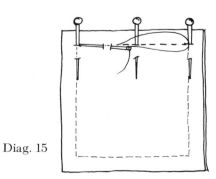

Diag. 15

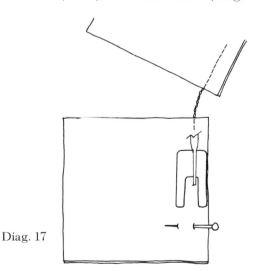

Diag. 17

machines have a marginally wider pressure foot than others, but as long as you're consistent this will not matter. Feed the pairs of patches through one after another. Your machine will form a chain between the patches. Sew from one edge of the patch to the other, and finger-press the seams to one side.

When you sew lines of squares together, pin the seams as described for hand-piecing.

There are various other forms of piecing, such as strip-piecing, seminole-piecing, and other quick-piecing methods, which you might find useful for backgrounds, but which we do not have enough space to cover here. You will find many books available on the subject at your local quilt store.

9. SEWING BIAS STRIPS

This is a useful technique for making narrow flower stems, or for running vines on borders, but you will need it here specifically, for the Courtly Fan (pattern 5). Cut bias strips ¾-inch (2cm) wide, and whatever length you need. Fold the strip in half with the right side out and press it. Lay it on your block and stitch through the center (diag. 18), following the

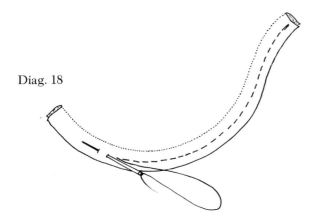

Diag. 18

marked line of the design. Then turn the folded side over so that it covers the raw edges of the strip and hem this in place (diag. 19). If necessary, trim the raw edges as you sew.

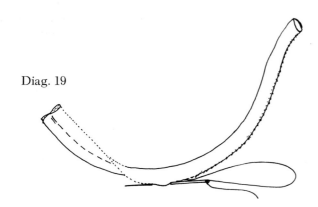

Diag. 19

10. CIRCULAR BLOCKS

For a scattered marumon quilt, always make your circular patterns on square pieces of muslin, as this avoids stretching the bias edges (diag. 20). Cut them out, leaving a ¼-inch (7mm) seam allowance (diag. 21), and you can then play around with your design before sewing the patterns to your quilt top. Use this method even with wreath patterns, where the leaves or blossoms extend beyond the edge of the circular stem.

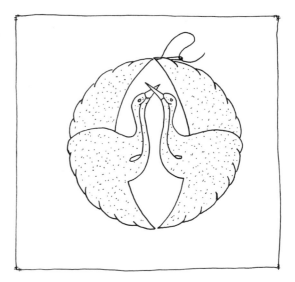

Diag. 20

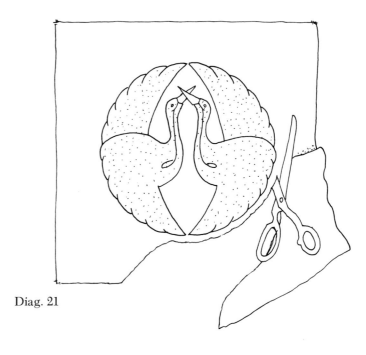

Diag. 21

11. HOW TO APPLY CIRCLES AND SNOW-RINGS

This method will ensure that your circles and snow-rings are accurately centered on your block.

a. First make yourself a template following the directions given in patterns 29a and 30b.

b. Cut two squares of fabric the size of the proposed block, *including seam allowances.* One square will be your background fabric and the other will be for your circle. Fold the fabric for the circle in half and then in quarters, and finger-press the crease lines.

c. Pin this to your background square. Then place your circle template on top, matching the marked lines on your template to the crease marks on the fabric, and draw around the circle in pencil being careful not to drag the fabric (diag. 22).

d. Baste through the center of the drawn circle all the way around (diag. 23), then cut away the surplus fabric from both

94

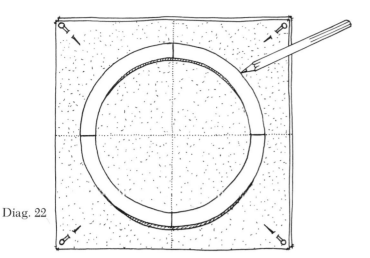

Diag. 22

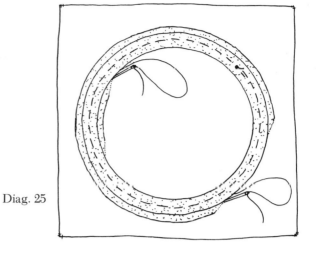

Diag. 25

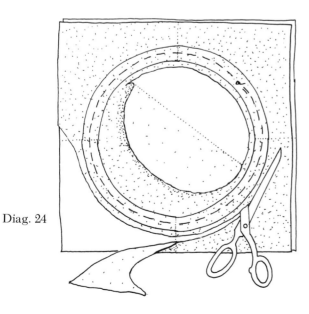

Diag. 23

inside and outside the circle, leaving a ³/₁₆-inch (5mm) seam allowance (diag. 24). Needle-turn both seam allowances (diag. 25).

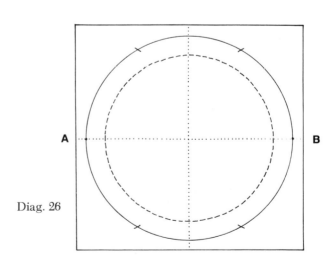

Diag. 24

e. You can, of course, trace the circle from a paper pattern. Pin the circle fabric to your pattern, matching center markings, trace off, and then follow step (d) above.

Sometimes you will need to insert parts of the pattern under the rim of the circle—flower stems for example. Either do this before hemming your ring, or leave a gap, and then tuck in the stems and complete the stitching.
f. Apply snow-rings in the same way.

12. HOW TO CUT YOUR OWN SNOW-RING

You may prefer to cut your own snow-ring, so here is a method given to us by Jenni Dobson.
a. Cut a square of greaseproof paper and fold it in half vertically and then horizontally to find the center.
b. Using a compass, draw two concentric rings 1 inch (2.5cm) apart (or more if you want a deeper snow-ring).
c. Keeping your compass at the same radius as the outer ring, put the point of the compass where the center horizontal line bisects the drawn circle (A). Draw a small arc across the outer line, above and below. Repeat on the opposite side (B). See diagram 26.

A   B

Diag. 26

d. Cut carefully around the outer edge of the circle and fold it in half horizontally through A and B (diag. 27).

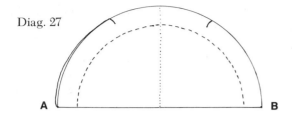

Diag. 27

e. Fold the paper again through the first arc and match A to the arc above B (diag. 28). Then turn the paper over and fold B up to make a wedge. The edges must form a zigzag (diag. 29).

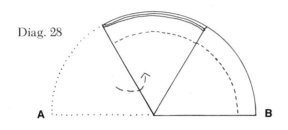

Diag. 28

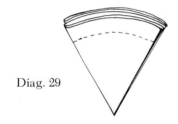

Diag. 29

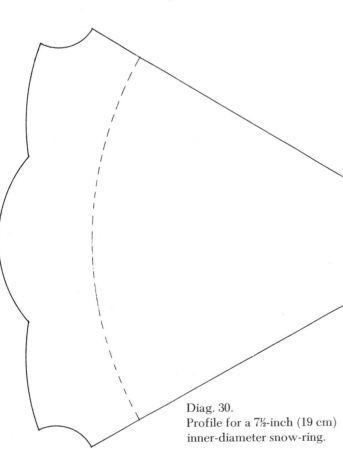

Diag. 30.
Profile for a 7½-inch (19 cm) inner-diameter snow-ring.

f. Now draw the profile of the snow-ring (diag. 30) on the outer edge of the circle. The notches should be at the folded sides of your wedge (diag. 31). When you unfold the snow-

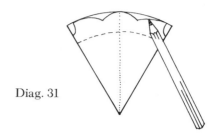

Diag. 31

ring after cutting, you may find that some of the notches that were on the inside will be smaller than others. Trim these to match.

g. To make a template, paste the snow-ring on a card, and then cut away the middle of the ring.

h. Apply snow-rings like circles (see section 11). Snow-rings and ordinary rings are a marvelous way of enclosing a piece of pretty fabric or just a single element from one of the patterns, such as a spray of bamboo.

13. EMBROIDERY

Embroidery adds texture to a block, and although you may prefer to quilt leaf veins, etc. to give a three-dimensional look, there are a number of patterns where embroidery is necessary. Here are some basic stitches that you may need:

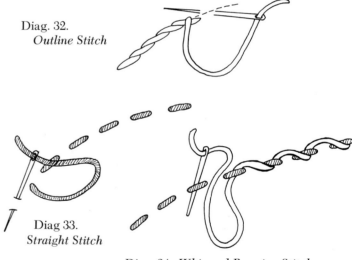

Diag. 32.
Outline Stitch

Diag 33.
Straight Stitch

Diag. 34. *Whipped Running Stitch.*
This is a way of embellishing and giving depth to the ordinary straight stitch.

Diag. 35.
Satin Stitch

Diag. 36.
French Knots

Embroidery is best done *before* you cut away surplus fabric from behind your blocks (see section 14), as the work will be more evenly tensioned if you work through two layers of fabric.

14. CUTTING AWAY BEHIND YOUR BLOCKS
Cutting away surplus fabric from behind the design before quilting is important with appliqué patterns because you often have layers of fabric piling up one on top of another. This step is essential when you make up marumon blocks on squares of muslin.

Having pressed your blocks, turn them over and carefully snip away the muslin leaving a ¼-inch (7mm) seam allowance (diag. 37). Then tackle the appliqué pieces. It is not

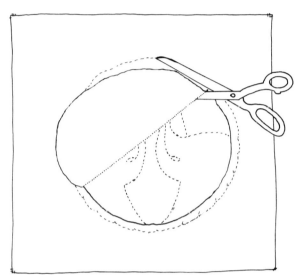

Diag. 37

necessary to cut away from behind every small leaf or petal, but make sure you cut away any dark fabrics that are likely to show through on the front. And also make sure that you snip away all those bits of surplus thread that have an unhappy knack of revealing themselves once you have the quilt top marked and basted ready for quilting!

Be careful when you cut; it is all too easy to snip through the front and ruin your block. A useful trick is to stick a pin into the layer of fabric you are cutting and use the pin to pull it up so that you can see where to make the first snip (diag. 38).

Snip here

Diag. 38

15. BORDERS
The Japanese often use elaborately patterned fabric for their borders, obi silk for example, which adds a richness to their quilts. If you do not plan to quilt your borders, you might like to consider using furnishing fabrics such as chintz, for example. Borders should not be too dominating, but they are

meant to be a frame for your work and as such should be chosen as carefully as a frame for a painting.

Ideally, borders should be cut in one piece so that there are no joins. In practice this is often wasteful, and you can save fabric by cutting them across the width of the fabric and seaming the pieces together to make the length you want. Remember to allow extra fabric if you need to match the pattern.

The most attractive configuration is to join the borders sides first and then the top and bottom as this avoids the tedious business of mitering the corners (diag. 39). If you

Diag. 39

choose this formula, however, you *must put on each border separately.*

Rather than binding the quilt to finish it, you might like to turn the edges of the borders over to the back instead. If so, allow an extra 1 inch (2.5cm) on the border width. If you want a puffy border, allow extra batting and double this over before hemming the back.

16. MARKING YOUR QUILT
You will have seen from the quilt illustrations how effective Japanese sashiko patterns look as background quilting designs. They create a wonderfully rich, tactile surface and once you have tried them, you will find conventional cross-hatching very dull by comparison.

Whether you wish to use them for quilting, or for traditional sashiko, the method of marking is the same.

First, make a pattern of the right size. Because of space considerations, we can only give a small sample of each sashiko pattern, but they are easy to trace, and by tracing them, and matching up the pattern, you will learn their structure and so how to stitch them. You will be surprised how easy most of them are.

An alternative method is to take nine photocopies and tape them together. This is an expensive and wasteful method because you lose so much of the photocopy when you match the pattern (some patterns are worse then others), but it is speedy. Nine copies of each design will make a minimum 14-inch (35.6cm) square; some will be even larger.

Having made your pattern the required size, there are two ways of transferring it to the quilt.

a. If your background fabric is light enough, trace the pattern following the directions in section 5, using a light source if necessary.

b. With very dark fabrics such as navy blue, or traditional Japanese indigo-dyed cotton, it is often impossible to see through it even with a powerful light source. Therefore, you must use dressmaker's carbon (dressmaker's tracing paper is another name for it). Choose a color that will show up on your fabric, but is not too strong a contrast and *test it on your chosen fabric*. Some of the colors are difficult to wash out if you make a mistake.

c. Press your block, or quilt top, before you start marking. Do not iron it after you have marked if you can possibly avoid it. Ironing has a knack of permanently setting the marking medium.

d. If you are marking a quilt top, divide it into manageable sections and make a pencil mark on the edges of the top to act as a guide. It is vital that you keep the pattern straight!

e. Tape or clip the quilt top (or block) to your work table, so that it can't move, with a couple of sheets of paper underneath to give a slightly padded surface. You can use bull-dog clips, or the kind of clips that are used to hold tablecloths in windy weather, or you can buy professional curtain-makers' clamps that are like a second pair of hands. They hold fabric absolutely steady and are invaluable tools.

f. Place the carbon paper with the colored, or greasy side *face down* on your fabric, then put the paper pattern on top.

g. Pin the pattern and the fabric together, *but do not pin the dressmaker's carbon* because you may need to pull it away to check whether or not the pattern is coming through (diag. 40).

h. Trace the design with a ball-point pen in a color that you can see clearly on the pattern, using a ruler if the pattern requires it. Rosemary Muntus, a British sashiko teacher, suggests using a *spent* ball-point because she finds that the ink runs and messes up her paper pattern. (An alternative is to use a stylus or the point of a short knitting needle such as a sock needle.) But with these complex grids, you need to keep track of where you mark—supposing the phone rings in the middle!—so keep several ball-points on hand and keep changing them over. You can always make two or three photocopies of your pattern.

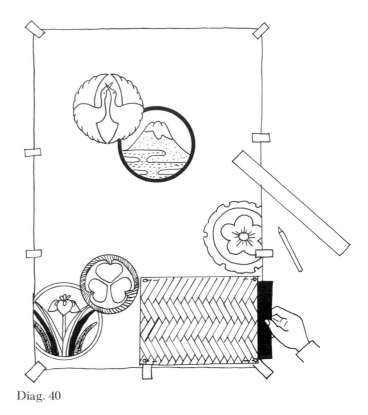

Diag. 40

For cross-hatching or straight lines, place strips of masking tape on the top and quilt down either side.

17. BASTING AND QUILTING

Your backing fabric should not be too tightly woven. Some books recommend sheeting, but the thread count is too high and if you are using a sashiko pattern, the last thing you want is to add to your labors!

a. Cut your backing fabric 3–4 inches (8–10cm) larger than your quilt top and trim off the selvedges. Lay this on your table, or on the floor, and anchor it securely with tape, clips, or pushpins.

b. Smooth the batting over it and trim it to match the backing. Lay your pressed and marked quilt on top and pin, and then baste it both lengthwise and crosswise. Some quilters baste diagonally as well, but this means working across the bias and it is an old dressmaking trick never to touch the bias of a piece of fabric if you can help it as it distorts so easily.

If you are not anchoring the quilt in a large frame, add a grid of basting stitches 4 inches (10cm) apart. Turn the backing over to the front of the quilt, tuck in the batting, and baste that too (diag. 41).

You can use safety pins if you prefer, and remove them as you quilt.

c. Whether or not you use a frame is up to you. Some people are expert at working in their hands, others prefer a hoop, but aim to get your work as flat as possible. There is nothing worse than bunched quilting.

d. Pull approximately 20 inches (50cm) of quilting thread off the spool and cut it diagonally. Thread this end through your needle and knot it. The diagonal cut will pop through the needle's eye easily, and you will be sewing the way the thread came off the spool, which helps it not to tangle. Thread several needles before you start.

c. Start quilting by pulling the knot through to the batting with a little tug. Unless you are an expert quilter, aim for even stitches rather than very small stitches. End off by taking a small back-stitch and running the last bit of your thread through the batting in the opposite direction to that which you have been quilting.

f. Outline quilt around each pattern piece.

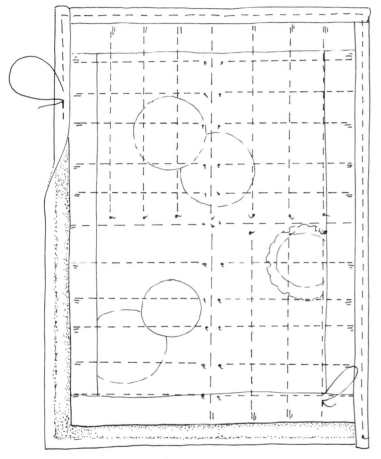

Diag. 41

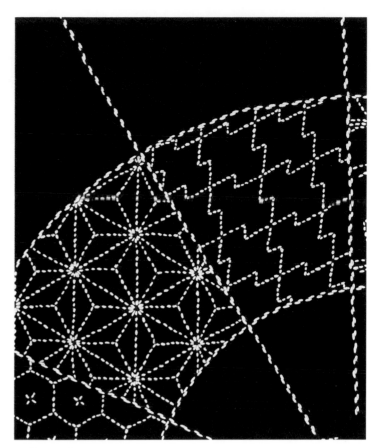

Diag. 42

18. SASHIKO-STITCHING

Sashiko-stitching can add sparkle and texture to a quilt, either interwoven as part of the design, or as alternate blocks. There are eight sashiko patterns in the PATTERN INDEX, but you could sashiko-stitch any of the appliqué patterns as well. (See section 5 and section 16 for marking methods.)

Genuine sashiko is done with white stranded cotton, and the stitch is larger than the quilting stitch, approximately ⅛-inch (3mm) long (diag. 42). As in quilting, you should try and keep your stitches as even as possible. The proper stranded cotton is difficult to get, so some sort of embroidery thread or crochet cotton would be good substitutes.

If you work sashiko through all three layers, there is a danger of the batting coming through, so you might like to

Diag. 43

copy Jenni Dobson's sashiko that she has used on the quilts illustrated in figures 34 and 63. She uses ordinary quilting thread but just makes a larger stitch (diag. 43).

Traditionally, sashiko was done in white on a blue ground, but nowadays you see a variety of colors used.

19. BINDING AND FINISHING

The moment when the last quilting stitch is done is a great moment. This quilt, this incubus that you have been nurturing all these months has finally made it. You will probably feel an enormous sense of anticlimax, and wonder why you ever felt so excited about the project in the first place. So take out the basting threads and lay it on a bed for twenty-four hours to let it (and you) recover from the labor. When you pick it up again, it will twinkle at you, and then your family and friends will praise it, and you will suddenly realize that these months of work have produced a masterpiece!

All that remains is to finish the edges. You can either turn an inch or so of the border over to the back, and blindstitch it down, having trimmed away the excess batting and backing fabric, or you can bind it.

Unless you have rounded the corners of your quilt, there is no need to use bias strips for binding. Cut straight strips of fabric 3 inches (7.6cm) wide and the length of the side borders. Fold the strips in half and press them.

Baste round the raw edges of the quilt with matching thread to hold them together. Then with the raw edges together, machine the side strips to your quilt, using a ¼-inch (7mm) seam allowance (or a fraction more if you like). Turn the folded edge of the strips to the back of the quilt and blindstitch in place.

Repeat with the top and bottom strips.

Finally, don't forget to put a label on the back giving as much information as possible to assist the quilt historians of the future!

Pattern Index

A NOTE ABOUT THE PATTERNS

- In this Pattern Index, you will find many of the patterns that you have already seen on the quilt pages, or similar ones, and they are presented with an explanation of their symbolism.

- The majority are 12-inch (30.5cm) appliqué patterns and with the exception of Pattern 22, Noshi, they are given full-size so that you can see what they will look like when they are made up. If the block size differs, this is noted at the top of the page.

- Comprehensive directions are given with each pattern but if a special technique is necessary, you will be referred to the Tips and Techniques section. The templates that you will need are marked with a darker line than the rest of the pattern, and do *not* include seam allowances. Each pattern piece has been given a number. The numbers represent the sequence in which the pieces should be sewn.

- The big wreath patterns have been drawn in two parts to avoid your having to work over the centerfold of the book. We recommend that you always make a complete tracing of the pattern before you start, as this not only helps you to understand the construction but also gives you a paper pattern from which to trace the outline on your background fabric. Some of the patterns are fairly complex, and it is easier to sew the appliqués in the proper position if you have a traced outline of the design to follow (see Tips and Techniques 5).

- Some of the stems on the wreath patterns are shown with a dotted line on the pattern itself, and some are given on a separate page. The pattern directions will make this clear.

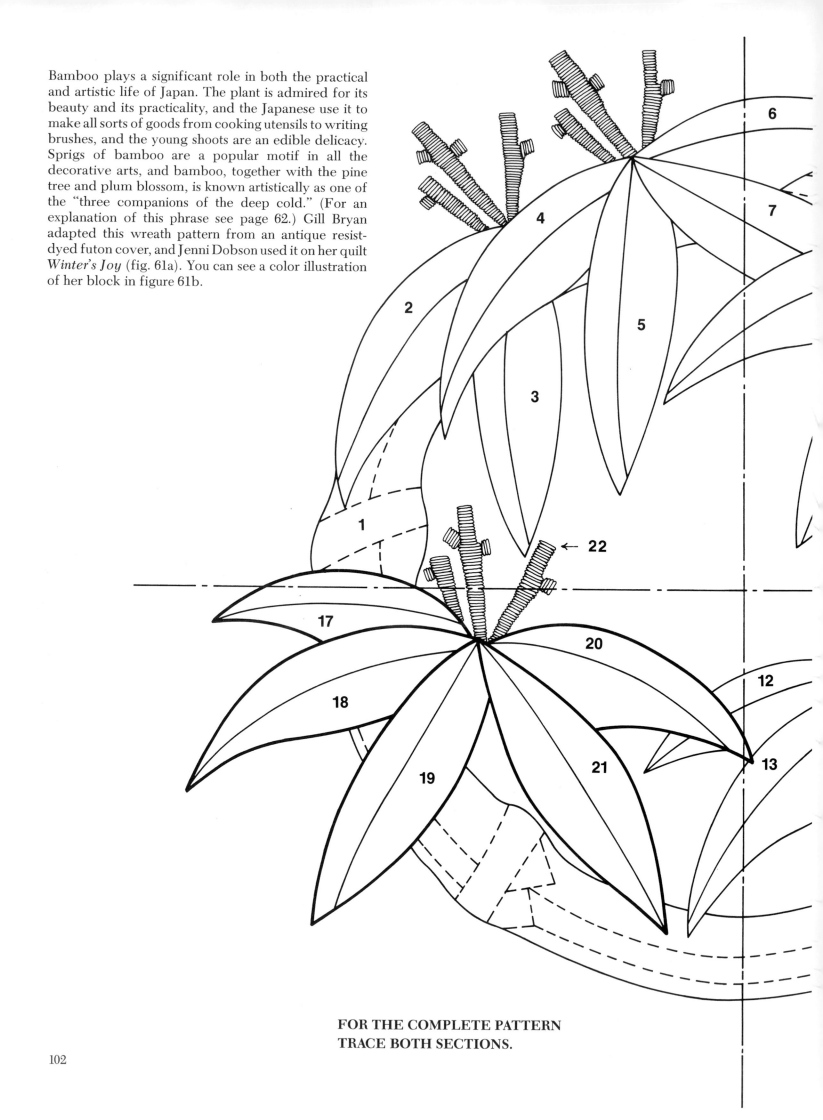

Bamboo plays a significant role in both the practical and artistic life of Japan. The plant is admired for its beauty and its practicality, and the Japanese use it to make all sorts of goods from cooking utensils to writing brushes, and the young shoots are an edible delicacy. Sprigs of bamboo are a popular motif in all the decorative arts, and bamboo, together with the pine tree and plum blossom, is known artistically as one of the "three companions of the deep cold." (For an explanation of this phrase see page 62.) Gill Bryan adapted this wreath pattern from an antique resist-dyed futon cover, and Jenni Dobson used it on her quilt *Winter's Joy* (fig. 61a). You can see a color illustration of her block in figure 61b.

**FOR THE COMPLETE PATTERN
TRACE BOTH SECTIONS.**

1. Bamboo Wreath (*Take*)

12-inch (30.5cm) block
Add ¼-inch (7mm) seam allowances

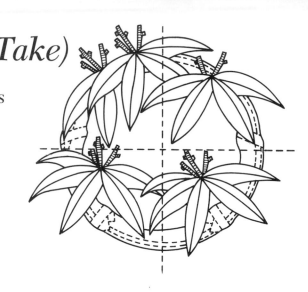

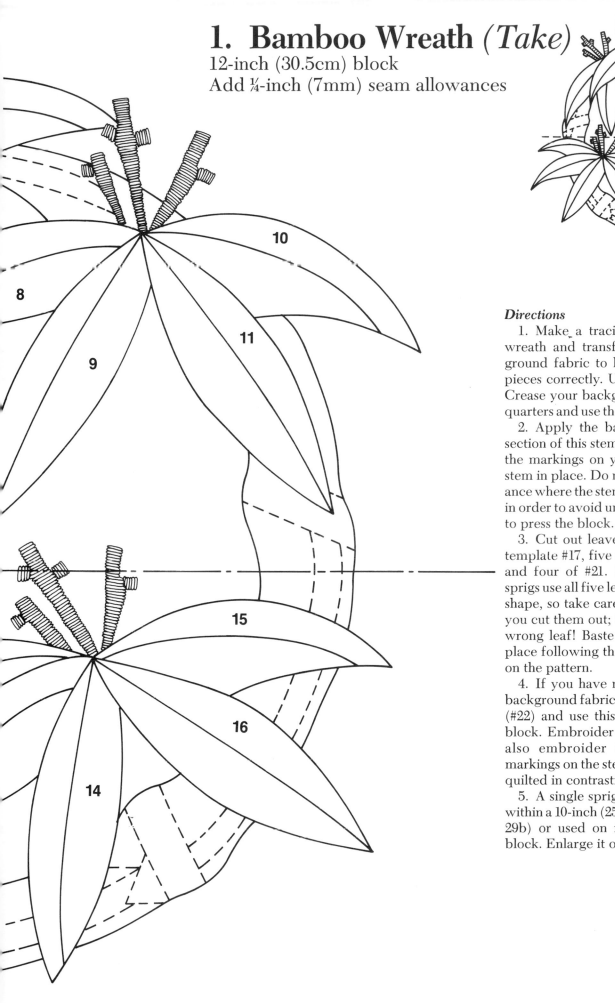

Directions

1. Make a tracing of the complete bamboo wreath and transfer the outline to your background fabric to help you position the pattern pieces correctly. Use a light source if necessary. Crease your background fabric in half and then quarters and use these creases to align the pattern.

2. Apply the bamboo stem #1 first. A half-section of this stem is given in Pattern 29b. Trace the markings on your fabric before sewing the stem in place. Do not turn under the seam allowance where the stem is covered by bamboo leaves in order to avoid unsightly ridges when you come to press the block.

3. Cut out leaves next. You will need two of template #17, five of #18, five of #19, four of #20 and four of #21. (*Note:* Only the bottom two sprigs use all five leaves.) The leaves are similar in shape, so take care to keep them separate when you cut them out; it is all too easy to pick up the wrong leaf! Baste seam allowances and sew in place following the numerical sequence marked on the pattern.

4. If you have not traced the design on your background fabric, make a template for the twigs (#22) and use this to draw the outline on your block. Embroider twigs in satin stitch. You can also embroider the leaf divisions and the markings on the stem, but they look equally good quilted in contrasting thread.

5. A single sprig of bamboo leaves can be set within a 10-inch (25.5cm) diameter circle (Pattern 29b) or used on its own to ornament another block. Enlarge it on a photocopier if necessary.

2. Blue Wave (*Seigaiha*)

The Blue Wave pattern reaches back into Japan's prehistory. It was etched on prehistoric pottery and also on the clothing of clay figurines found in fifth-century tombs. Here are two versions, a diamond-shaped patchwork version similar to the pattern used by Emiko Toda Loeb on her quilt, *Sounds of the Sea* (fig. 73), and a simpler version of Sanae Hattori's classic clamshell pattern shown on her quilt, *Thousand Waves* (fig. 38).

Directions

1. Directions for piecework are given in Tips and Techniques 8. To make one block, cut two of template #1, two of #2, two of #3, two of #4, and one of #5, varying the colors of each patch.

2. Piece together in two halves following numerical sequence given on the pattern. Stitch the two halves together and inset bottom diamond (template #5). See piecing diagram.

3. Stitch completed blocks together in diagonal rows. Larger or smaller versions of this block can easily be drawn with isometric graph paper available at good stationery stores. A quilt setting that uses this pattern appears in Pattern Projects 5.

DIAMOND WAVE

5⅞-inch x 10¼-inch (15 x 26cm) block
Add ¼-inch (7mm)
seam allowances

Stitch completed blocks together in diagonal rows.

CLAMSHELL WAVE

4⅞-inch (12.3cm) block
Add ¼-inch (7mm) seam allowances

1. This block is divided into three sections, but do not try to piece it. Make three complete clamshell templates, #1, #2, and #3. Baste the top curved edge of each piece.

2. To make up the clamshells, lay piece #1 on a flat surface and apply piece #2, matching lower edges. Sew top curve. Repeat with piece #3.

3. To apply finished clamshells, draw horizontal lines 2¼ inches (5.5cm) apart on your background fabric (or use masking tape), and set the base of the clamshell on these lines. Work in rows; blindstitch the top curve only.

Sew clamshells down in horizontal rows.

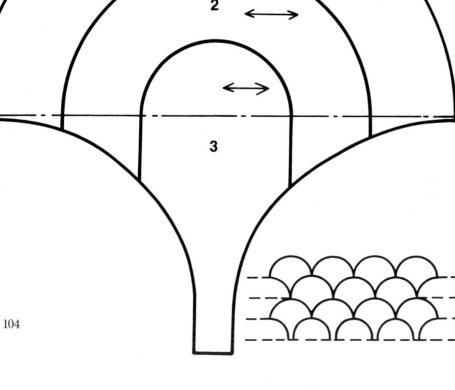

104

3. Bush Clover *(Hagi)*

12-inch (30.5cm) block
Add ¼-inch (7mm) seam allowances

This graceful pattern is symbolic of Autumn. It is much admired by the Japanese and is one of the "Seven Grasses of Autumn," a decorative combination that is often to be found on textiles, porcelain, and lacquer ware. It is one of Jenni Dobson's patterns taken from a kamon. You can see an illustration of it in figure 61h.

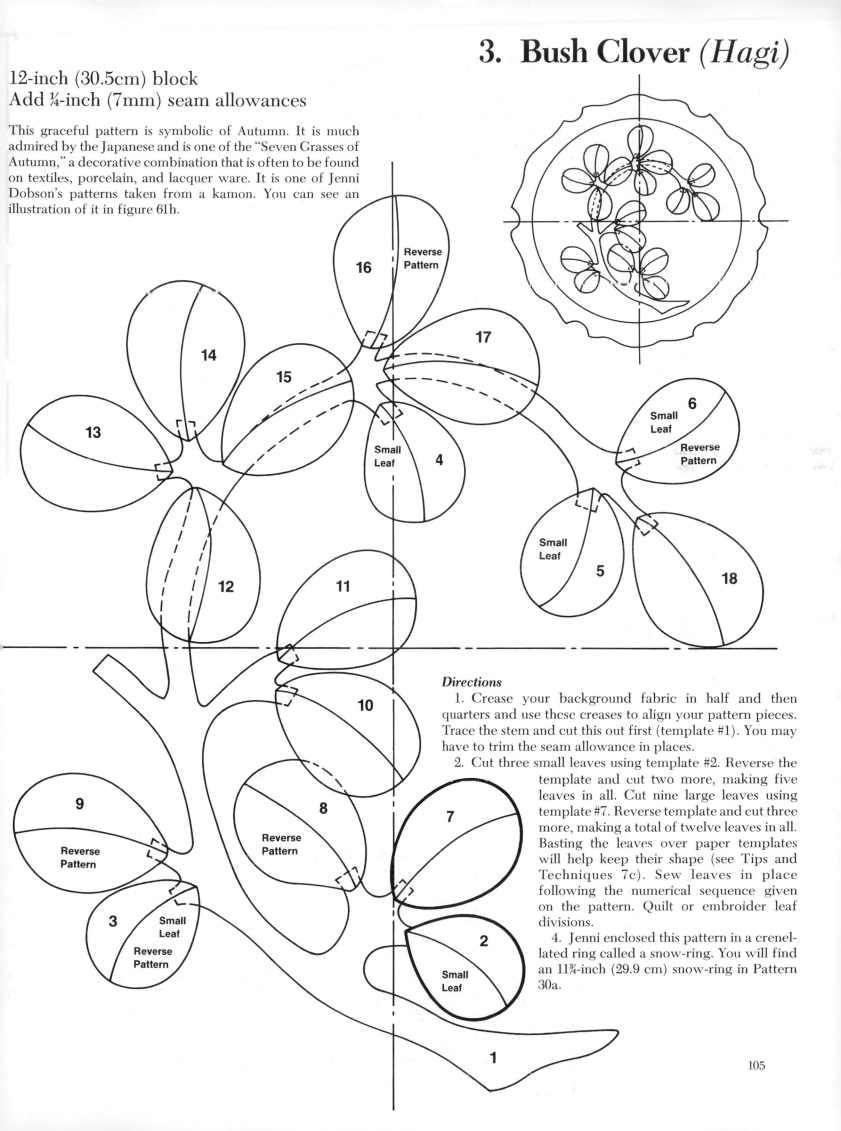

Directions

1. Crease your background fabric in half and then quarters and use these creases to align your pattern pieces. Trace the stem and cut this out first (template #1). You may have to trim the seam allowance in places.

2. Cut three small leaves using template #2. Reverse the template and cut two more, making five leaves in all. Cut nine large leaves using template #7. Reverse template and cut three more, making a total of twelve leaves in all. Basting the leaves over paper templates will help keep their shape (see Tips and Techniques 7c). Sew leaves in place following the numerical sequence given on the pattern. Quilt or embroider leaf divisions.

4. Jenni enclosed this pattern in a crenellated ring called a snow-ring. You will find an 11¾-inch (29.9 cm) snow-ring in Pattern 30a.

Cherry blossom is the national flower of Japan, and the ceremony of cherry blossom–viewing is one of the highlights of the year. The cherry-blossom pattern is often confused with plum blossom, also a popular motif, but you can tell the difference because cherry blossom has indentations on the petals and the plum has not. The tree is native to Japan, and the pattern became a favorite with the nobility in the tenth century. Both the designs shown here are taken from kamon.

SMALL CHERRY BLOSSOM

5½-inch (14cm) block
Add ¼-inch (7mm) seam allowances

Cut this blossom from one piece of fabric (template #4). Apply center circle #5. Quilt or embroider petal divisions. Embroider stamens.

SIDE-VIEW CHERRY BLOSSOM

5-inch (12.5cm) block
Add ¼-inch (7mm) seam allowances

The two side petals on this pattern are not symmetrical so you will have to cut one each of templates #6 and #7. Cut one of template #8, and one each of the stalk and leaf #9 and #10. Baste seam allowances and sew in place following the numerical sequence shown on the pattern. Embroider markings on the petals.

4. Cherry Blossom *(Sakura)*
12-inch (30.5cm) block
Add ¼-inch (7mm) seam allowances

Directions

1. A single blossom set within a circle is a well-known family crest. You will find a pattern for an 11-inch (28cm) circle in pattern 29a. Apply this to your background fabric first (see Tips and Techniques 11). Crease your background fabric in half and then quarters to help you to center the blossom correctly.

2. You can either cut the blossom (template #1) from one piece of fabric and quilt or embroider the petal divisions, or you can apply each petal separately (template #3). If you use different subtle shades of fabric for each petal, it creates movement and interest. Baste seam allowances and sew in place. Mark the stamens ready for embroidering.

3. Cut center circle #2. Basting over a paper template will keep it in shape. Embroider stamens in outline stitch finishing with a bar (a small stitch) at the top.

4. If you wish to scatter individual blossoms on your quilt, like Utako Fujiwara's quilt, *Weeping Cherry Blossom* (fig. 21), use template #4 and cut from one piece of fabric. Apply center circle #5, quilt or embroider petal divisions, and embroider stamens.

5. The side-view version (templates #6 through #10) can be used in conjunction with this smaller cherry-blossom pattern, or on its own.

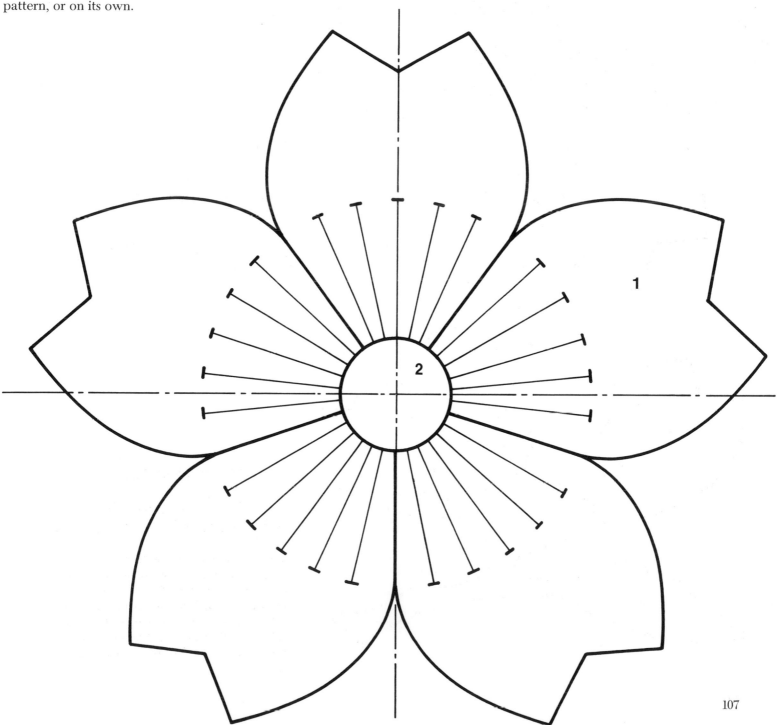

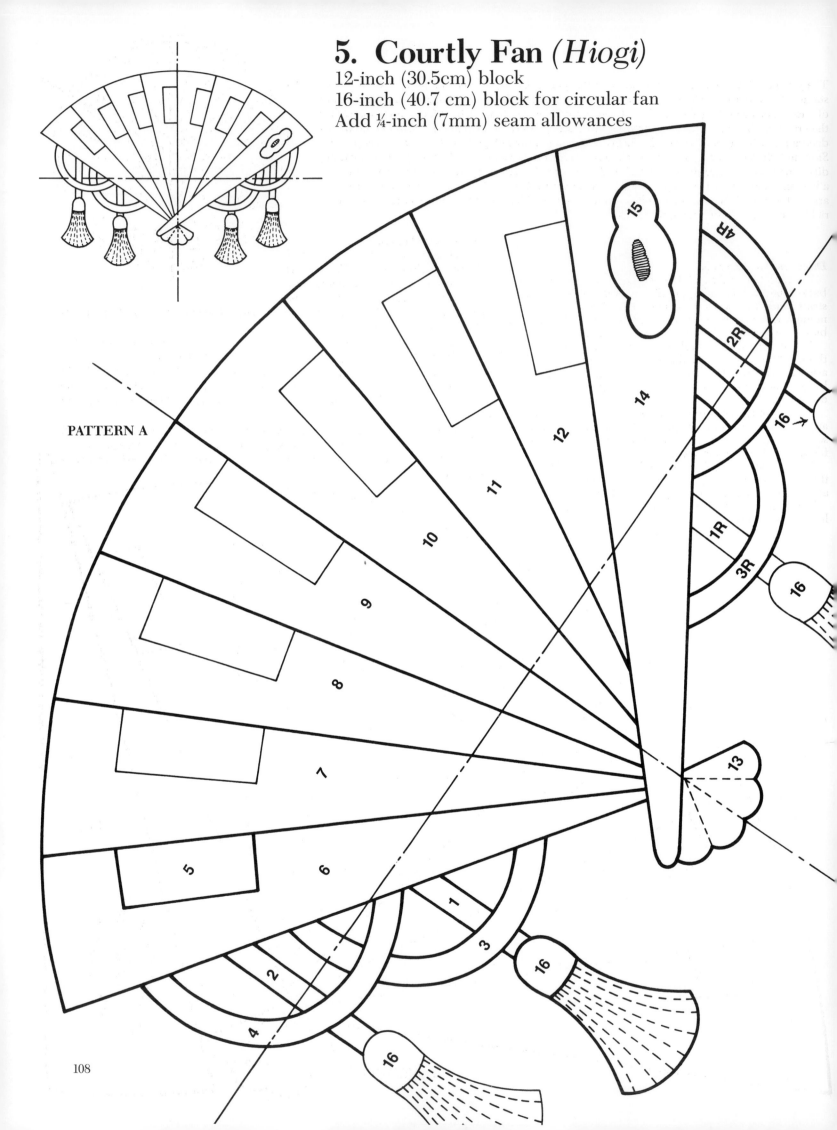

5. Courtly Fan (*Hiogi*)

12-inch (30.5cm) block
16-inch (40.7 cm) block for circular fan
Add ¼-inch (7mm) seam allowances

PATTERN A

The Japanese invented the folding fan, and this particular slatted version became an object of status. The emperor and his courtiers carried fans as part of their official regalia, and the number of slats varied according to rank. Court ladies were forbidden to show their faces to any man other than relatives (lovers were excluded from this ban!), so they hid behind beautifully painted fans decorated with cords and tassels. Barbara Holmes designed pattern A for the group quilt, *Summer's Splendor*, and you can see in figure 34c how she created the effect of painting by using different colored fabrics for each slat. We also give you the circular pattern of three fans based on a kamon in Pattern B. The shape of this fan differs from Pattern A because it has to fit within the arc of the circle. Three of them will fit inside a 14-inch (35.5cm) circle. See also Sanae Hattori's richly patterned circular fan quilt in figure 24b.

Directions for Pattern A

1. Trace the outline of the fan and the cords on your background fabric and apply the cords first using two bias strips ¾ inch x 18 inches (2 x 46cm) folded in half. Follow the numerical sequence given on the pattern when sewing the bias. (See Tips and Techniques 9 for method.)

2. Cut cord-slots (template #5) and slats (templates #6 through #12). The slats should be pieced together, but as they are *not* symmetrical in shape, you must reverse the templates by placing them *face down* on the back of your fabric to draw around them.

3. Mark the position of the cord-slots on each slat and then apply the cord-slots before piecing the slats together. Baste seam allowances except on the right side of slat #12, and stitch fan to your background fabric.

4. Cut end-piece, handle, and motif (templates #13 through #15) and apply motif to handle. Baste seam allowances. Apply end-piece (#13) and then the handle.

5. Cut four tassels from template #16 and mark quilting lines. Sew in position.

6. Embroider center of handle motif in satin stitch.

Directions for Pattern B

We give a quarter section of a 14-inch (35.6cm) circle in pattern 30b, but we advise you to draw up the circle yourself to ensure accuracy. The inner radius should be 6⅜ inches (16.1cm) and the outer radius 7 inches. (17.8cm). See pattern 30b for further instructions.

1. Cut a 16-inch (40.7cm) square of fabric, fold in half and then quarters and apply the circle first (see Tips and Techniques 11 for method).

2. Lightly mark the Y-shaped division shown on the small-scale diagram in the center of the circle (your crease lines must be accurate), and extend the lines to the inner edge of the circle. *These angles are always the same whatever the size of your block.*

3. Make fans following directions 2 through 4 above. One fan will fit into each of the three divisions with the sides touching and the end-pieces fitting snugly against one another (see diagram). The top of the fans should lie against the inner rim of the circle.

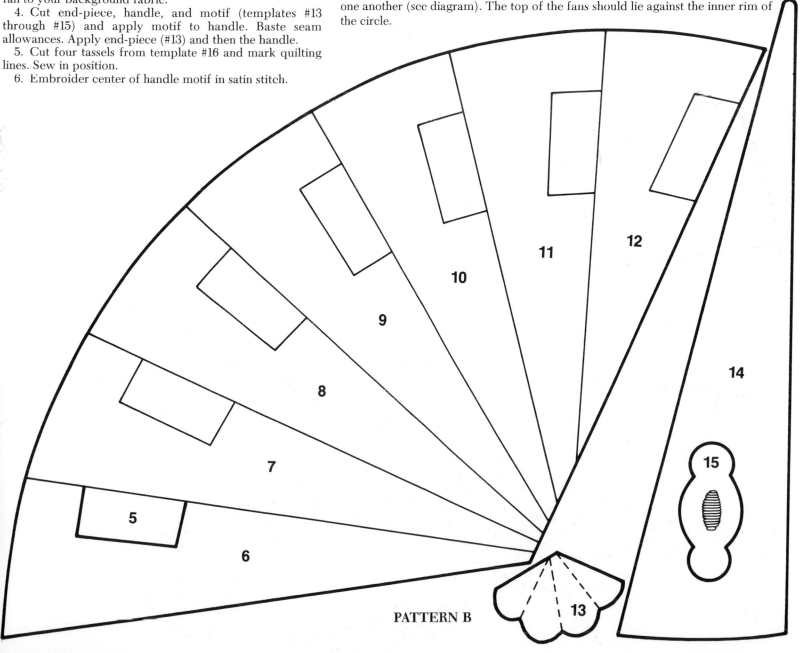

PATTERN B

The pattern that all quilters know as Dresden Plate is the crest of the Japanese imperial family. Chrysanthemums are associated with long life, because legend has it that if you eat the flowers or drink the water into which chrysanthemum petals have fallen, you will live forever. This particular version of the pattern was adapted from a Japanese New Year's card by Jenni Dobson, and it appears in a smaller size than we give here on her quilt, *Winter's Joy* (fig. 61a). She reduced the pattern on a photocopier to measure 8 inches (20cm) in diameter. There is a color illustration of her block in figure 61d.

SIDE PETAL TEMPLATES

MAIN PETAL TEMPLATE

PERFECT POINTS

Cut petals and fold in half vertically, wrong side out (diag. A). Seam top edge using ¼-inch seam allowance (diag. B). Trim seam allowance, turn right side out and press carefully (diag. C).

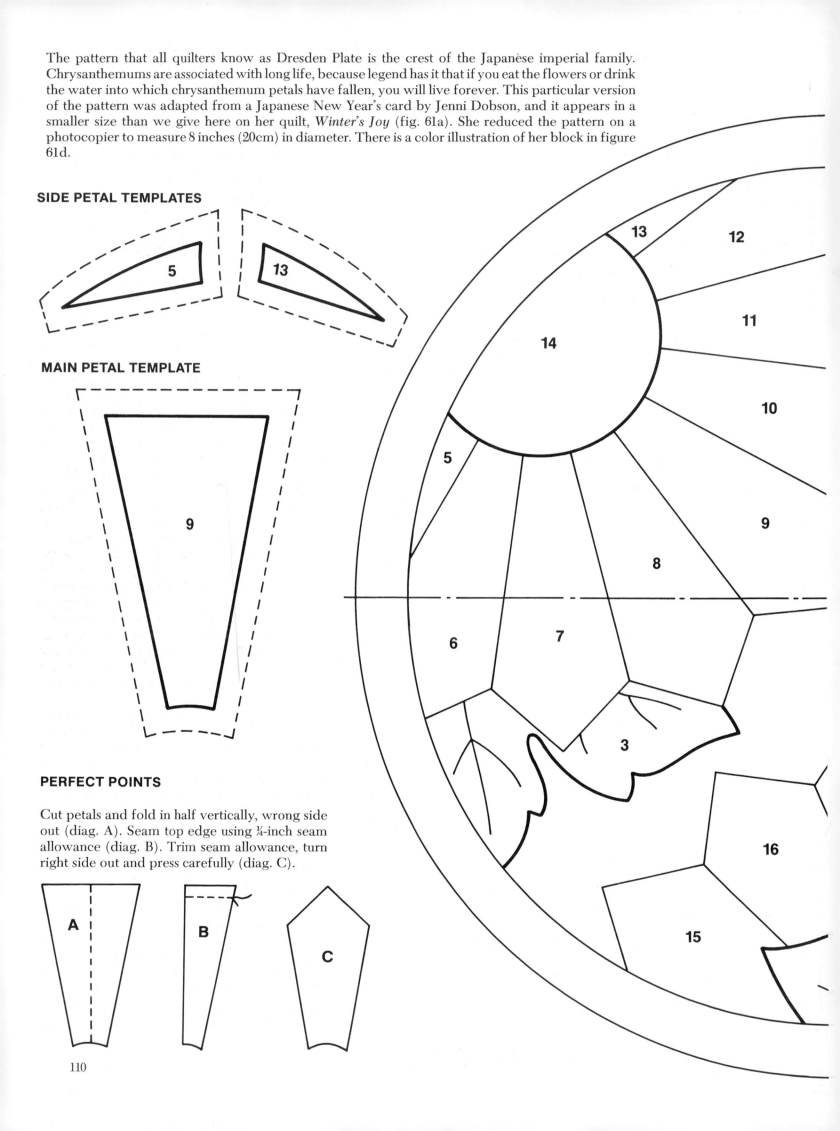

6. Chrysanthemum *(Kiku)*

12-inch (30.5cm) block
Add ¼-inch (7mm) seam allowances

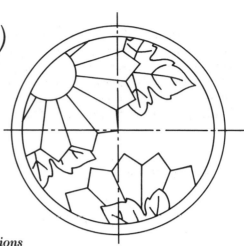

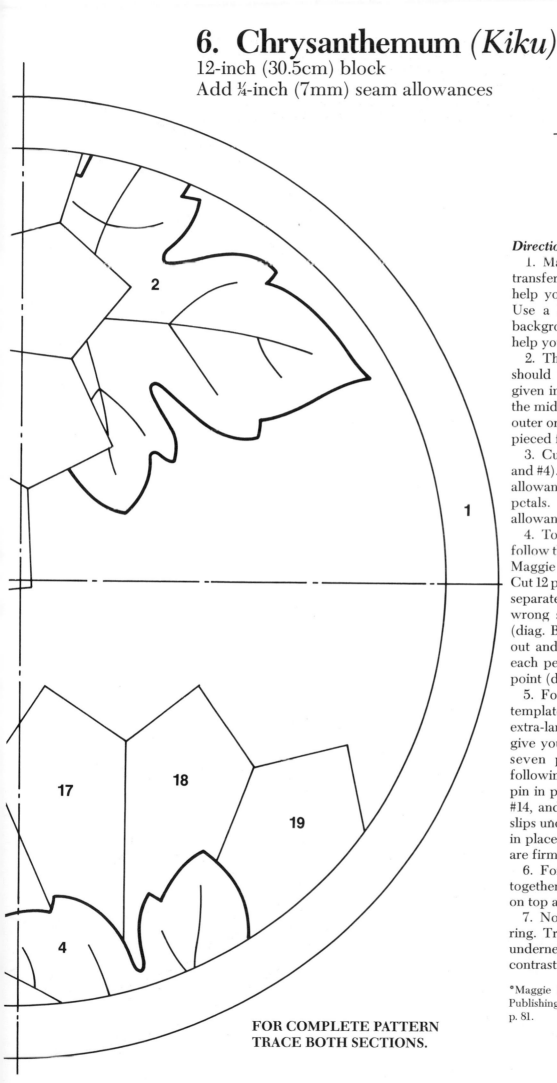

Directions

1. Make a tracing of the complete block and transfer the outline to your background fabric to help you position the pattern pieces correctly. Use a light source if necessary. Crease your background fabric in half and then quarters to help you align the pattern.

2. The 10-inch (25.5cm) ring (template #1) should be applied first following the method given in Tips and Techniques 11. Baste through the middle of the ring, but do not sew either the outer or the inner rim as you will need to slip the pieced flowers and leaves underneath it.

3. Cut out the leaves next (templates #2, #3, and #4). Make sure that you add on enough seam allowance to slip under the ring and the flower petals. Mark the leaf-veins and baste seam allowances. Pin leaves #2 and #3 in position.

4. To make automatic points on your petals, follow the following neat technique suggested by Maggie Malone in her book *Quilting Shortcuts*. Cut 12 petals from template #9 (*Note:* this is given separately) and fold each one in half vertically, wrong side out (diag. A). Seam the top edge (diag. B). Trim seam allowance, turn right side out and press carefully, and you will find that each petal has miraculously acquired a perfect point (diag. C)!

5. For the big flower, cut two part-petals from templates #5 and #13. (*Note:* We have marked extra-large seam allowances on these templates to give you enough to tuck under the ring.) Piece seven petals and two part-petals together following numerical sequence on the pattern and pin in position. Cut center circle from template #14, and baste seam allowance except where it slips under the ring. Stitch the flower and leaves in place making sure that your seam allowances are firmly tucked under the ring.

6. For the small flower, piece five petals together. Pin in position. Place leaf (template #4) on top and sew in place.

7. Now sew the inner and outer edges of the ring. Trim any bulky seam allowances that lie underneath it. Embroider or quilt leaf-veins in contrasting thread.

°Maggie Malone, *Quilting Shortcuts*, New York: Sterling Publishing Co., Inc., and Dorset, England: Blandford Press, p. 81.

**FOR COMPLETE PATTERN
TRACE BOTH SECTIONS.**

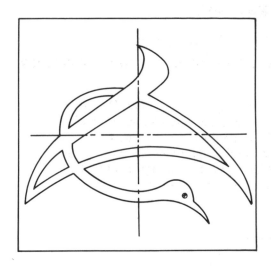

7, 8, and 9. Crane (*Tsuru*)

The crane is admired for its elegance, but it is also an auspicious motif because it represents 1000 years of life and is consequently much favored for bridal wear. Many samurai families, seeking immortality, adopted various crane patterns as their kamon. The designs that you see on these three pages are all heraldic emblems. In Japanese art and textile design the crane is often associated with pine, plum, and bamboo patterns.

7. CALLIGRAPHY CRANE

12-inch (30.5cm) block
Add ¼-inch (7mm) seam allowances

Directions

Jenni Dobson chose a crane pattern in calligraphic form for her kimono on page 60, and has allowed us to reproduce it here. She worked her design in reverse appliqué, but you could also apply it with the needle-turn method (see Tips and Techniques 7e and 7b). Make a tracing of the complete pattern and transfer this to your fabric using a light source if necessary. An illustration of Jenni's calligraphy crane is also on page 60.

**FOR COMPLETE PATTERN
TRACE BOTH SECTIONS**

Directions

1. This is an easy block to sew. Crease your background in half and then quarters and use these crease marks to align the pattern pieces correctly. Cut the right-hand crane from template #1. Reverse the template and cut the left-hand crane. Trace the markings on the wings and bodies, using a light source if necessary.

2. Because of all the curves along the outer edges of the wings, you might find it easier to baste the cranes to your background fabric and needle-turn the seam allowances under, clipping the curves as you go.

3. Cut two beaks from template #2. Baste seam allowances (you will have to trim some of the fabric away at the point of each beak), or use the needle-turn method here too. Overlap the right beak over the left beak.

4. Embroider or quilt the markings in contrasting thread.

8. FACING CRANES

10-inch (25.5cm) block
Add ¼-inch (7mm) seam allowances

This pattern appears on Jenni Dobson's quilt, *Winter's Joy*, on page 66, but she had it enlarged on a photocopier to measure 12 inches (30.5cm) in diameter. An illustration of the block appears in figure 61e. The design is taken from a kamon.

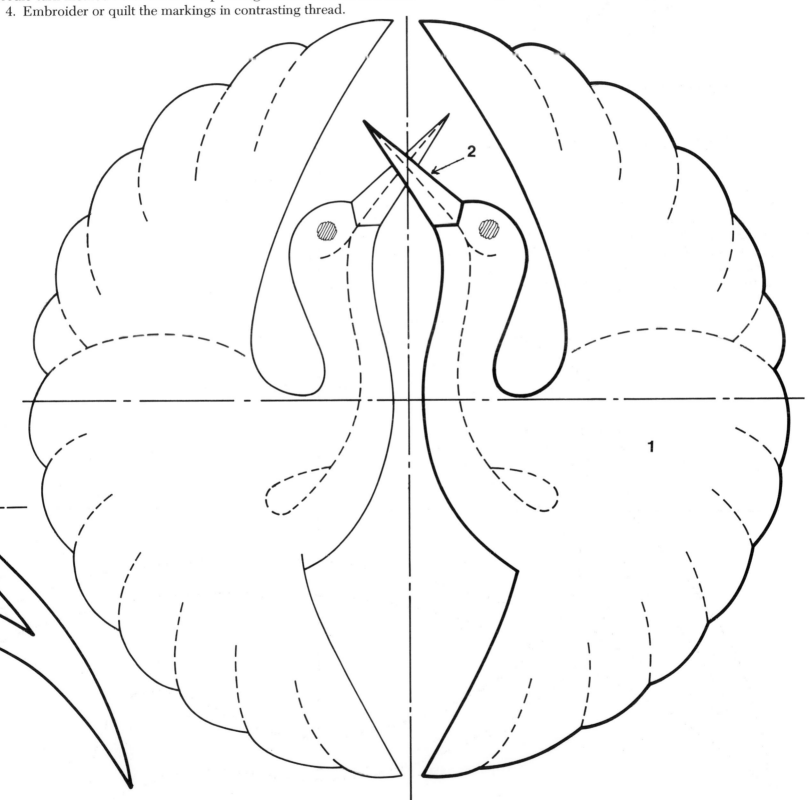

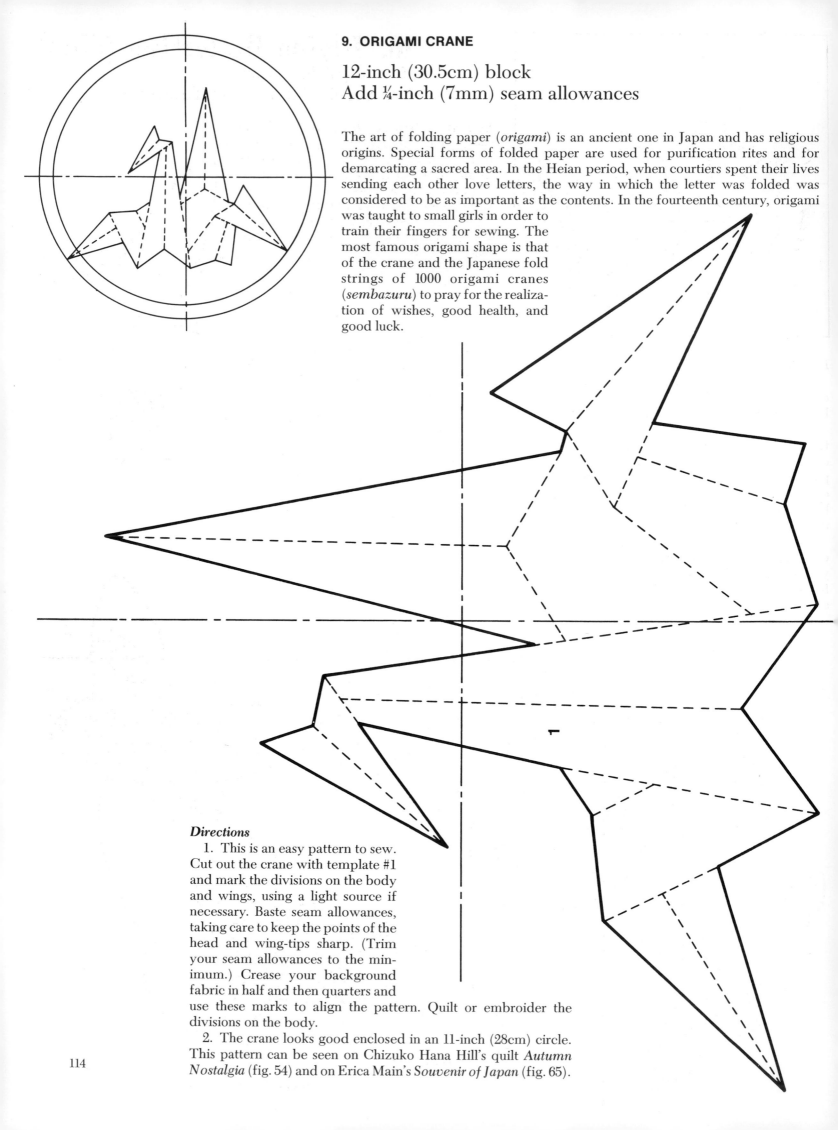

9. ORIGAMI CRANE

12-inch (30.5cm) block
Add ¼-inch (7mm) seam allowances

The art of folding paper (*origami*) is an ancient one in Japan and has religious origins. Special forms of folded paper are used for purification rites and for demarcating a sacred area. In the Heian period, when courtiers spent their lives sending each other love letters, the way in which the letter was folded was considered to be as important as the contents. In the fourteenth century, origami was taught to small girls in order to train their fingers for sewing. The most famous origami shape is that of the crane and the Japanese fold strings of 1000 origami cranes (*sembazuru*) to pray for the realization of wishes, good health, and good luck.

Directions

1. This is an easy pattern to sew. Cut out the crane with template #1 and mark the divisions on the body and wings, using a light source if necessary. Baste seam allowances, taking care to keep the points of the head and wing-tips sharp. (Trim your seam allowances to the minimum.) Crease your background fabric in half and then quarters and use these marks to align the pattern. Quilt or embroider the divisions on the body.

2. The crane looks good enclosed in an 11-inch (28cm) circle. This pattern can be seen on Chizuko Hana Hill's quilt *Autumn Nostalgia* (fig. 54) and on Erica Main's *Souvenir of Japan* (fig. 65).

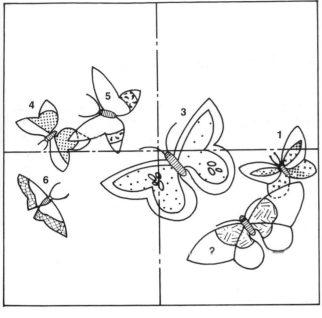

10. Flying Butterflies (Cho)
12-inch (30.5cm) block
Add ¼-inch (7mm) seam allowances

Butterfly patterns speak to all nations, but to the Japanese they have a special, aristocratic appeal. In olden times, warriors displayed butterfly patterns on their armor and many versions appear as family crests. Gill Bryan drew an elegant flight of butterflies for her quilt, *Summer's Splendor*; you can see this block in color with her quilt (figs. 34a, 34d).

Directions

1. Fold your background fabric in half and then quarters and use the crease marks to align your butterflies. Refer to the diagram for placement.

2. Cut the basic shape of each butterfly from one fabric and let your imagination run riot for the decoration on the wings. Choose colorful, large-patterned fabrics in contrasting colors, embellish with embroidery, and try reverse appliqué. Hem the butterflies in position following numerical sequence on the pattern.

3. Satin-stitch the bodies, or you could use fabric for butterfly 3 if you prefer. Make French knots for eyes, and outline-stitch the antennae.

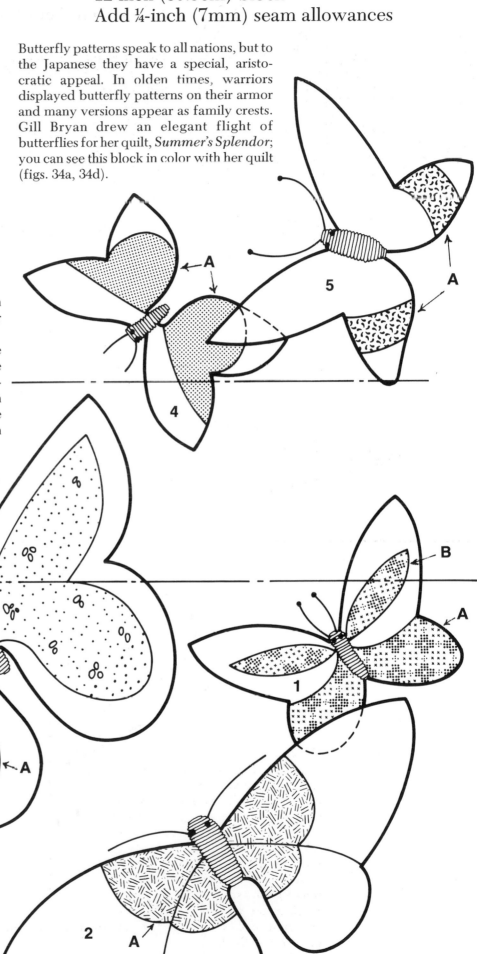

115

Flower arranging in Japan was originally a religious custom, confined to offertory flowers in temples. In the fifteenth century, encouraged by an aesthetic shogun, it became fashionable to arrange flowers in the home—the birth of Japanese ikebana. Wheels have always been associated with good fortune in Japan, and as the giving and receiving of flowers gained popularity, a charming design of flower-filled carts was devised that is still popular today. Gill Bryan adapted this pattern from the kimono in figure 29, and she made it the focal point of her quilt design for *Summer's Splendor* (fig. 34a.) She set it on a 14-inch (35.5cm) block, and you can see an illustration of it in figure 34b.

Directions

1. Make a tracing of the complete pattern and transfer the outline to your background fabric to help you position the pattern pieces correctly. Use a light source if necessary. Crease your background fabric in half and then quarters to help you align the pattern.

2. Make the wheels (see directions below) and hem wheel B and then wheel A in place.

3. Cut out three long leaves from template #5, then reverse it and cut out four more. Baste seam allowances and sew in place.

4. Cut out three peony leaves from template #6, then reverse it and cut out two more. Mark veins and baste seam allowances. Sew in place. (*Note:* We have not marked a sewing sequence for these leaves on the pattern. All long leaves are marked #5 or #5r, and all peony leaves are marked #6 or #6r.)

5. Cut out two each of the five peony petals (templates #7 through #11). You will find it easier to manipulate the curves on the petals if you use fine 100% cotton. Vary the coloring to add interest. Baste seam allowances; you could use paper templates for greater accuracy. Stitch the lower blossom in place first, following the numerical sequence given on the pattern. Repeat for the upper blossom.

6. Embroider or quilt the division on petals (template #11.)

Directions for Wheels

1. Make wheel A on a 7-inch (18cm) background square of muslin. Cut out and baste the outer rim first (template A1), but do not stitch it down until you have made the patchwork spokes.

2. Cut four light and 4 medium spokes (template A2). Patch these together, alternating the colors until you have a complete circle. Press carefully.

3. Slip the outer edge of your patched spokes under the unsewn edge of the wheel's rim, pin or baste in place. Make sure you have centered it correctly.

4. Sew the inner and outer edges of the rim (clip the inner seam allowance in place), making sure that you catch the patched spokes. Work on a flat surface to prevent wrinkles.

5. Cut out center of wheel (template A3) and stitch in place.

6. Now cut out the wheel from the muslin backing, leaving a ¼-inch (7mm) seam allowance round the outside. Baste this down. Cut away as much of the muslin backing from behind the wheel as you can without weakening the structure.

7. For wheel B, follow the directions above but *omit* steps 2 and 5. Use template B4 to cut the inner circle. Trim away the unwanted part of wheel B after pinning wheel A in place.

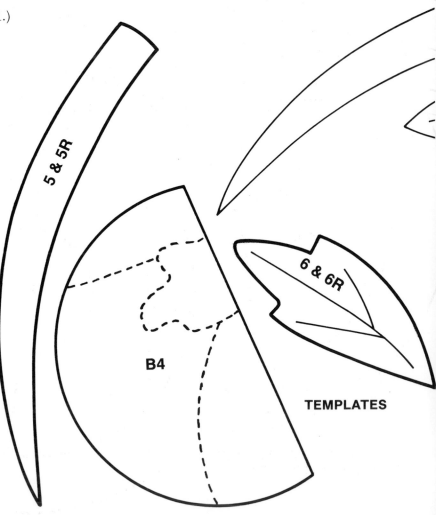

5 & 5R

6 & 6R

B4

TEMPLATES

11. Flower Cart
(*Hana Garuma*)

12-inch (30.5cm) or 14-inch (35.5cm) block
Add ¼-inch (7mm) seam allowances

5R

5R

5

6R

6

7

8

11

5

5R

9

10

6R

7

5

11

10

8

6R

5R

6

A1 & B1

9

A2

B4

A3

**FOR COMPLETE PATTERN
TRACE BOTH SECTIONS.**

117

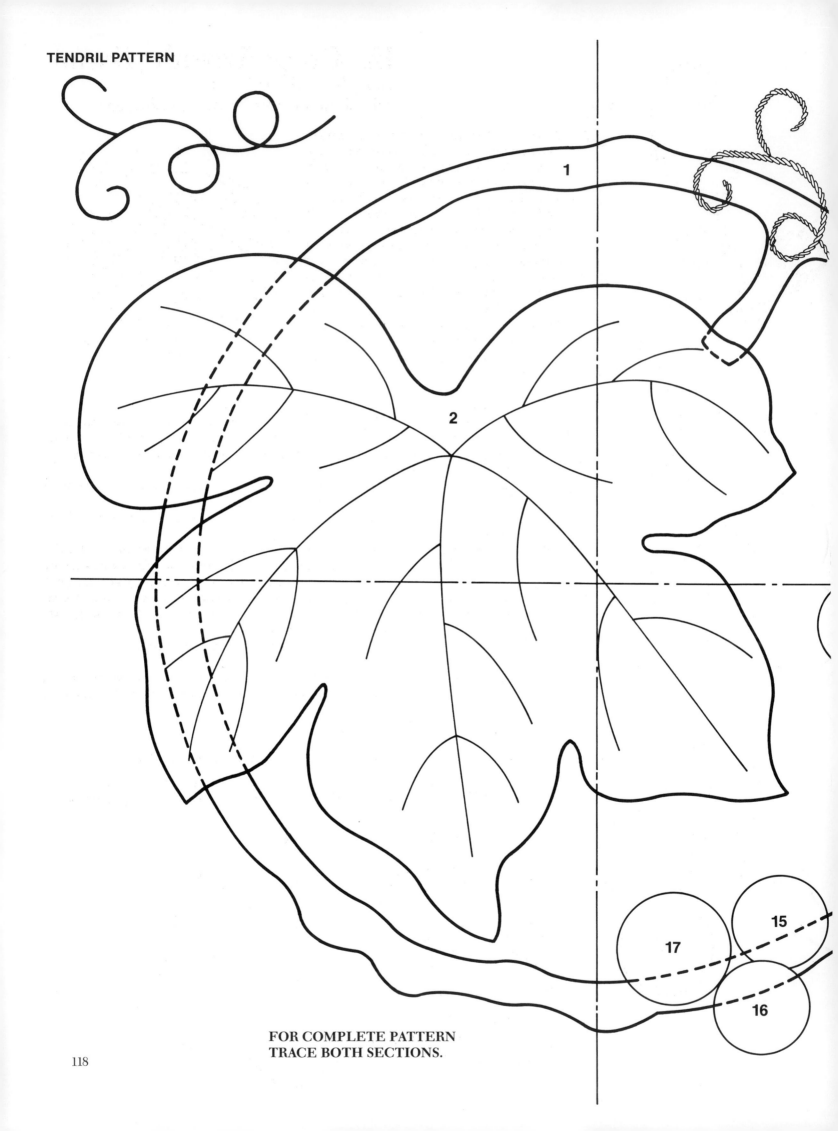

TENDRIL PATTERN

1

2

15

17

16

**FOR COMPLETE PATTERN
TRACE BOTH SECTIONS.**

118

12. Grape Wreath (Budo)
12-inch (30.5cm) block
Add ¼-inch (7mm) seam allowances

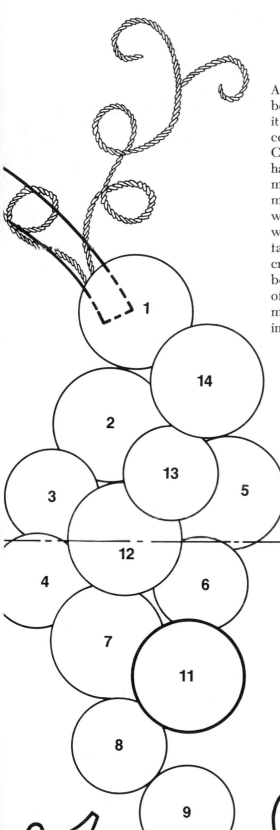

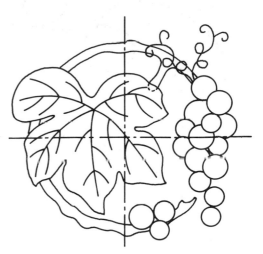

A pattern of grapes and leaves has always been admired by the Japanese ever since it came to Japan, via China, in the eighth century, when it was thought to be a Christian pattern. Echoes of Christianity had reached Japan by then. The vine itself may have arrived later and, until the modern era, was never associated with wine-drinking, for the native wine is sake, which is made from rice. A few samurai families chose grape designs for their family crest, probably out of deference to its beauty rather than its Christian antecedents, of which this pattern is one. It appears on my quilt, *The Vintage*, which you will find in figure 53.

Directions

1. Make a tracing of the complete design first in order to obtain the pattern for the circular stem. (*Note* that it appears in dotted form under the leaf.) Crease your background fabric in half and then quarters and use the crease marks to help you align the pattern pieces.

2. Apply the stem first (template #1), baste in position, and needle-turn the seam allowances except where the stem is covered by the leaf.

3. Cut out leaf (template #2) and mark the veins. Baste seam allowances and sew in position.

4. Cut nine grapes from template #10 and eight grapes from template #11. Use a variety of solid and patterned fabrics to add interest. (Sachiko Gunji's use of different patterned fabrics adds such richness to the bunches of grapes on her quilt, *Bird Mandala—Grapes*, in figure 52.) Baste grapes over paper (or use freezer paper) to get perfect circles (see Tips and Techniques 7c). Sew the grapes following the numerical sequence given on the pattern.

5. Mark and embroider tendrils. Quilt or embroider leaf veins.

Template #18 is an extra leaf that I used in various sizes on my quilt mentioned above. I also scattered the big leaf, reversing some of them to create a sense of movement.

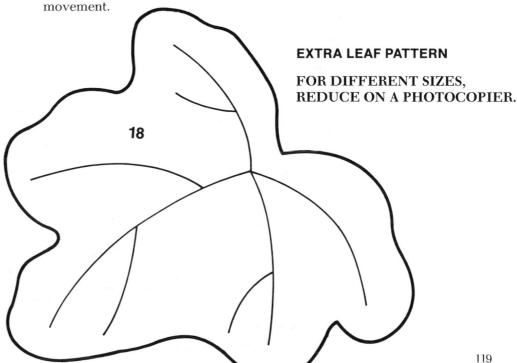

EXTRA LEAF PATTERN

FOR DIFFERENT SIZES, REDUCE ON A PHOTOCOPIER.

**FOR COMPLETE PATTERN
TRACE BOTH SECTIONS.**

120

13. Hollyhock (Aoi)
12-inch (30.5cm) block
Add ¼-inch (7mm) seam allowances

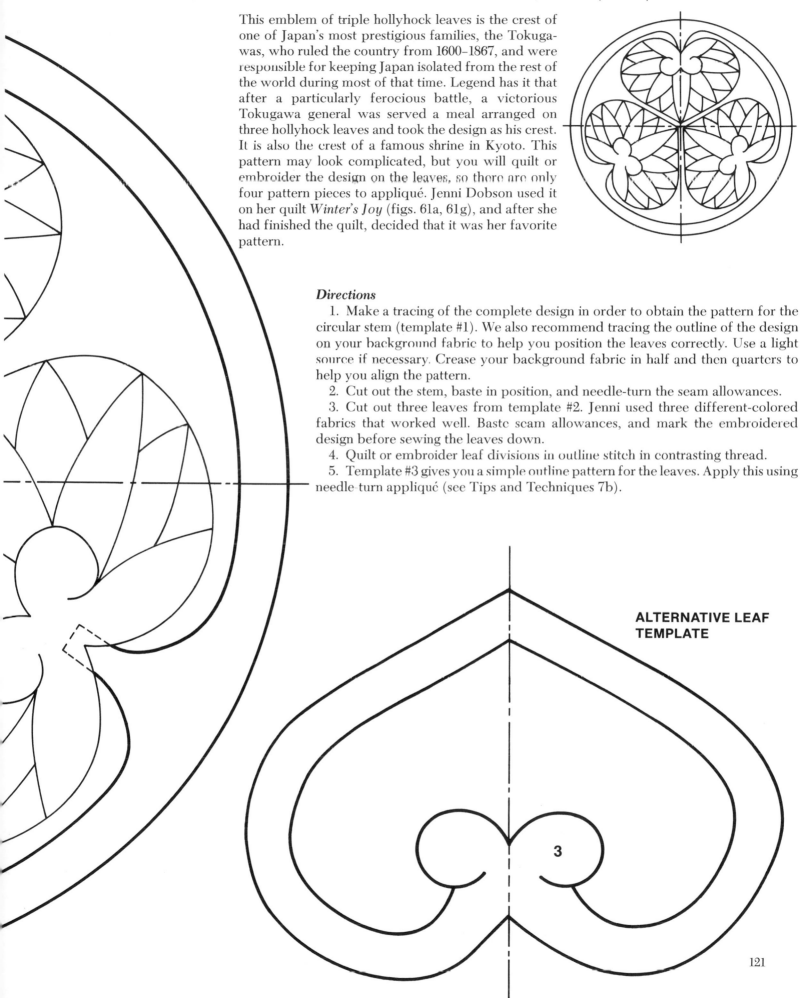

This emblem of triple hollyhock leaves is the crest of one of Japan's most prestigious families, the Tokugawas, who ruled the country from 1600–1867, and were responsible for keeping Japan isolated from the rest of the world during most of that time. Legend has it that after a particularly ferocious battle, a victorious Tokugawa general was served a meal arranged on three hollyhock leaves and took the design as his crest. It is also the crest of a famous shrine in Kyoto. This pattern may look complicated, but you will quilt or embroider the design on the leaves, so there are only four pattern pieces to appliqué. Jenni Dobson used it on her quilt *Winter's Joy* (figs. 61a, 61g), and after she had finished the quilt, decided that it was her favorite pattern.

Directions

1. Make a tracing of the complete design in order to obtain the pattern for the circular stem (template #1). We also recommend tracing the outline of the design on your background fabric to help you position the leaves correctly. Use a light source if necessary. Crease your background fabric in half and then quarters to help you align the pattern.

2. Cut out the stem, baste in position, and needle-turn the seam allowances.

3. Cut out three leaves from template #2. Jenni used three different-colored fabrics that worked well. Baste seam allowances, and mark the embroidered design before sewing the leaves down.

4. Quilt or embroider leaf divisions in outline stitch in contrasting thread.

5. Template #3 gives you a simple outline pattern for the leaves. Apply this using needle-turn appliqué (see Tips and Techniques 7b).

ALTERNATIVE LEAF TEMPLATE

3

121

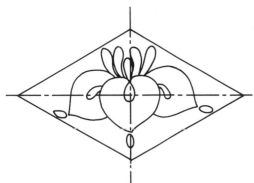

14. DIAMOND IRIS

Diamond-shaped patterns are traditionally Japanese, and Sanae Hattori has kindly agreed to let us feature her unique design of a diamond-block quilt (fig. 31). The directions are given in Pattern Projects.

1. This iris pattern will fit on the 12¼-inch (31cm) diameter diamond-block given in Pattern 30b, or you can use it as an individual motif—as a border pattern, for example.

2. Cut out three flower petals from templates #1, #2, and #8. You can embroider the markings, or make them in contrasting fabric as Sanae has done on her quilt. (You could also try reverse appliqué.) Cut out top petals, templates #3 through #7, in toning or contrasting colored fabrics. Baste seam allowances except where they tuck under the big petals. Sew in position following the numerical sequence on the pattern.

3. The little "drops" (templates #9, #10, and #11) at the tip of each petal can either be done with appliqué or embroidered in satin stitch.

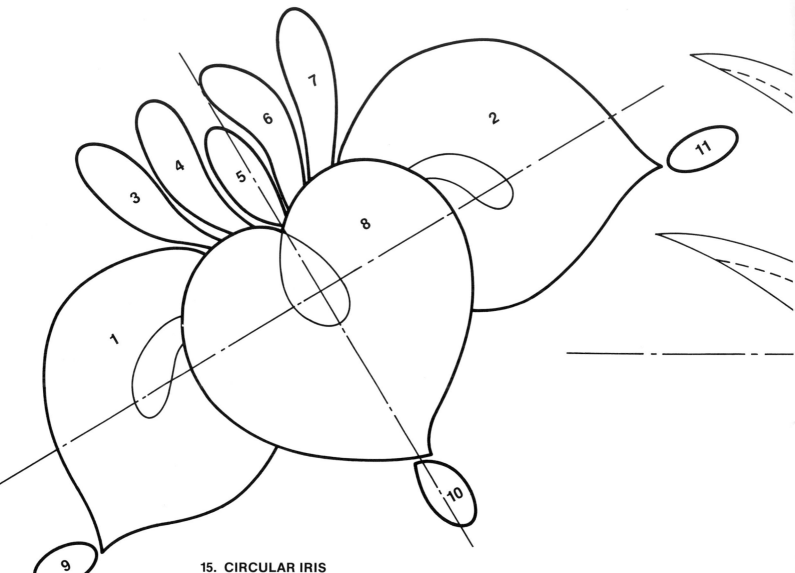

15. CIRCULAR IRIS

1. This pattern fits inside an 11-inch (28cm) circle (see pattern 29a). Crease your background fabric in half and then quarters and apply the circle first (see Tips and Techniques 11). *Note:* Do not sew the inside edge on the bottom part of the circle as you will be tucking the lower ends of the stalk and leaves underneath it.

2. Cut out the stalk (template #1), and three leaves from each of templates #2, #3, and #4. Reverse your leaf templates for the left side (flip them over when drawing around them). Baste seam allowances except on bottom edges, and pin the stalk in position on the center fold. Align your leaves on each side, being careful to tuck the seam allowances under the inner rim of the circle. Sew down following the numerical sequence on the pattern. As you can see from the diagram, the tips of the topmost leaves will lie over the edge of the circle. Finish sewing the circle.

3. Cut out three flower petals using templates #5, #6, and #8. Baste seam allowances except where the two side petals tuck under the main flower petal. You can either embroider the markings on the petals, or make them from contrasting fabric. Cut out the top petal (template #7) using a different tone or colored fabric, and mark the divisions which can be either embroidered or quilted in contrasting thread. Sew petals in position following the numerical sequence on the pattern.

4. Embroider or quilt markings on petals and leaves in contrasting thread.

The Japanese love their irises almost as much as they love their cherry blossom. The flower has been the idol of poets and painters since ancient times, and an annual festival used to be held on May 5th, when people decorated their houses with irises, believing that the scent would drive away evil spirits. Today, the Japanese celebrate the Boy's Day festival on May 5th, the day they fly the huge carp-shaped windsocks from flagpoles on their houses, but irises are still associated with this festival (see fig. 30). Both the designs on these pages are taken from kamon.

14 and 15. Iris (*Ayame*)
12-inch (30.5cm) block
Add ¼-inch (7mm)
seam allowances

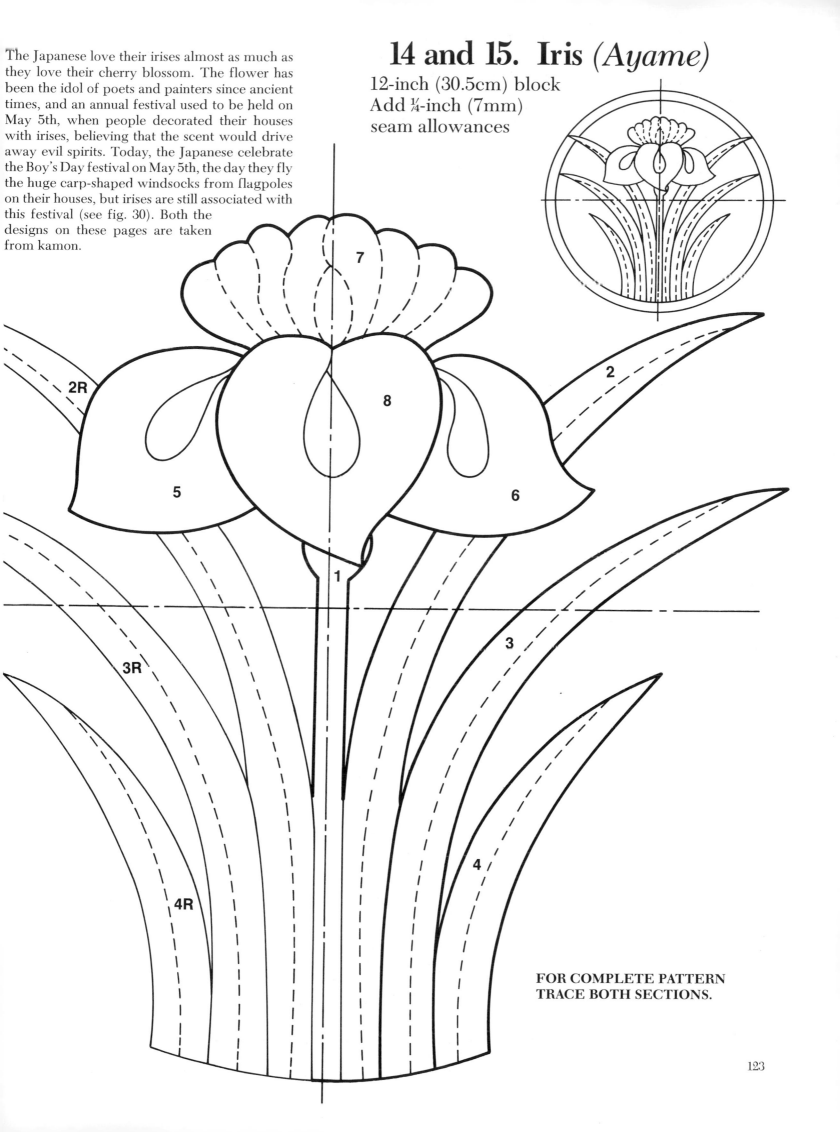

**FOR COMPLETE PATTERN
TRACE BOTH SECTIONS.**

123

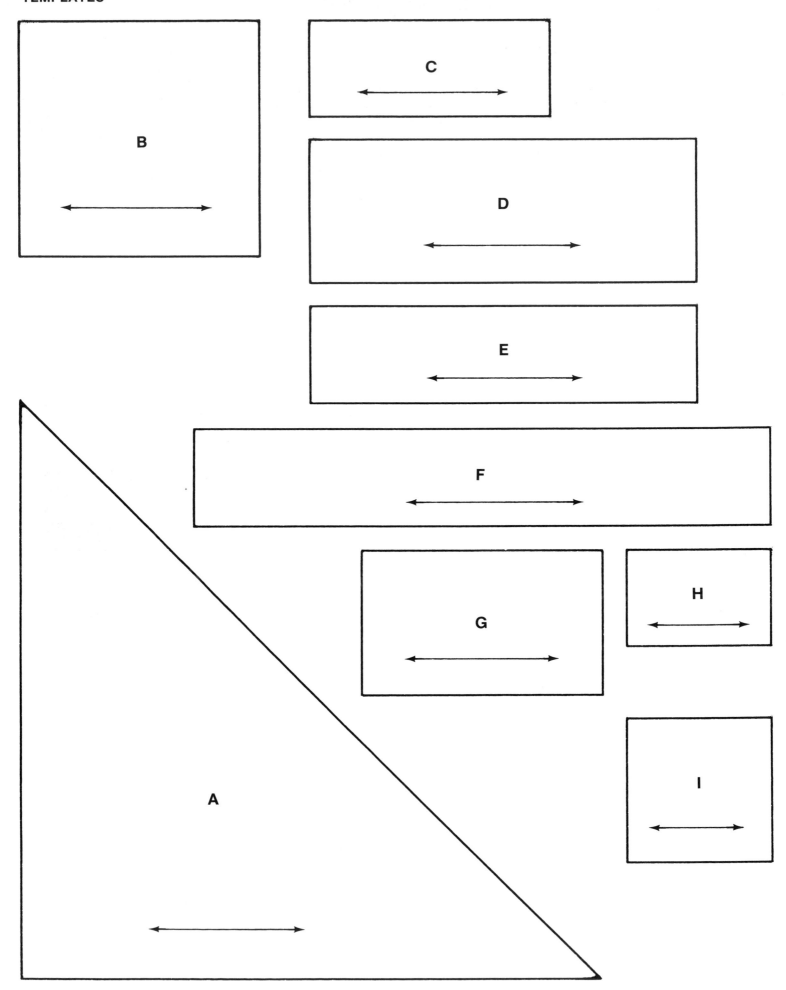

16. Interlocking Squares (*Kuginuki*)
12-inch (30.5cm) block
Add ¼-inch (7mm) seam allowances

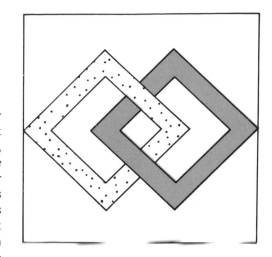

This pattern is a kamon, and the design is known in Japanese as *kuginuki*, which actually means "nail extractor" because it looked like the tip of a carpenter's tool, possibly some sort of crowbar. It was a popular motif among the samurai who liked the implications of power, but a continuous pattern of interlocking squares is an old one that is found in all the decorative arts. Yukiko Endo's design for her quilt, *Interlocking Squares* (fig. 72), for example, was taken from the type of inlaid woodwork done in the Mount Fuji area, but as we illustrate in figure 69, it was also used by tie-dye craftsmen for kimono. Yukiko has generously let us give the pattern for her quilt (see Pattern Projects 4), but the block construction for continuous interlocking squares used there is different from the one shown here. We thought this version might provide you with an interesting contrast to applique floral blocks for an album quilt.

Directions
Each block requires 4 white A, 2 white B, 2 dark print C, 3 medium print C, 2 white D, 2 dark print E, 1 medium print E, 1 medium print F, 1 dark print F, 2 white G, 1 medium print H, 1 white I.

Directions for piecing are given in Tips and Techniques 8.

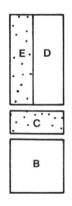 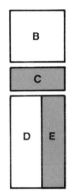

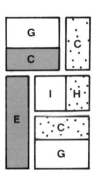

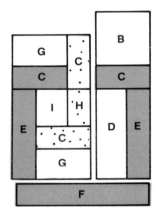

UNIT 1
Make one unit
following diagram.

UNIT 2
Make one unit
following diagram.

UNIT 3
Make one unit
following diagram.

UNIT 4
Piece unit 3 to unit 2
Add dark print F,
following diagram.

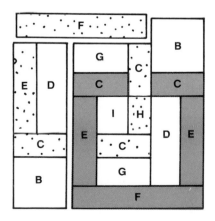

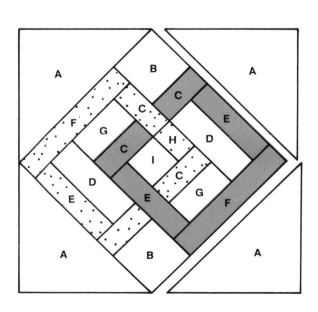

UNIT 5
Piece unit 1 to left-hand side
of unit 3/2 and insert one
F patch following diagram.

UNIT 6
Turn completed unit on point
and sew one Triangle A to
each corner following diagram 6.

125

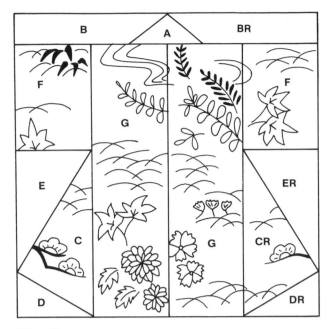

17. Kimono
10-inch (25.4cm) block
Add ¼-inch (7mm) seam allowances

Once the everyday costume of both men and women in Japan, the beautiful kimono is now rarely worn except for ceremonial occasions. Traditional kimono fabric is only 14 inches (36cm) wide, and it is woven to accommodate the various parts of the garment. The Japanese dislike wasting fabric, so apart from the collar and collar band, there is no tailoring, and the fabric is cut into standard lengths and sewn together along the selvedges with a running stitch.

All kimono are the same size—if you are very short, you take in a tuck around the waist—and the fabric is sold in rolls of 1 *tan* (approximately 12½ yards; 11.70 meters), which is enough for one garment. Sawako Tsurugiji has kindly given us permission to feature her kimono pattern from her quilt, *Kimono*, illustrated in figure 39.

Directions

For piecing instructions see Tips and Techniques 8, but remember to place your templates *face down* on the wrong side of your fabric because templates C, D, and E are not symmetrical. Make templates and cut one A, one each of B and Br (flip your template over for the Br), one each of C and Cr, one each of D and Dr, one each of E and Er, two F and two G. Sew together in the following order.

1. Sew B and Br to A to make collar panel.

2. Sew C to D and Cr to Dr.

3. Sew these two units to an E and Er to make lower side panels (see diagram for placement).

4. Sew these two units to F to make complete side panel.

5. Seam two Gs together vertically.

6. Sew completed side panel to each side of Gs (see diagram for placement).

7. Sew this unit to collar panel, B/A/Br to finish the block.

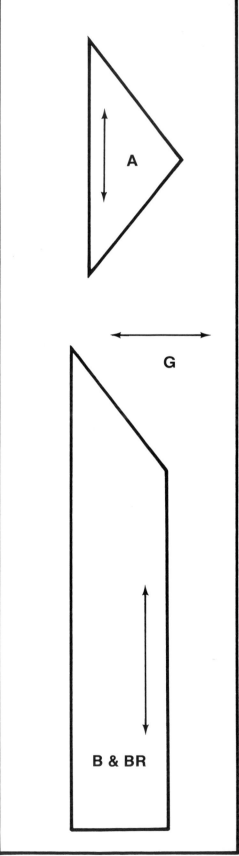

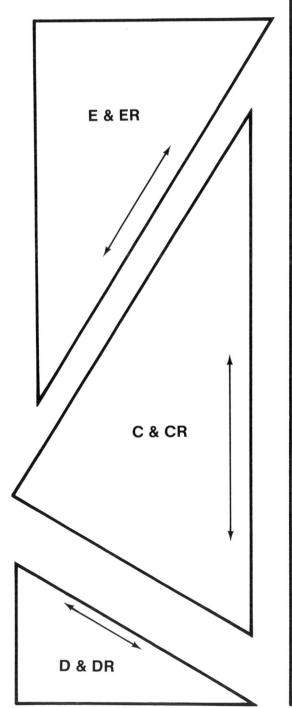

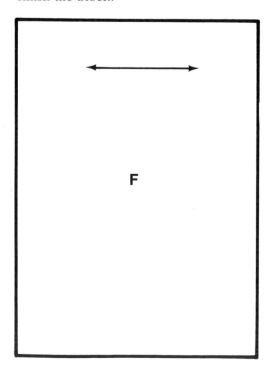

18. Knotted Square (*Musubikaku*)

12-inch (30.5cm) block
Add ¼-inch (7mm) seam allowances

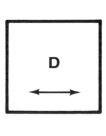

In common with other countries, the Japanese have a variety of geometric patterns based on squares. This interwoven pattern is a kamon that Emiko Toda Loeb adapted for her quilt, *Knotted Square*, illustrated in figure 74, which she has kindly given us permission to include here. If you look at her quilt, you will see that Emiko has colored each of her blocks differently, which makes this pattern an ideal candidate for a scrap quilt.

Directions

Each block requires 4 light solid A, 9 light solid B, 4 light solid C, 4 light solid D, 8 dark print C, 4 dark print D, 12 medium print C.

Directions for piecing are given in Tips and Techniques 8.

1. Make four units following diagram 1.
2. Make four units following diagram 2.
3. Piece units together following diagram 3, giving each unit 1 a quarter turn to create the pattern.
4. Turn block on point to create the pattern and stitch blocks together in diagonal rows.

BLOCK PIECING DIAGRAM 3

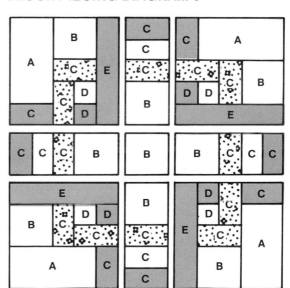

DIAGRAM 1

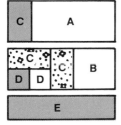

DIAGRAM 2

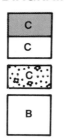

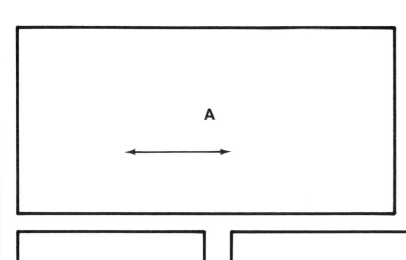

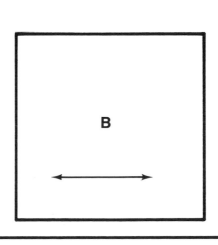

19. Mandarin Ducks (*Oshidori*)
12-inch (30.5cm) block
Add ¼-inch (7mm) seam allowances

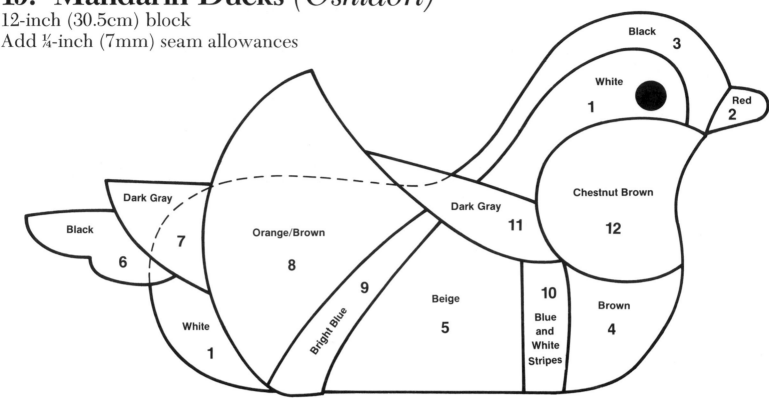

In both China and Japan, a pair of mandarin ducks is a symbol of marital fidelity, despite the fact that in nature the birds change their partners each year. Japanese artists in the past delighted in featuring these attractive little birds—the handsome drake with his colorful plumage and a suitably deferential female dressed in drab grays. They appear in all the decorative arts, but particularly as embroidered motifs on textiles, and always in association with some sort of water pattern (see fig. 2). These mandarins appear on Sachiko Gunji's quilt, *Midsummer* (fig. 16d), and she has kindly given us permission to reproduce them here.

Directions

1. Unless you plan to use the ducks in a block, you would be wise to make each one on a scrap of muslin. Then cut it out, leaving a ¼-inch (7mm) seam allowance all around, and sew it in place on your quilt. The correct coloring of the plumage is given on the pattern, but allow yourself some artistic license and use different patterned fabrics to suit your color scheme. The drake will fit on the diamond block given in pattern 30b.

2. THE DRAKE

Cut out the shape of the duck's body except for the beak and tail feathers, in white fabric (template #1), and trace each section of plumage on this basic shape to assist placement. Make templates for each section of plumage and study the pattern carefully to see which seam allowances need to be basted, and which will be covered by another patch. Apply plumage following the numerical sequence given on the pattern. Embroider the eye in satin stitch.

3. FEMALE DUCK

Trace the shape of the duck on a scrap of muslin and then apply each section of plumage following the numerical sequence given on the pattern. Embroider eyes of both ducks in satin stitch.

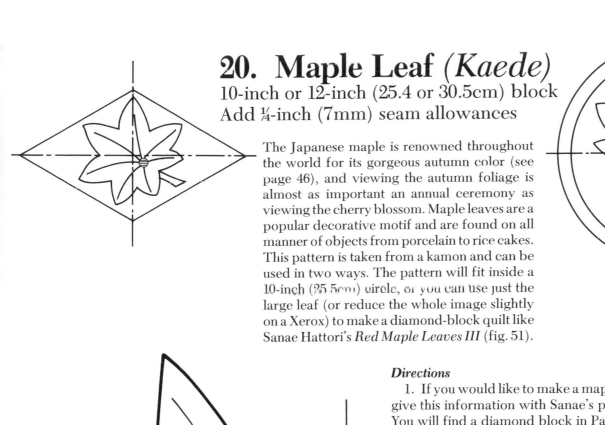

20. Maple Leaf (*Kaede*)
10-inch or 12-inch (25.4 or 30.5cm) block
Add ¼-inch (7mm) seam allowances

The Japanese maple is renowned throughout the world for its gorgeous autumn color (see page 46), and viewing the autumn foliage is almost as important an annual ceremony as viewing the cherry blossom. Maple leaves are a popular decorative motif and are found on all manner of objects from porcelain to rice cakes. This pattern is taken from a kamon and can be used in two ways. The pattern will fit inside a 10-inch (25.5cm) circle, or you can use just the large leaf (or reduce the whole image slightly on a Xerox) to make a diamond-block quilt like Sanae Hattori's *Red Maple Leaves III* (fig. 51).

Directions

1. If you would like to make a maple-leaf diamond block quilt, we give this information with Sanae's permission in Pattern Projects 1. You will find a diamond block in Pattern 30b.

2. If you plan to enclose maple leaves in a circle, use pattern 29b and apply this first (see Tips and Techniques 11). Crease your background fabric in half and then quarters to help you align the pattern.

3. Cut out two leaves from templates #1 and #3. Cut the stalk from template #2. Mark leaf veins and baste seam allowances.

4. Apply motifs to background fabric following the numerical sequence given on the pattern.

5. Quilt or embroider leaf veins in contrasting thread, but as the center circle (#4) is so small, we suggest you do this in satin stitch and outline-stitch around it afterwards.

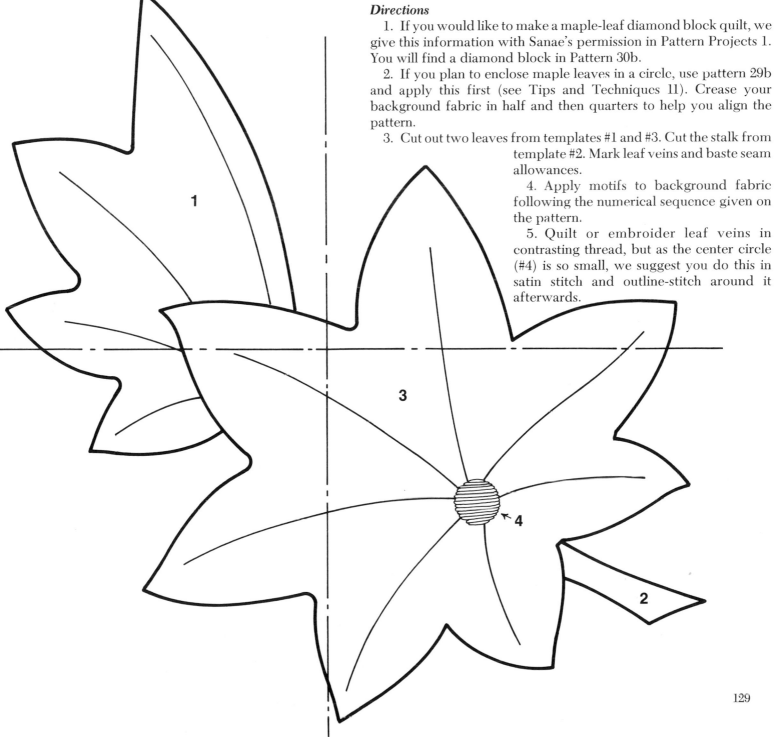

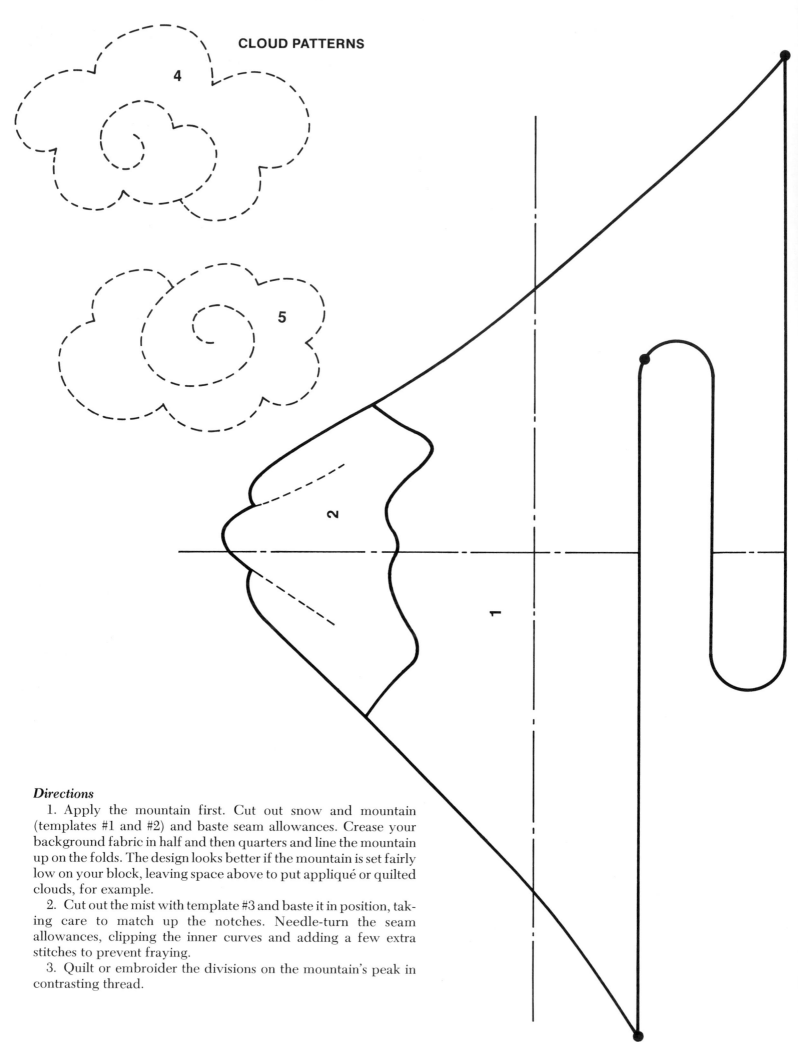

CLOUD PATTERNS

4

5

2

1

Directions

1. Apply the mountain first. Cut out snow and mountain (templates #1 and #2) and baste seam allowances. Crease your background fabric in half and then quarters and line the mountain up on the folds. The design looks better if the mountain is set fairly low on your block, leaving space above to put appliqué or quilted clouds, for example.

2. Cut out the mist with template #3 and baste it in position, taking care to match up the notches. Needle-turn the seam allowances, clipping the inner curves and adding a few extra stitches to prevent fraying.

3. Quilt or embroider the divisions on the mountain's peak in contrasting thread.

21. Mount Fuji and Mist
12-inch (30.5cm) block
Add ¼-inch (7mm) seam allowances

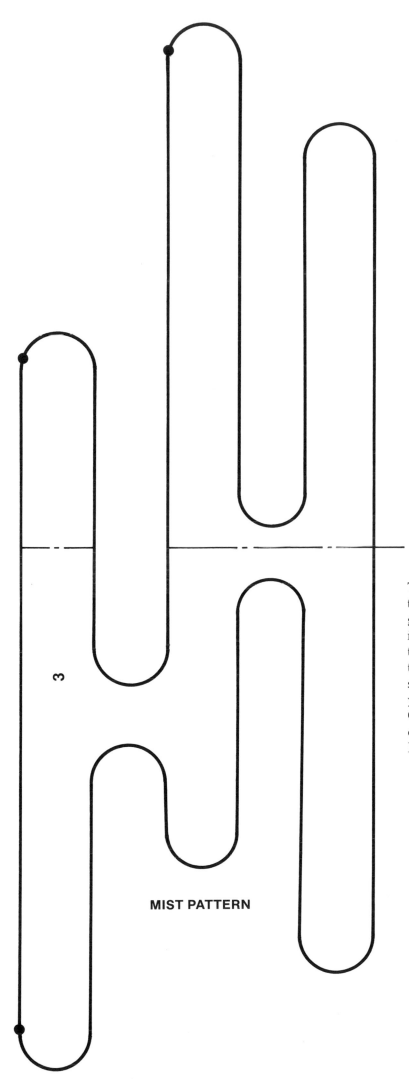

3

MIST PATTERN

To most foreigners, Mount Fuji is the symbol of Japan, and to the Japanese it is one of their most sacred icons. Mountains are generally considered auspicious. Primeval, massive, unyielding, they represent the male force of the universe, the *yang* to the feminine softness and fluidity of water (*yin*). In this pattern, taken from a kamon, Mount Fuji rises out of bands of mist. This stylized method of depicting mist is typical of Oriental art, and you will find it on Chinese and Japanese scroll paintings. Catherine Felix features this pattern on one of her floor cushions (fig. 48a), and a similar pattern appears on Jenni Dobson's kimono (fig. 56a).

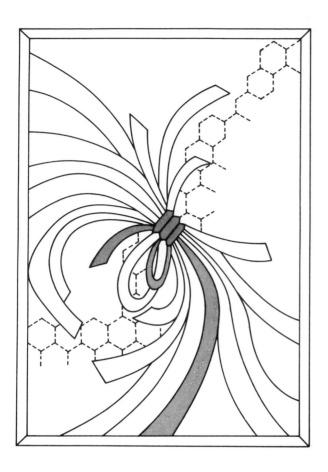

Because this gorgeous design of flying streamers is uniquely Japanese, we have not attempted to translate the name into English. It is a form of talisman, but this is no ordinary talisman such as you might buy at a souvenir shop. The Noshi reaches back into Japan's primitive past, when the only offering people had to make to their gods were the gifts of nature. (For an explanation of the emblem's origins and symbolism, see the caption to the kimono illustrated in figure 3.) We give you two versions of the design drawn over a grid so that you can enlarge it to whatever size you want. Permission to reproduce the Japanese version (the one contained within the inner rectangle) was kindly given to us by Hiroko Oyama, and you can see her quilt in figure 68. But for those of you who might prefer to feature the entire design like I did on my quilt (fig. 67), we have extended the streamers on the diagram with dotted lines.

Directions

1. You will need to make a full-scale drawing in order to make your templates. On our diagram, each square represents 2 inches (5cm), but you can, of course, make this 3 inches or even 4 inches if you want to make a larger quilt. Following our measurements, for Hiroko's "Japanese" version, you will need to cut a piece of paper 22 x 30 inches (56 x 76cm) and divide it into 2-inch (5cm) squares. Draw the Noshi square by square and then transfer the design to your background fabric using a light source if necessary. For the "complete" version, you will need a piece of paper 34 x 36 inches (86.3 x 91.5cm).

2. On the diagram, you will see that we have given each streamer a number and a letter, A or B. The top parts of each streamer, i.e. those above and to the left of the knot, are given the letter A, and those to the right and below the knot are given the letter B. This makes the streamers much more manageable and allows you to cut them in two sections. You will cover the ends of each streamer section with the knot. *Note* that the knot has four parts, which are numbered 11a, 11b, 11c, and 11d.

3. Make a template of each streamer section, numbering them carefully, and when you cut each one out, write the number and letter on the back of the fabric.

4. Baste seam allowances and sew in place following the traced outline on your background fabric. *Note:* On this particular pattern, the numbers on each streamer do *not* represent the sequence in which they should be sewn. You will have to gauge this for yourself by looking at your full-scale drawing.

5. Hiroko quilted the background with a hexagon pattern (template #12). The hexagon represents a tortoise in the Orient, and symbolizes 10,000 years of life, consequently it is always shown standing on one of its points so that it resembles a tortoise shell. Alternatively, you could choose another sashiko pattern; see SASHIKO-PATTERN INDEX.

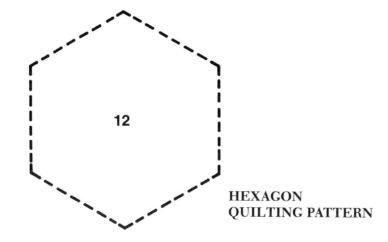

12

HEXAGON QUILTING PATTERN

22. Noshi

Scale: ½ inch equals 2 inches.
Japanese version: 22 x 30 inches (56 x 76cm)
Complete version: 34 x 36 inches (86.3 x 91.5cm)
Add ¼-inch (7mm) seam allowances

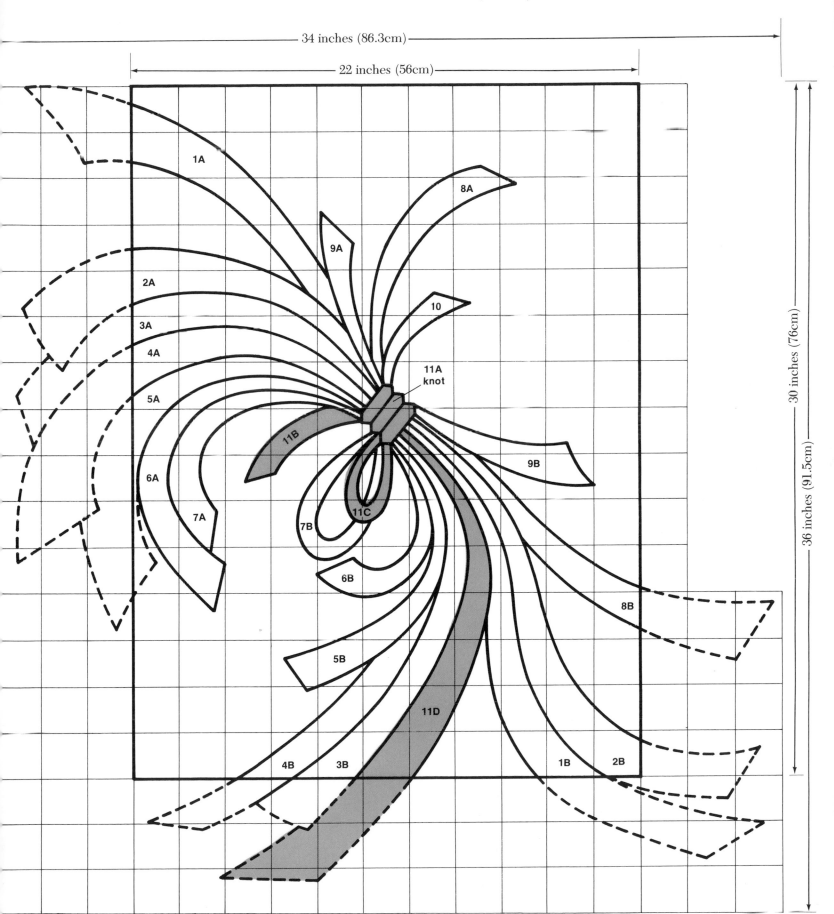

Boxes represent 2 in. squares or 5cm squares

The beautiful peony, known as the "queen of flowers," is a favorite subject in both Chinese and Japanese art, and it is often paired with the lion, the "king of beasts." The plant was imported from China in the eighth century, and it was grown originally for its medicinal properties (an infusion made from the root apparently cured stomach ache, fever, arthritis, and headaches), but the blooms soon came to be admired for their beauty alone. In Japanese heraldry, the peony was a prestigious crest and ranked almost as high as the chrysanthemum and the hollyhock. This pattern was taken from a kamon and made up by Mary Herrold for the group quilt *Japanese Flower Garden* (figs. 33a, 33b).

Directions

1. You will need to make a tracing of this design in order to obtain complete templates as some have been cut in half by the division of the pattern. We also suggest you transfer the design to your background fabric to make it easier to position the stem and the flower petals correctly. Use a light source if necessary.

2. Cut out the stem (template #1) and baste in position. Note that part of the stem is shown as a dotted line under the large leaf. Do not sew it down until you have positioned the large leaf and the flower petals.

3. Cut out the two leaves next (templates #2 and #3) and baste seam allowances. Note that leaf #2 overlaps part of the stem.

4. Make templates for each of the eight petals (templates #4 through #11). Cut these out, using several different tones of fabric, and baste seam allowances except where they tuck under the top of the stem. Blindstitch in place following the numerical order given on the pattern.

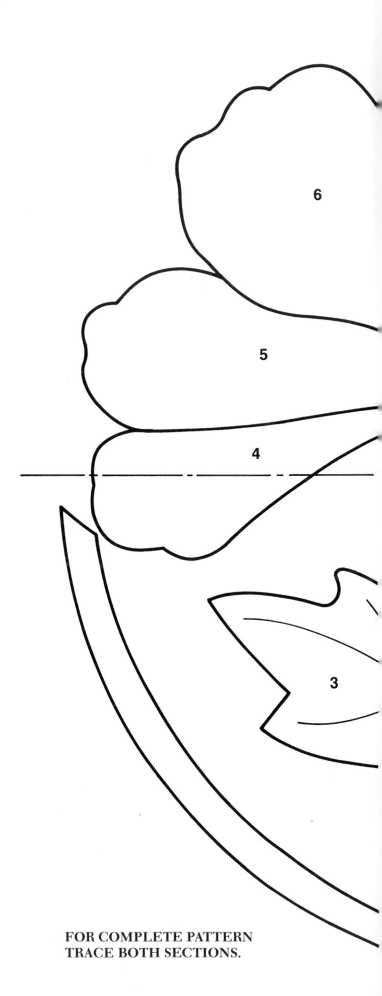

FOR COMPLETE PATTERN TRACE BOTH SECTIONS.

23. Peony (*Botan*)
12-inch (30.5cm) block
Add ¼-inch (7mm) seam allowances

135

24. Plum Blossom Wreath (*Ume*)

12-inch (30.5cm) block
Add ¼-inch (7mm) seam allowances

The Japanese admire plum blossom, not only for its beauty but also because it symbolizes constancy and endurance. The tree is purely ornamental (it is a form of *prunus*), and as it flowers in February, a time of winter chill, it joins the pine and the bamboo as one of the "three companions of the deep cold." The symbolism is explained by the fact that the blossom survives severe weather conditions, and remains on the tree for several weeks. This makes the plum a much more auspicious motif for bridal couples than the fickle cherry blossom that drops at the first hint of a storm! Jenni Dobson adapted this pattern from a nineteenth-century futon cover, probably part of a bridal trousseau, for her quilt, *Winter's Joy* (figs. 61a, 61f).

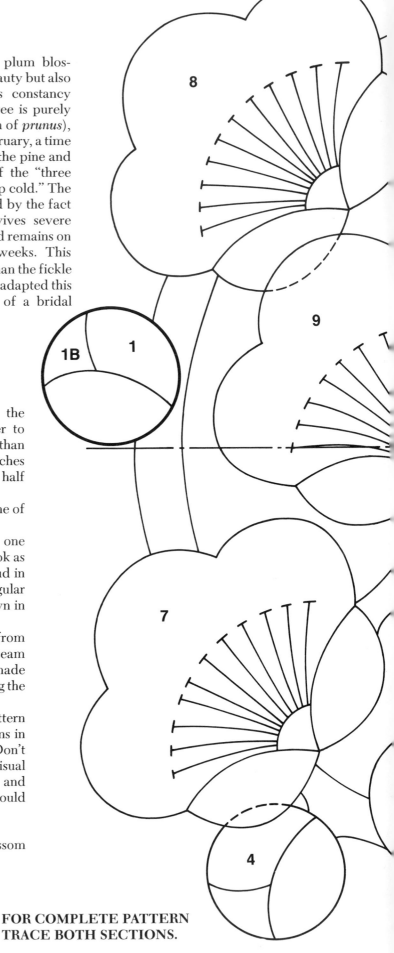

Directions

1. Pattern 29a gives you the pattern and directions for half the circular stem. Follow the directions carefully, because in order to complete the stem, you need to *swivel* the half section, rather than reverse it in the usual way. This puts the two protruding branches diagonally opposite each other. Fold your background fabric in half and then quarters and apply the stem first.

2. Make a tracing of the complete pattern and transfer the outline of the blossoms to your fabric to help you with the positioning.

3. Cut four buds from template #1. You can either make them one color and embroider the divisions, or if you want to make them look as if they are about to burst into flower, cut the lower part of the bud in green fabric and insert a scrap of pink or white fabric into the triangular section (template #1b). Baste seam allowances and sew buds down in the same numerical sequence given on the pattern.

4. Cut three blossoms from template #11 and five blossoms from template #12. Mark the stamens using a light source and baste seam allowances. The two side petals (templates #12a and b) can be made from a different shade of fabric if you wish. Sew blossoms following the numerical sequence given on the pattern.

5. The amount of embroidery looks daunting, but it gives the pattern great delicacy (see Jenni's block in figure 61f). Embroider stamens in outline stitch, finishing with a tiny bar—a single stitch—at the top. Don't worry if your stitching varies from flower to flower, it will add visual interest. You can either embroider the centers of blossoms #5, #6, and #11 in satin stitch and then outline-stitch them afterward, or you could use tiny circles of contrasting fabric.

You can see three enlarged versions of the partially opened blossom (template #12) on Erica Main's quilt, *Souvenir of Japan* (fig. 65).

**FOR COMPLETE PATTERN
TRACE BOTH SECTIONS.**

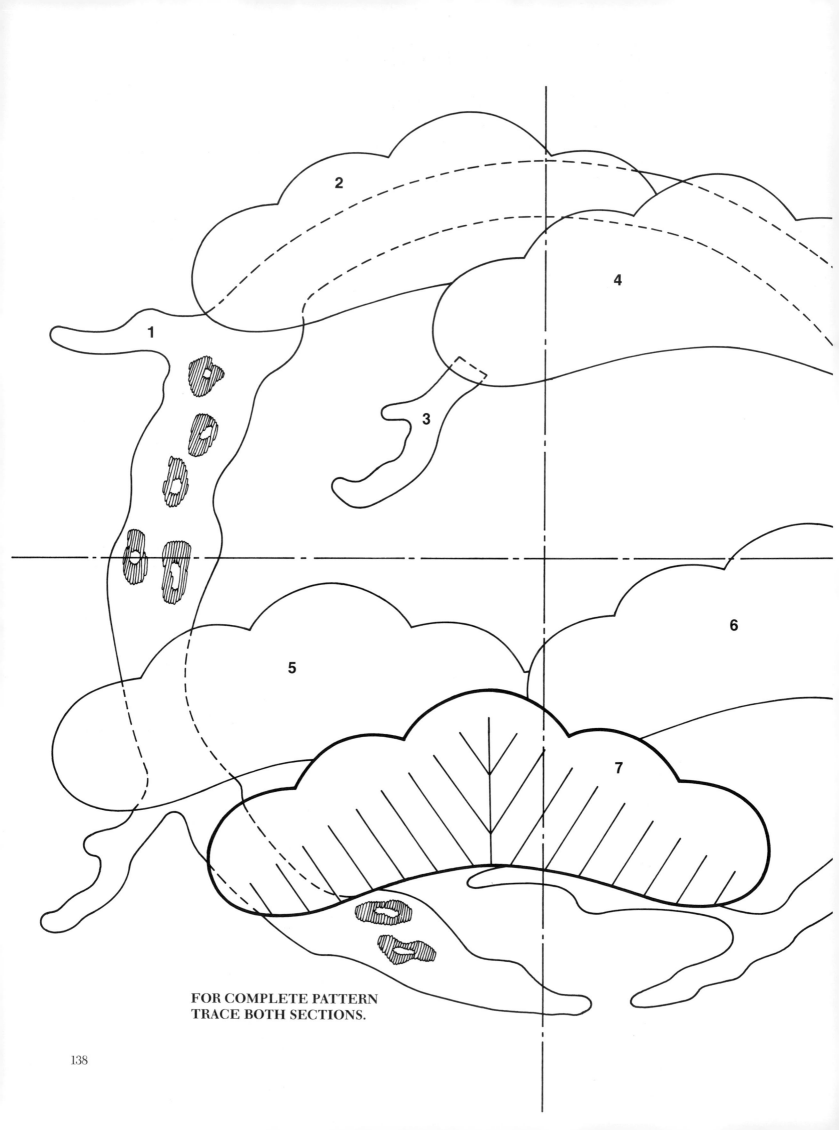

**FOR COMPLETE PATTERN
TRACE BOTH SECTIONS.**

25. Pine Wreath (*Matsu*)
12-inch (30.5cm) block
Add ¼-inch (7mm) seam allowances

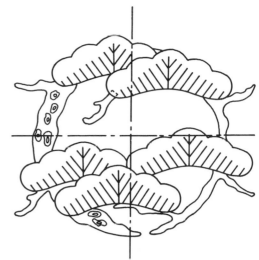

Here is the pine-wreath pattern, the third member of that decorative trio, "the three companions of the deep cold." (See page 62 for an explanation of this phrase.) The shape represents both the tree itself, and the way the clusters of needles grow on the branches. You will find similar stylized interpretations in both Chinese and Japanese art. Because pine trees resist the elements and are long-lived, the pine is considered doubly auspicious. The Japanese decorate their front doors with pine branches at New Year, and the pine was a popular motif for a family crest. We feature a crest pattern overleaf, but this wreath design was adapted by Jenni Dobson from an antique resist-dyed futon cover. It appears on her quilt, *Winter's Joy* (figs. 61a, 61c).

Directions

1. You will need to make a tracing of the complete design in order to obtain the pattern for the stem. *Note* that it is shown in some places as a dotted line under the pine shapes. Crease your background fabric in half and then quarters and use the crease marks to help you align the pattern pieces. Apply the stem first (template #1), marking the whorls ready for embroidering, and baste in position. Needle-turn the seam allowances *except* where the stem is covered by a pine shape. *Note* that there is a separate bit of stem which is template #3.

2. Cut out five pine shapes using template #7. Vary the tones of your fabrics to add depth and interest to the block. We give two methods of decorating these pine shapes. One can either be quilted or embroidered with contrasting thread (template #7), and the other is a reverse-appliqué design (template #8). Of the two methods, the embroidered version is the most traditional.

3. You will need to mark your chosen decoration on the pine shapes before stitching them down. If you are using reverse appliqué, pin or baste a strip of contrasting fabric to the back of each shape (see Tips and Techniques 7e). Sew pine shapes in place following the numerical sequence given on the pattern.

4. For the reverse-appliqué decoration, snip along the dotted line (the "pin" method described in Tips and Techniques 14 is a help here), and needle-turn the seam allowance under to reveal the contrasting fabric underneath.

5. Jenni Dobson embroidered some of her pine shapes with whipped running stitch (see Tips and Techniques 13) and used satin stitch for the whorls on the stem.

REVERSE-APPLIQUÉ DECORATION

Mark the design and baste a strip of contrasting fabric behind each pine-shape before sewing down. Snip along dotted line and needle-turn seam allowance under.

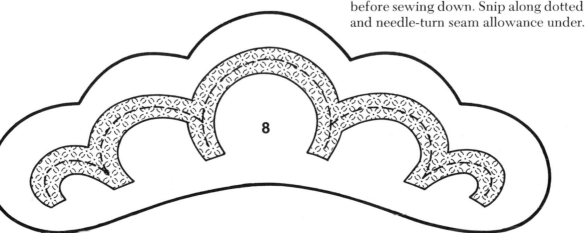

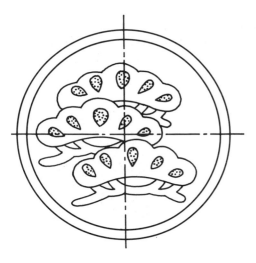

26. Pine Trees (*Matsu*)

12-inch (30.5cm) block
Add ¼-inch (7mm) seam allowances

Directions

1. Here is another traditional pine pattern given to us by Jenni Dobson. She drew it up from a kamon for her quilt, *The Three Companions of the Deep Cold* (fig. 63). The design will fit nicely into a 10-inch (25cm) circular enclosure or a snow-ring (patterns 29b and 30a). If you plan to use a circle or a snow-ring, apply this to your background fabric first (see Tips and Techniques 11). Crease your background fabric in half and then quarters and use these marks to help you align the pattern pieces correctly.

2. Cut out three pine trunks using template #1 and sew in position. Do not bother to turn under seam allowances where the trunks are covered by pine shapes.

3. Cut three pine shapes from template #6. We suggest a reverse-appliqué design, but alternative decorative ideas are shown on pattern 25. If you use reverse appliqué, pin or baste a strip of contrasting fabric to the back of the pine shapes and then sew them down following the numerical sequence given on the pattern. Snip away the centers of the tear-drop design leaving a ³/₁₆-inch (5mm) seam allowance. Clip in places and needle-turn to reveal your contrasting fabric underneath.

4. You can use one pine tree (templates #1 and #6) by itself in a diamond-shaped block like Sanae Hattori's quilt, *Dancing Pine Tree* (fig. 62). Enlarge the image on a photocopier to fit the diamond block given in pattern 30b.

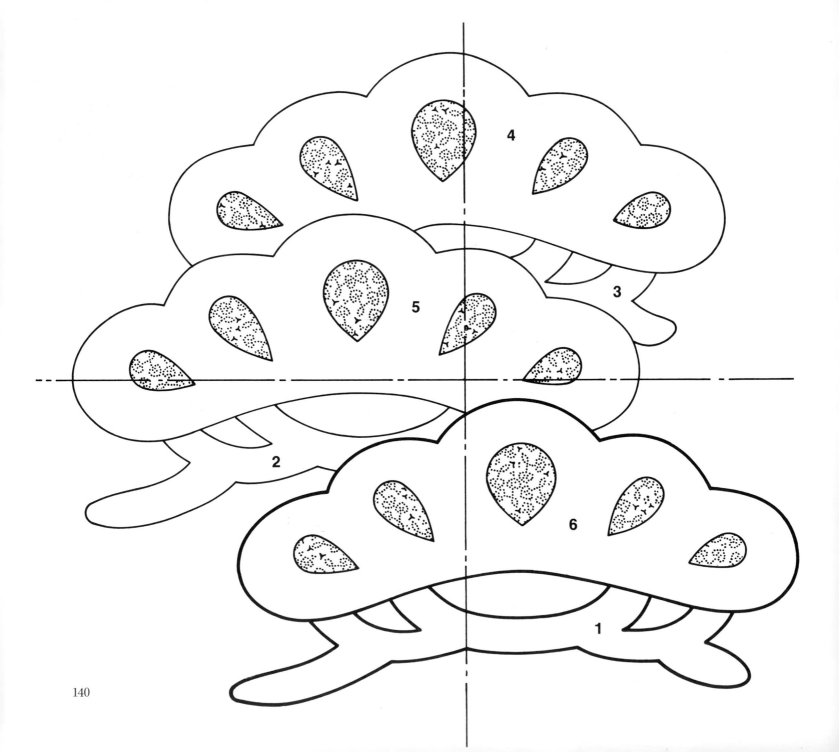

27. Vegetables (*Yasai*)
Add ¼-inch (7mm) seam allowances

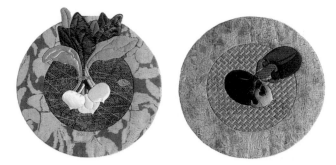

Buddhist philosophy, which prevailed until the modern era, does not allow the eating of meat, so vegetables have always formed a major part of the Japanese diet, and the delight the Japanese take in artistically presenting fresh, seasonal vegetables is evident in Sachiko Gunji's series of ravishing mandala quilts illustrated in figures 42a through 42f. She is happy to share her vegetable patterns with us, and we thought you would enjoy creating your own versions of her charming "Japanese plates." You could lay the vegetables on blue-and-white fabric plates for a true Oriental look, or you could pile them all up on a big platter and make a colorful wall-hanging for your kitchen. The pumpkin, shown on this page, might form a centerpiece of a child's Halloween quilt, while on the overleaf you will find a feast of turnips, carrots, eggplants, and leeks—ideal candidates for placemats and napkins.

Directions
Make templates and cut out the various parts of the vegetables. Sew in place following the numerical sequence given on the patterns.

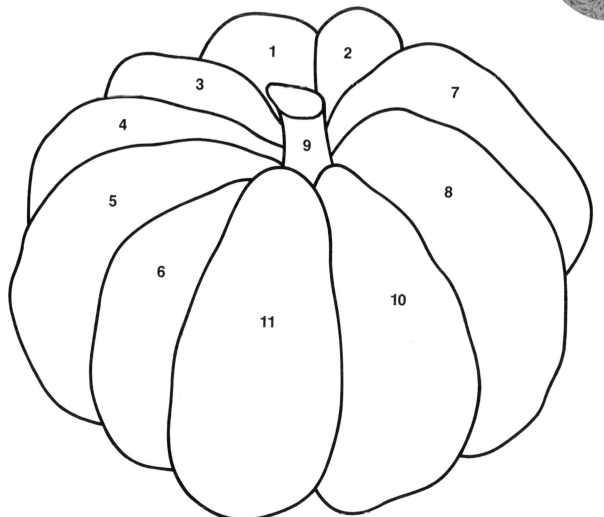

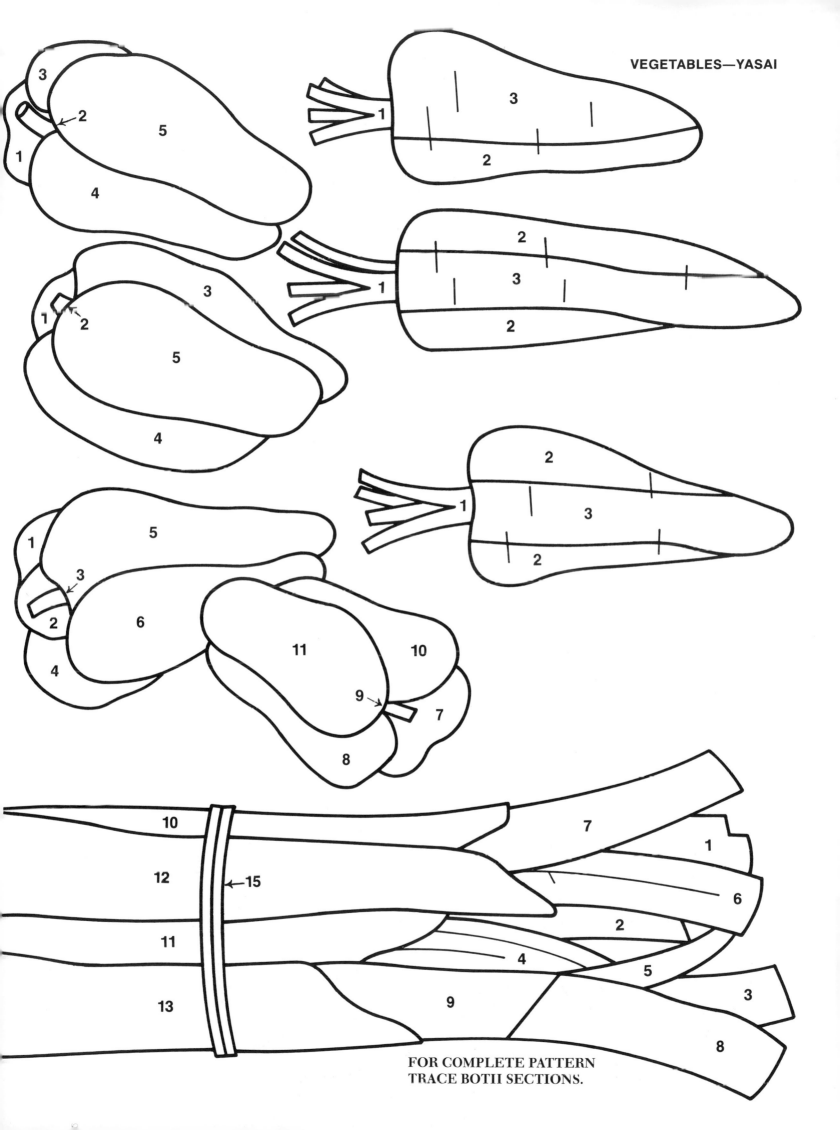

VEGETABLES—YASAI

FOR COMPLETE PATTERN
TRACE BOTH SECTIONS.

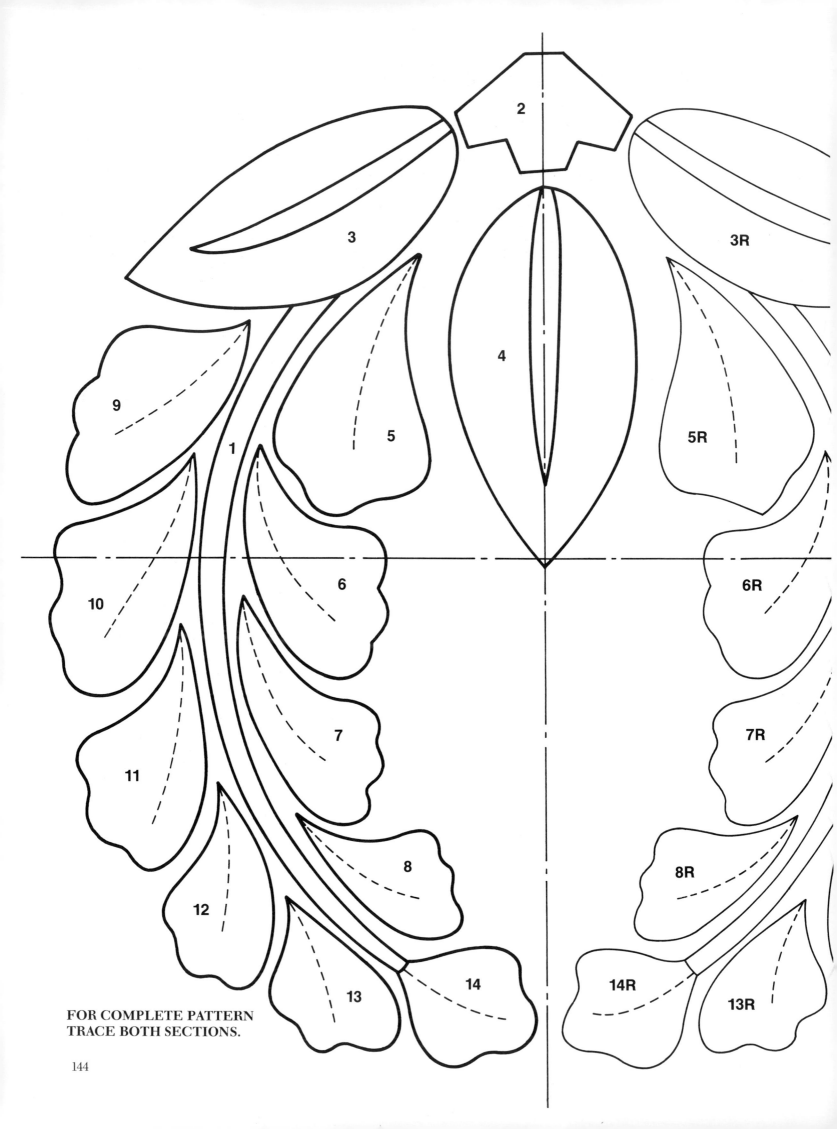

FOR COMPLETE PATTERN
TRACE BOTH SECTIONS.

144

28. Wisteria Wreath (*Fuji*)

12-inch (30.5 cm) block
Add ¼-inch (7mm) seam allowances

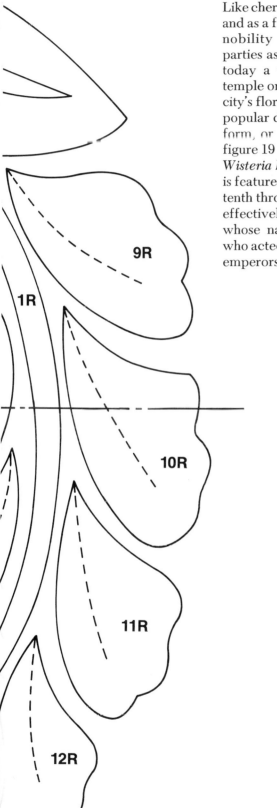

Like cherry blossom, wisteria is native to Japan and as a flower, it is just as much admired. The nobility began holding wisteria-viewing parties as early as the ninth century, and even today a visit to see wisteria in bloom at a temple on the outskirts of Tokyo is part of that city's floral calendar. The graceful wisteria is a popular decorative motif, both in this circular form, or as a frond as seen on the kimono in figure 19 and in Sanae Hattori's stunning quilt, *Wisteria Like a Fall* (fig. 23), a detail of which is featured on the cover of this book. From the tenth through the twelfth centuries, Japan was effectively ruled by one family, the Fujiwara, whose name means "field of wisteria," and who acted regents to a succession of powerless emperors. Although relatively few descen-

dants of this family actually used a wisteria crest, it was adopted by many other families, who doubtless chose it because of its prestigious associations. This pattern was adapted from one of those kamon. Sanae Hattori's version is illustrated in figure 24c.

Directions

1. Make a tracing of the complete wisteria wreath and transfer this to your background fabric to help you with the positioning. Crease your background fabric in half and then quarters and use these creases to align the pattern correctly.

2. Apply the stems first (templates #1 and #1r). You can either do these in reverse appliqué or with bias. You will need two strips ¾ inch x 12 inches (2 x 30.5cm) folded in half (see Tips and Techniques 7e or 9). Cut out top stem (template #3) in the same fabric.

3. The leaves (templates #3, #3r, and #4) are done in standard appliqué, but you could do the slits in reverse appliqué to match the color of the stems.

4. The flowers (templates #5 and #5r through #14 and #14r) can be cut from a medley of colored prints (see Sanae Hattori's quilts mentioned above for ideas), or you could restrict yourself to deep mauves. Baste seam allowances and sew in place following the numerical sequence on the pattern.

5. Quilt or embroider the marks on the flowers with contrasting thread.

145

29a. 11-inch (28cm) Diameter Circle

Stem for Plum Blossom Wreath (Pattern 24)

Add ¼-inch (7mm) seam allowances

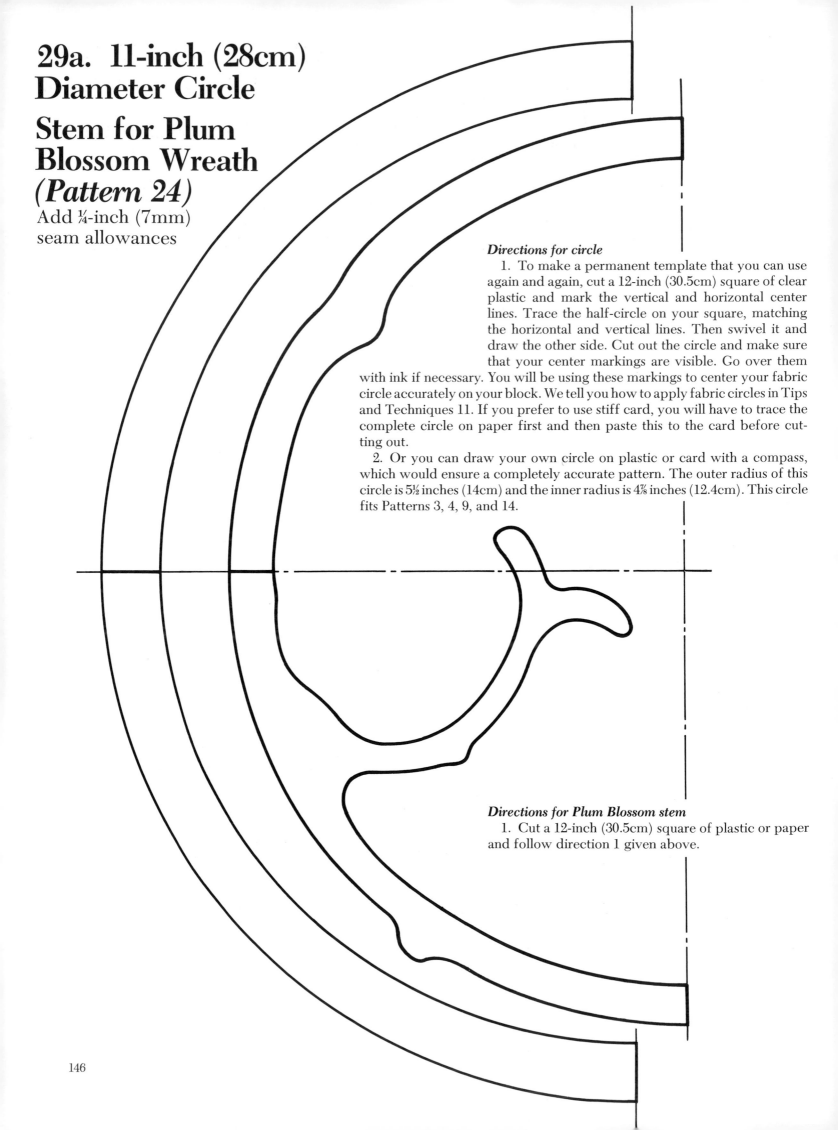

Directions for circle

1. To make a permanent template that you can use again and again, cut a 12-inch (30.5cm) square of clear plastic and mark the vertical and horizontal center lines. Trace the half-circle on your square, matching the horizontal and vertical lines. Then swivel it and draw the other side. Cut out the circle and make sure that your center markings are visible. Go over them with ink if necessary. You will be using these markings to center your fabric circle accurately on your block. We tell you how to apply fabric circles in Tips and Techniques 11. If you prefer to use stiff card, you will have to trace the complete circle on paper first and then paste this to the card before cutting out.

2. Or you can draw your own circle on plastic or card with a compass, which would ensure a completely accurate pattern. The outer radius of this circle is 5½ inches (14cm) and the inner radius is 4⅞ inches (12.4cm). This circle fits Patterns 3, 4, 9, and 14.

Directions for Plum Blossom stem

1. Cut a 12-inch (30.5cm) square of plastic or paper and follow direction 1 given above.

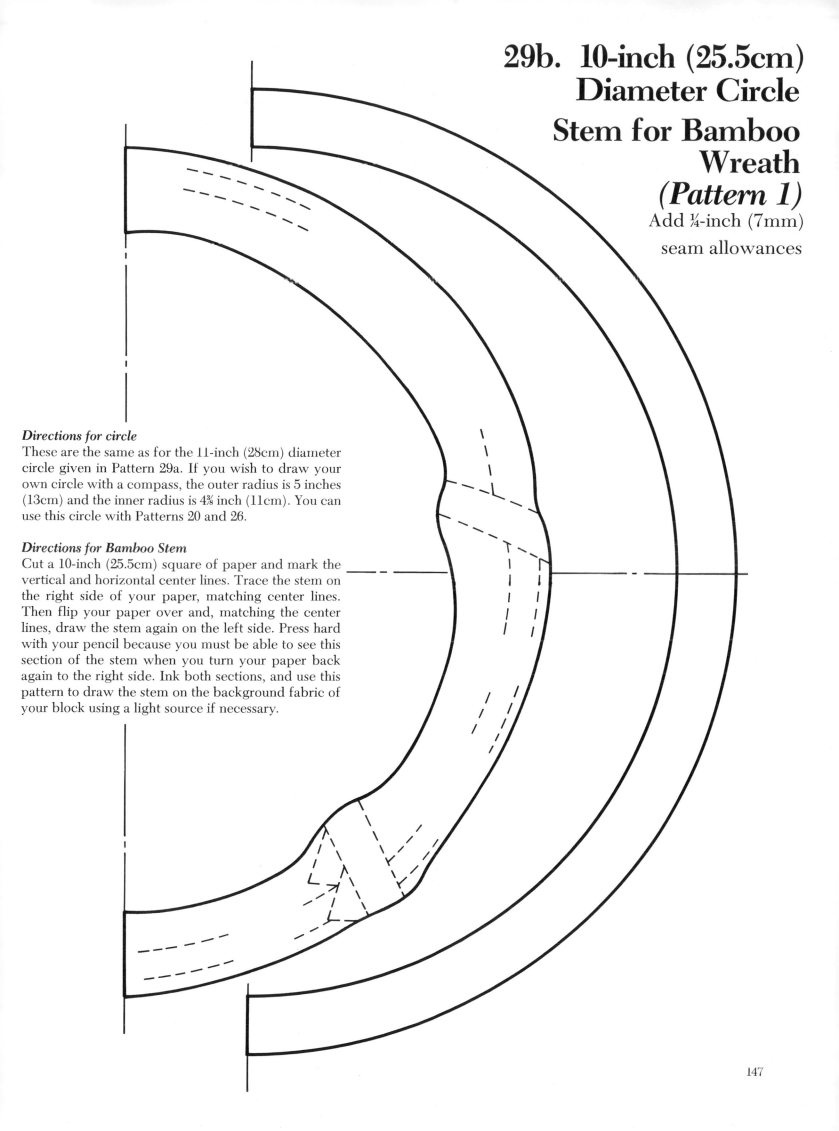

29b. 10-inch (25.5cm) Diameter Circle Stem for Bamboo Wreath (Pattern 1)

Add ¼-inch (7mm) seam allowances

Directions for circle

These are the same as for the 11-inch (28cm) diameter circle given in Pattern 29a. If you wish to draw your own circle with a compass, the outer radius is 5 inches (13cm) and the inner radius is 4⅜ inch (11cm). You can use this circle with Patterns 20 and 26.

Directions for Bamboo Stem

Cut a 10-inch (25.5cm) square of paper and mark the vertical and horizontal center lines. Trace the stem on the right side of your paper, matching center lines. Then flip your paper over and, matching the center lines, draw the stem again on the left side. Press hard with your pencil because you must be able to see this section of the stem when you turn your paper back again to the right side. Ink both sections, and use this pattern to draw the stem on the background fabric of your block using a light source if necessary.

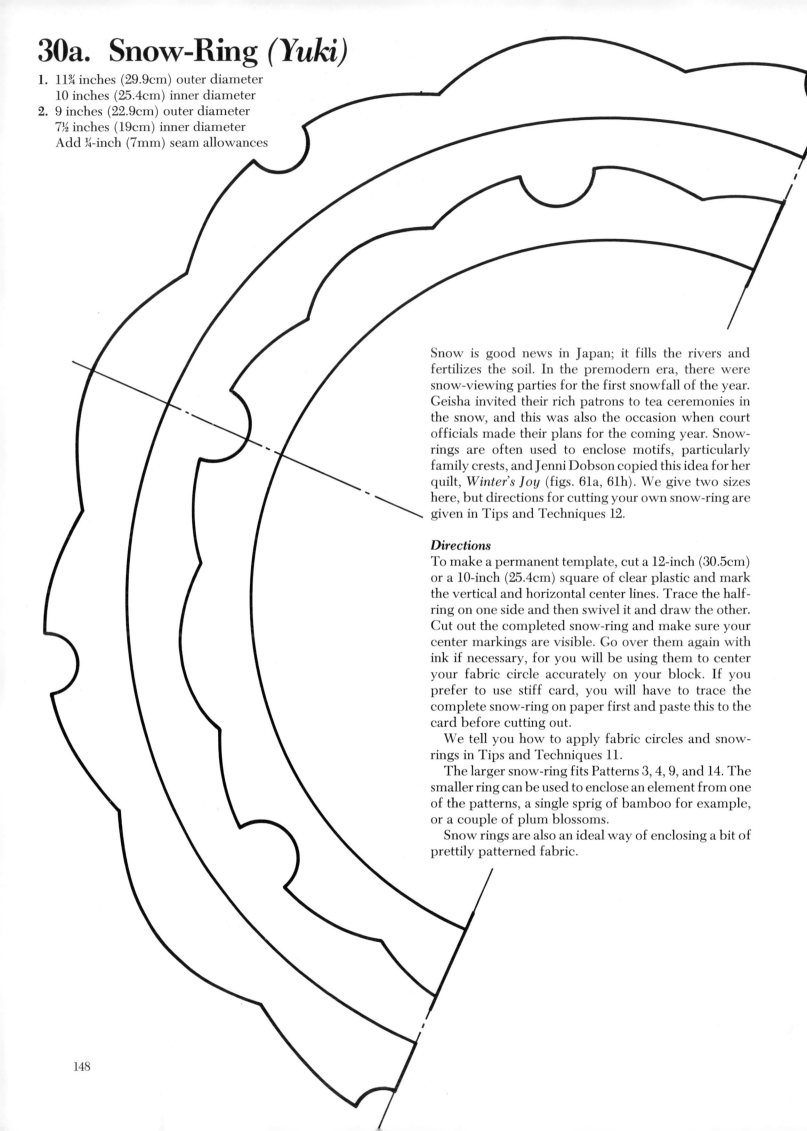

30a. Snow-Ring (*Yuki*)

1. 11¾ inches (29.9cm) outer diameter
   10 inches (25.4cm) inner diameter
2. 9 inches (22.9cm) outer diameter
   7½ inches (19cm) inner diameter
   Add ¼-inch (7mm) seam allowances

Snow is good news in Japan; it fills the rivers and fertilizes the soil. In the premodern era, there were snow-viewing parties for the first snowfall of the year. Geisha invited their rich patrons to tea ceremonies in the snow, and this was also the occasion when court officials made their plans for the coming year. Snow-rings are often used to enclose motifs, particularly family crests, and Jenni Dobson copied this idea for her quilt, *Winter's Joy* (figs. 61a, 61h). We give two sizes here, but directions for cutting your own snow-ring are given in Tips and Techniques 12.

Directions

To make a permanent template, cut a 12-inch (30.5cm) or a 10-inch (25.4cm) square of clear plastic and mark the vertical and horizontal center lines. Trace the half-ring on one side and then swivel it and draw the other. Cut out the completed snow-ring and make sure your center markings are visible. Go over them again with ink if necessary, for you will be using them to center your fabric circle accurately on your block. If you prefer to use stiff card, you will have to trace the complete snow-ring on paper first and paste this to the card before cutting out.

We tell you how to apply fabric circles and snow-rings in Tips and Techniques 11.

The larger snow-ring fits Patterns 3, 4, 9, and 14. The smaller ring can be used to enclose an element from one of the patterns, a single sprig of bamboo for example, or a couple of plum blossoms.

Snow rings are also an ideal way of enclosing a bit of prettily patterned fabric.

30b. Diamond Block (*Hishi*)

12¼ inches wide x 7³⁄₁₆ inches high (31 x 18.3cm)
14-inch (35.6cm) circle for Circular Fan Pattern 5
Add ¼-inch (7mm) seam allowances

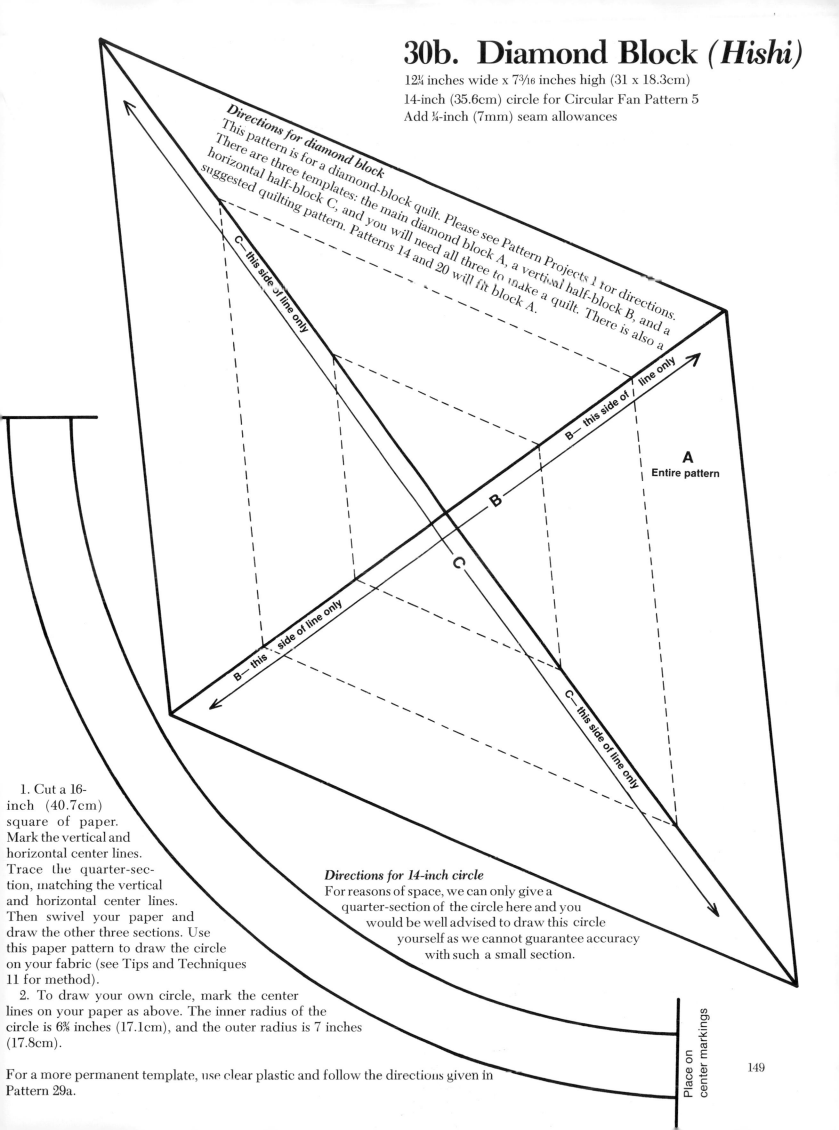

Directions for diamond block
This pattern is for a diamond-block quilt. Please see Pattern Projects 1 for directions. There are three templates: the main diamond block A, a vertical half-block B, and a horizontal half-block C, and you will need all three to make a quilt. There is also a suggested quilting pattern. Patterns 14 and 20 will fit block A.

C— this side of line only

B— this side of / line only

B— this side of line only

B— this side of line only

C— this side of line only

A
Entire pattern

B

C

Directions for 14-inch circle
For reasons of space, we can only give a quarter-section of the circle here and you would be well advised to draw this circle yourself as we cannot guarantee accuracy with such a small section.

1. Cut a 16-inch (40.7cm) square of paper. Mark the vertical and horizontal center lines. Trace the quarter-section, matching the vertical and horizontal center lines. Then swivel your paper and draw the other three sections. Use this paper pattern to draw the circle on your fabric (see Tips and Techniques 11 for method).

2. To draw your own circle, mark the center lines on your paper as above. The inner radius of the circle is 6⅝ inches (17.1cm), and the outer radius is 7 inches (17.8cm).

For a more permanent template, use clear plastic and follow the directions given in Pattern 29a.

Place on center markings

149

Sashiko Patterns

How to use these patterns

• The eight sashiko patterns we give here have all appeared either in traditional sashiko, or as quilting designs on quilts featured in this book.

• Traditional sashiko done with white stranded cotton can add a sparkle and texture to a quilt, either as alternate blocks, or interwoven as part of the design. The quilts illustrated in the section called Geometric Patterns will give you ideas, and Tips and Techniques 18 tells you how to do sashiko. But it is really as background quilting grids that these designs make their greatest impact.

• The Japanese love the movement and depth created by contrasting geometric patterns with floral or other motifs. You can see this from the kimono shown in figures 6, 57, 59, and 69, where the patterns have been woven or resist-dyed on the fabric and then overlaid with scattered flowers or wreaths. You could reproduce these geometric grounds by quilting them with sashiko patterns.

• Background quilting gives a quilt movement and depth, for it throws pieced or appliqué blocks into relief, enhances quilted motifs like flowers or feathers, and creates a wonderfully rich, tactile surface. Once you have used these sashiko grids as background quilting patterns, you will find standard cross-hatching very dull by comparison. Directions for marking these grids on your quilt top are given in Tips and Techniques 16.

• If you are making a circular-block quilt, you can fill one or two of the circles with sashiko quilting instead of an appliqué pattern, or the patterns would make interesting alternate quilted blocks for a Japanese album quilt. Try stitching them in contrasting thread to give a sashiko effect.

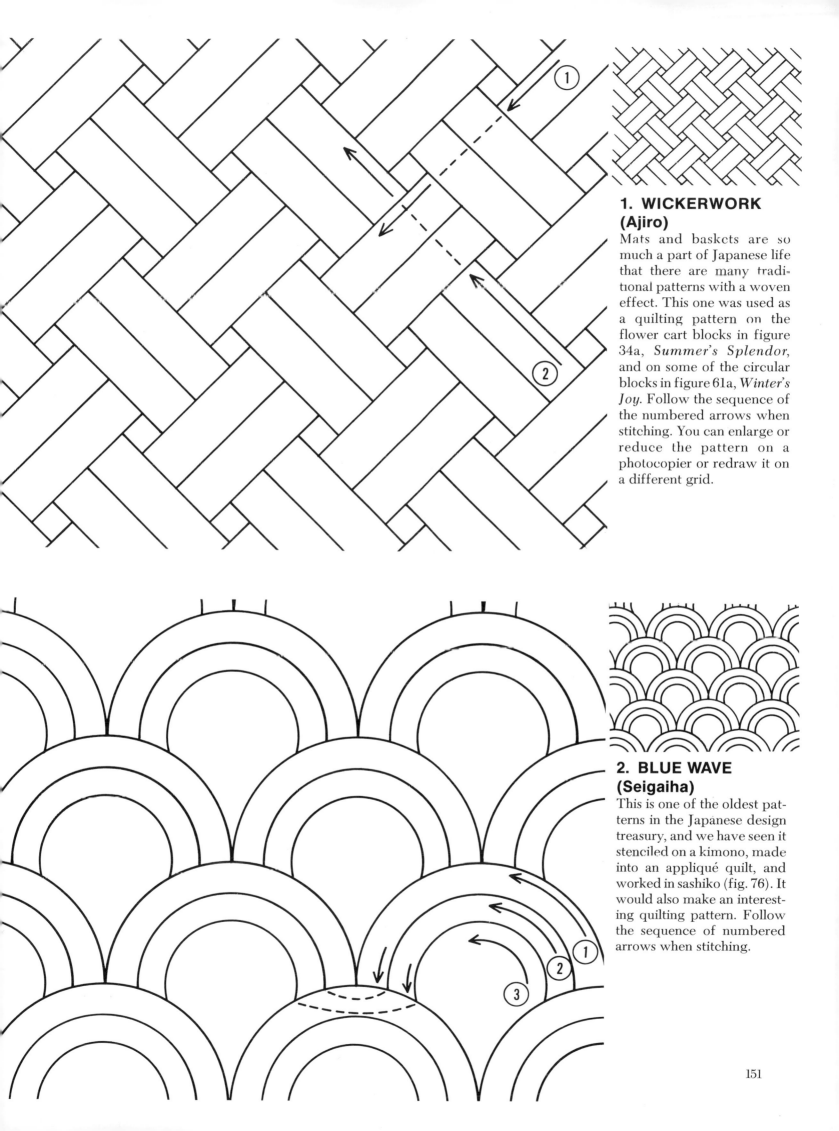

1. WICKERWORK (Ajiro)

Mats and baskets are so much a part of Japanese life that there are many traditional patterns with a woven effect. This one was used as a quilting pattern on the flower cart blocks in figure 34a, *Summer's Splendor*, and on some of the circular blocks in figure 61a, *Winter's Joy*. Follow the sequence of the numbered arrows when stitching. You can enlarge or reduce the pattern on a photocopier or redraw it on a different grid.

2. BLUE WAVE (Seigaiha)

This is one of the oldest patterns in the Japanese design treasury, and we have seen it stenciled on a kimono, made into an appliqué quilt, and worked in sashiko (fig. 76). It would also make an interesting quilting pattern. Follow the sequence of numbered arrows when stitching.

151

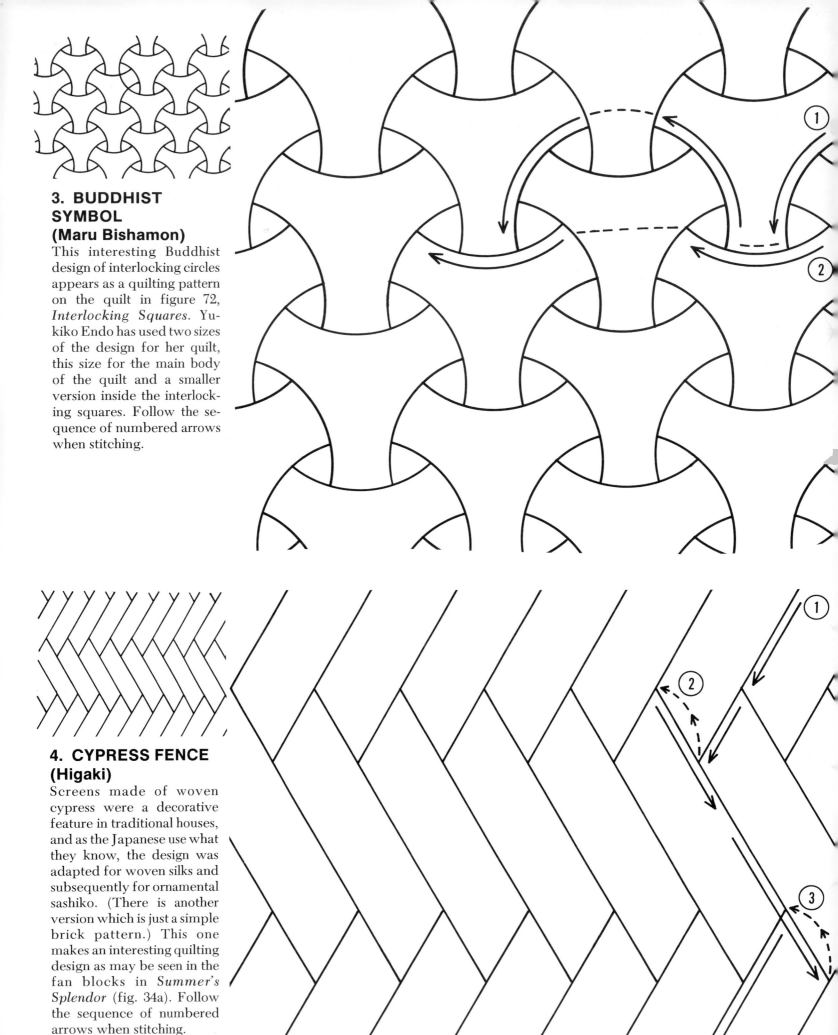

3. BUDDHIST SYMBOL (Maru Bishamon)

This interesting Buddhist design of interlocking circles appears as a quilting pattern on the quilt in figure 72, *Interlocking Squares*. Yukiko Endo has used two sizes of the design for her quilt, this size for the main body of the quilt and a smaller version inside the interlocking squares. Follow the sequence of numbered arrows when stitching.

4. CYPRESS FENCE (Higaki)

Screens made of woven cypress were a decorative feature in traditional houses, and as the Japanese use what they know, the design was adapted for woven silks and subsequently for ornamental sashiko. (There is another version which is just a simple brick pattern.) This one makes an interesting quilting design as may be seen in the fan blocks in *Summer's Splendor* (fig. 34a). Follow the sequence of numbered arrows when stitching.

152

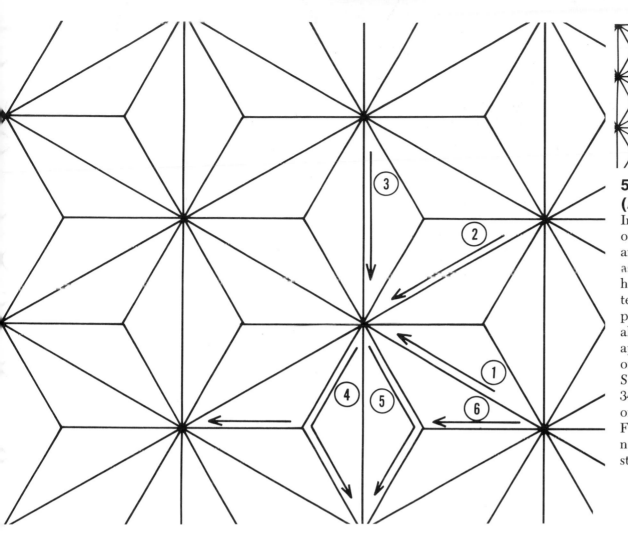

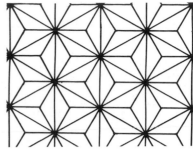

5. HEMP LEAF (Asanoha)

In ancient Japan, hemp was one of the five basic crops and was used to make cloth as well as ropes. It seems to have become a popular pattern for tie-dyeing, and it is probably the best known of all the sashiko designs. It appears as a quilting pattern on the butterfly blocks in *Summer's Splendor* (fig. 34a) and worked in sashiko on *Tama (Jewel)* (fig. 78). Follow the sequence of numbered arrows when stitching.

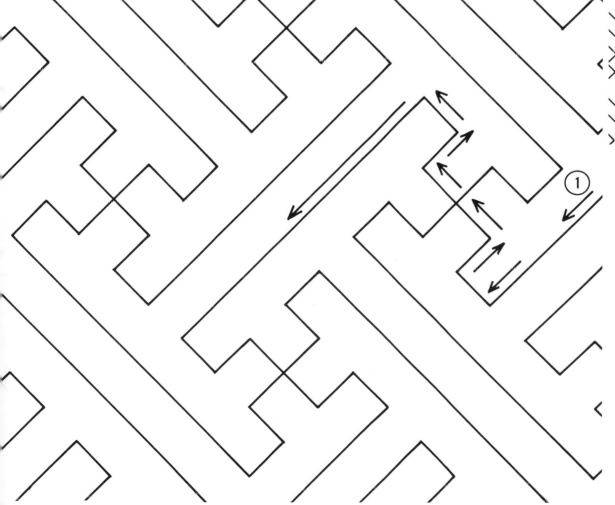

6. KEY-FRET (Sayagata)

This is an ancient Chinese design that is found in all the Japanese decorative arts. It is often used as a woven design for silks and is popular for sashiko, but it also makes a marvelously rich quilting pattern (see fig. 61a). It is easier than it looks; you can keep going for as long as your thread lasts. Follow the sequence of numbered arrows when stitching.

153

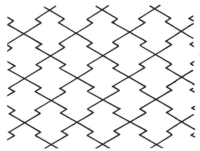

7. PINE BARK DIAMOND (Matsukawabishi)

This is another ancient Chinese design—a fragment of cloth woven in this pattern was found in a tomb dating to 200 B.C. It became popular in Japan, where it is thought to look like the pattern on the bark of a pine tree. It is easy to quilt, but see it used as a sashiko pattern in figure 63, *The Three Companions of the Deep Cold.* Follow the sequence of numbered arrows when stitching.

8. LINKED PLOVERS (Chidori Tsunagi)

Here is another easy pattern to quilt, and a rollicking one at that. The Japanese are particularly attached to a design of flying plovers, of which this is an abstraction. You can see it used as a quilting pattern in figure 73, *Sounds of the Sea*, and in sashiko in figure 79, *My Grandmother.* Follow the sequence of numbered arrows when stitching.

154

Pattern Projects

Now that you have admired the quilts and inspected the patterns, we felt that you might like a project to get you started. Five quiltmakers, whose work appears in the quilt sections, have very kindly given us permission to feature their work as projects for you to make. Three are appliqué quilts and two are patchwork quilts, and all have some Japanese element in their design.

The instructions given are for making the top only. You will find all the information you need for marking the quilting pattern and sandwiching the three layers together in Tips and Techniques 15 through 17. Nor do the yardage requirements include the amount of fabric needed for the backing, the batting, or the binding as this information is also covered in Tips and Techniques.

1.
Sanae Hattori's Diamond Iris Quilt

102½ x 82½ inches (260 x 200cm)
12¼ x 7³/₁₆ inch (31.1 x 18.3cm) block
Add ¼-inch (7mm) seam allowances

Patterns—consult PATTERN INDEX
    14. Diamond Iris
    30b. Diamond Block

You will have seen Sanae's stunning diamond-block quilts in the Summer, Autumn, and Winter sections of this book, and she has very kindly agreed to let us give directions for you to make a similar quilt yourself.

Her Diamond Iris quilt shown in figure 31 measures approximately 75 x 75 inches (190 x 190cm), but we felt that you might prefer to make a full-size quilt, so we have changed her block size and added an extra row of diamonds to make a luxurious queen-size quilt (diag. 1).

Sanae uses two iris patterns. We give the pattern for only one of them (Pattern 14), but you could adapt the iris from Pattern 15 to make a spray like her second block, or you could use a different pattern altogether, a butterfly or a sprig of bamboo for example.

You will find the pattern for the diamond block itself in Pattern 30b.

FABRIC REQUIREMENTS AND CUTTING GUIDE

45-inch (115cm) fabric pre-washed and with the selvedges cut off. NOTE: All yardage measurements include ¼-inch (7mm) seam allowances. We have also allowed an extra 2 inches (5cm) on all border lengths for safety; you can trim to size later.

Blocks

The charm of all Sanae's diamond-block quilts is, of course, their beautiful color. She varies the tonal values and coloring of her diamonds, and uses many different prints for the patterns, which creates a wonderful sense of spontaneity and movement. As it would be impossible to give you specific color directions, we suggest that you take inspiration from Sanae's iris quilt and create a color scheme to suit your own taste. Therefore, the following requirements are based upon the *total amount of fabric* that will be needed for the diamond blocks only.

We suggest that when you appliqué a diamond block, you *always* work on a rectangle of fabric to avoid stretching the bias edges (diag. 2). Pattern 30b gives you the diamond template and the half-blocks for the sides and the top and bottom. (NOTE: You do not need to cut rectangles for the

Diagram 1

156

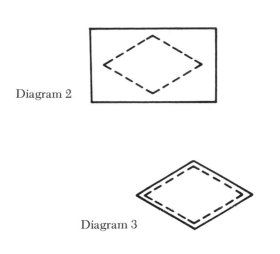

Diagram 2

Diagram 3

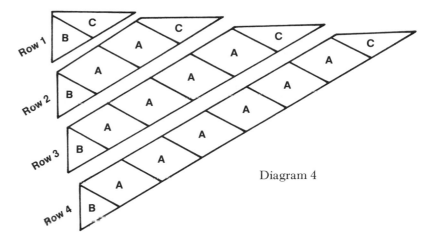

Diagram 4

half-blocks as these do not have appliqué patterns on them, but if you decide to cut the half-blocks together, you must add seam allowances to all *three* sides.

From 14 yards (13m) cut:

137 rectangles 14 x 9 inches (35.5 x 22.9cm) for the diamond blocks A.

26 vertical half-diamonds B for the sides.

12 horizontal half-diamonds C for the top and bottom edges.

Iris Patterns

For the appliqué irises you will need approximately 11½ yards (10.60m) of assorted prints and solids.

Borders

Fabric requirements for borders are based on cutting across the *width* of the fabric and seaming the pieces together. (NOTE: No allowance is made for matching pattern.) Sanae has turned the edges of her outer borders over to the back of the quilt to avoid binding, so we have added on an extra 1 inch (2.5cm) on the width measurement to allow for this.

Inner Borders

From ¾ of a yard (68.5cm) cut:

2 95½ x 2 inches (242.7 x 5cm) side borders

2 79 x 2 inches (200.7 x 5cm) top and bottom borders.

Outer Borders

From 1¼ yards (1.40m) cut:

2 98½ x 4½ inches (250.2 x 11.4cm) side borders

2 87 x 4½ inches (221 x 11.4cm) top and bottom borders.

DIRECTIONS

1. Trace each diamond A on the rectangle of fabric and stay-stitch the outline on your machine (diag. 2).

2. Stay-stitch the outline on the half-diamonds B and C to save the bias edges from stretching.

3. Appliqué irises following the directions given with Pattern 14.

4. When you have finished sewing the irises, cut out the diamonds leaving a ¼-inch (7mm) seam allowance (diag. 3),

and seam together in diagonal rows following diagrams 1 and 4. Use your stay-stitching as guide and machine-stitch just inside it so that it won't show on the front. Add half-blocks B and C where necessary.

5. Sew on side inner borders first, then top and bottom.

6. Sew on side outer borders first, then top and bottom.

7. Cut away excess fabric from behind each iris, and if you wish to quilt the background, you could use the quilting pattern shown in diagram 5. (You will find this marked on Pattern 30b.) Outline quilt around the irises and around each side of the inner borders.

8. Turn the edges of the outer borders over to the back and hem.

ALTERNATIVE DIAMOND IRIS QUILT

This design is for those who feel daunted by the thought of having to appliqué 137 irises. As you will see from diagram 5, this version needs only 57 appliqué blocks; the rest are quilted.

You could also make an attractive quilt by using two coordinated decorating or furnishing fabrics, one with a background print and one with a floral print.

This is a traditional design, in that it is an adaptation of two ancient Japanese patterns. A diamond lattice enclosing four small diamonds is a well-known woven pattern associated with the costumes of the Heian period. You can see it depicted on the outer robe worn by the court lady in figure 7.

The quilting design of concentric diamonds is a simplified version of the woven pattern on the fragment of kimono fabric shown in figure 59. You will find a pattern for it with Pattern 30b.

DIRECTIONS

1. Follow directions 1 and 2 above.

2. Appliqué 57 iris on to diamond blocks and mark the quilting pattern on the rest, including all the half-blocks.

3. Follow directions 4 through 8 above.

Alternative patterns for diamond-block quilts are the Maple Leaf (Pattern 20), or an enlarged version of the main pine tree in Pattern 26. See Sanae Hattori's *Red Maple Leaves 111* (fig. 51) and *Dancing Pine Tree 1* (fig. 62).

Diagram 5

2.
Gill Bryan's
Summer's Splendor

54 x 42 inches (137.2 x 106.7cm)
8-inch (20.3cm) block
12-inch (30.5cm) block
14-inch (36.2cm) block

Patterns—consult PATTERN INDEX
    5. Courtly Fan
   10. Flying Butterflies
   11. Flower Cart
Sashiko Patterns:
    1. Wickerwork
    4. Cypress Fence
    5. Hemp Leaf
    7. Pine Bark Diamond

Gill Bryan and her co-quilters, Violet Plume, Barbara Holmes, and Jenni Dobson, are pleased to share their attractive wall-hanging with you. The staggered placement of the blocks is an interesting construction that could be adapted for a full-size quilt. In our directions we have followed their original color scheme for the background blocks and borders, but have not specified any colors for the patterns. Look at the detail photos on page 36 for ideas.

FABRIC REQUIREMENTS AND CUTTING GUIDE

45-inch (115cm) fabric pre-washed and with selvedges cut off. NOTE: All yardage measurements include ¼-inch (7mm) seam allowances. We have allowed an extra 2 inches (5cm) on all the border lengths for safety; you can trim to size later. The *correct* measurement is given for the green framing strips for each block D, D, E, and F, and for the block joining strips G and H.

Blocks
From 1⅓ yards (1.2m) of cream fabric cut:
  2 8½ x 12½-inch (21.6 x 31.8cm) blocks for butterflies A and B.
  2 12½ x 12½-inch (31.8 x 31.8cm) blocks for cypress fans A and B.
  2 14½ x 14½-inch (36.8 x 36.8cm) blocks for flower carts A and B.
Assorted scraps for appliqués.

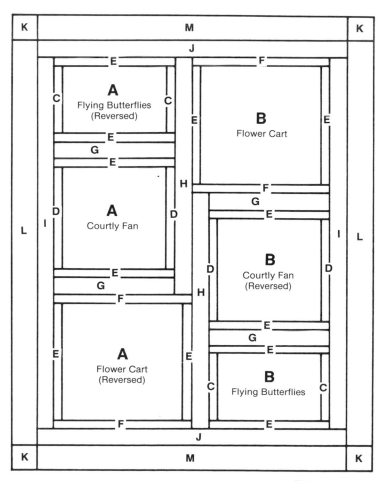

Diagram 1

Green framing strips
From ⅜ yard (.40cm) of green print cut:
  4 8½ x 1½-inch (21.5 x 3.8cm) strips C.
  4 12½ x 1½-inch (31.8 x 3.8cm) strips D.
  12 14½ x 1½-inch (36.8 x 3.8cm) strips E.
  4 16½ x 1½-inch (42 x 3.8cm) strips F.

Borders
Fabric requirements for borders are based on cutting across the *width* of the fabric and seaming the pieces together. NOTE: No allowance is made for matching pattern.

Inner black borders and joining strips
From ⅞ yard (.80cm) of black fabric cut:
  4 14½ x 2½-inch (36.8 x 6.4cm) strips G.
  2 28½ x 2½-inch (72.4 x 6.4cm) strips H.
  2 46 x 2½-inch (116.8 x 6.4cm) inner borders I.
  2 38½ x 2½-inch (97.8 x 6.4cm) inner borders J.

Red print outer borders
From ¾ yard (.70cm) of red print cut:
  2 48½ x 3½-inch (123.2 x 9cm) outer borders L.
  2 36½ x 3½-inch (92.7 x 9cm) outer borders M.
  4 3½-inch (8.9cm) border squares K. (NOTE: On the above quilt, these squares were actually cut from the batik border fabric that had butterflies already printed on it. You may wish to make the squares a different color and appliqué a butterfly from Pattern 10 instead.)

DIRECTIONS

1. Each pattern appears twice, once as shown on the pattern pages and once reversed. When marking the outline of the pattern on your background fabric, you will need to reverse it for the reverse blocks. To do this, trace the pattern on a piece of paper, turn it over and ink it in on this side as well. Mark all six patterns on your background blocks.

2. When cutting out your pattern pieces, remember to *reverse all your templates when cutting out the reverse blocks*. Appliqué according to the directions given with each pattern.

3. Sew green border strips to each block. The butterfly blocks will need two Cs and two Es. The fan blocks will need two Ds and two Es. The flower-cart blocks will need two Es and two Fs. Sew on the shorter side borders first, then the top and bottom ones.

4. Appliqué a butterfly on the four border squares K, if desired.

Assembling the Quilt

5. In order to join your blocks together correctly, lay them out on the floor following diagram 1. Make sure you put the reverse blocks in the right places (see diagram for placement). Then join one black strip G to the *bottom* of butterfly block A and fan block A. Join one black strip G to the *top* of butterfly block B and fan block B. Join blocks together making two sets, one being an A set and the other a B set.

6. Join one black strip H to the right side of the A set. Join one black strip H to the left side of the B set (diag. 1).

7. Sew flower cart A to the bottom of the A blocks and flower cart B to the top of the B blocks.

8. Join A and B sections together and add on the black inner borders. Sew the two side borders I on first and then the top and bottom borders J.

9. Sew on outer side borders L.

10. Sew one corner square K to each end of the outer top and bottom borders M and then, matching seams, sew these borders on last.

11. Cut away excess fabric from behind the appliqués and mark Sashiko Pattern 5, Hemp Leaf, on the two butterfly blocks, Sashiko Pattern 4, Cypress Fence, on the two fan blocks, and Sashiko Pattern 1, Wickerwork, on the two flower-cart blocks (see Tips and Techniques 16 for marking methods). Jenni also did some sashiko stitching on the black inner borders that you may like to try. She used Sashiko Pattern 7, Pine Bark Diamond.

12. Quilt the sashiko patterns on the blocks first and then outline quilt around the appliqués, around each side of the framing strips, and down the inside of the borders. Jenni used an ordinary quilting stitch on the blocks, but created the effect of sashiko on the inner black borders by using white thread and a larger stitch.

13. Bind to finish.

3.
Jenni Dobson's Winter's Joy

63 x 44 inches (160 x 111.7cm)

Patterns—consult PATTERN INDEX
1. Bamboo Wreath
3. Bush Clover
6. Chrysanthemums
8. Facing Cranes
13. Hollyhock
24. Plum Blossom Wreath
25. Pine Wreath
30a. Snow-Ring
Sashiko Pattern 6, Key-Fret.

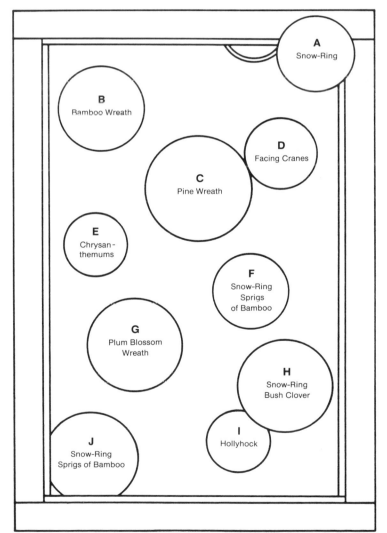

Diagram 1

Thanks to Jenni Dobson's generosity, here is your chance to try your hand at making a marumon quilt, one of the loveliest of all the traditional Japanese designs. By making this quilt, you will learn most of the design principles set out in Tips and Techniques 1—the value of space, asymmetry, scattering, and overlapping. Jenni's design also demonstrates the marvelously tactile effect of background sashiko quilting. The instructions cover the basic color scheme for the background and borders, but not for the patterns. Look at the detail photos of Jenni's blocks on pages 67 and 68 for ideas.

FABRIC REQUIREMENTS AND CUTTING GUIDE
45-inch (115cm) fabric pre-washed and with the selvedges cut off. NOTE: All measurements *include* ¼-inch (7mm) seam allowances. We have allowed an extra 2 inches (5cm) on all border lengths for safety; you can trim to size later.

Blocks
We recommend that you always appliqué your circular patterns on square pieces of fabric and then trim them later to prevent the bias edges from stretching (see Tips and Techniques 10). This means that you will work blocks B, C, D, F, G, and J on squares of fabric that are the *same* color as your background.

From 2½ yards (2.30m) of light terra-cotta fabric cut:
   1 inner panel 54½ x 34½ inches (138.4 x 87.6cm).
   1 15-inch (38cm) square for block C (Pattern 25).
   1 13-inch (33cm) square for block J (Pattern 30a).
   3 12½-inch (31.7cm) squares for blocks B, D, and G (Patterns 1, 8, and 24).
   1 10-inch (25.4cm) for block F (Pattern 30a).
You will also need:
   1 13-inch (33cm) square of navy for the snow-ring on block J (Pattern 30a).
   1 10-inch (25.4cm) green print for the snow-ring on block F (Pattern 30a).
   1 12½-inch (31.7cm) square of deep rust for block H (Pattern 3), and 1 12½-inch (31.7cm) square of turquoise for the snow-ring (Pattern 30a).
   1 10-inch (25.4cm) square of green print for block A and 1 10-inch (25.4cm) square of peach for the snow-ring (Pattern 30a).

The character for "Joy" is Jenni's "Oriental" signature, so you could substitute your own initial, or use a motif from another pattern.
   1 10-inch (25.4cm) square of navy for block E (Pattern 6) and 1 10-inch (25.4cm) square of green for the snow-ring (Pattern 30a).
   1 10-inch (25.4cm) square of pale ochre for block I (Pattern 13).

Patterns

Assorted scraps for the appliqué patterns and for the quarter-ring next to block A.

Borders

Fabric requirements for borders are based on cutting across the *width* of the fabric and seaming the pieces together. NOTE: No allowance is made for matching pattern. Jenni turned the edges of her outer borders over to the back of the quilt to avoid binding, so we have added on an extra 1 inch (2.5cm) on the width measurement to allow for this.

Inner border
From ¼ yard (22.8cm) of turquoise fabric cut:
   2 56½ x 1¼ inch (143.5 x 3.2cm) side borders
   2 38½ x 1¼ inch (97.8 x 3.2cm) top and bottom borders.

Outer borders
From 1 yard (91.5cm) of navy print fabric cut:
   2 58½ x 5 inch (148.6 x 12.7cm) side borders
   2 48 x 5 inch (122 x 12.7cm) top and bottom borders.

DIRECTIONS

When making a marumon quilt, it is essential to vary the sizes of your circular patterns to create contrast. Jenni used a photocopier to enlarge or reduce the diameter of the actual motif, *not* the given block size, on the following patterns:
   Block C, Pattern 25. Pine Wreath to 13 inches (33cm)
   Block D, Pattern 8. Facing Cranes to 10 inches (25.4cm)
   Block E, Pattern 6. Chrysanthemums to 8 inches (20.3cm)
   Block I, Pattern 13. Hollyhock to 8 inches (20.3cm)

1. Apply the circles and snow-rings first and then appliqué the motifs according to the directions given on each pattern. For blocks F and J, Jenni applied two sprigs of bamboo taken from pattern 1 inside each snow-ring. The empty ring beside block A is a quarter section cut from pattern 30b.

2. Cut out blocks leaving ¼-inch (7mm) seam allowance and baste.

3. Refer to diagram 1 and sew all blocks—except block A—in position on your background fabric. Don't forget to cut away excess fabric from behind the blocks and the larger pattern pieces (see Tips and Techniques 14).

4. Sew on side inner borders first, then top and bottom.

5. Sew on side outer borders first, then top and bottom.

6. Sew block A in position.

7. Mark the Sashiko Pattern 6 (Key-Fret) on the background (see Tips and Techniques 16). Jenni found it worked best to quilt the key-fret pattern first and then go back and outline quilt around the patterns. She says that if you do it the other way around, there is a danger that when you quilt the sashiko pattern it will not lie flat.

8. Turn the edges of the outer borders over to the back and hem. Quilt a line all the way around the border, approximately ½-inch (1.2cm) in from the edge.

4.
Yukiko Endo's
Interlocking
Squares

95 x 75 inches (241.3 x 190.5cm)
14-inch (35.6cm) block set on point
Add ¼-inch (7mm) seam allowances

Patterns
1. Interlocking Square (templates given below)
2. Sashiko Pattern 3, Buddhist Symbol.

The Japanese have an affection for large-scale patterns, and when Yukiko Endo adapted the popular design of interlocking squares to make her striking quilt, she enlarged the pattern so that just three squares would span the width of a double bed. She did not use a block construction, so when she kindly agreed to let us feature her design, we adapted it into a block form and lengthened it slightly to make a proper double-sized quilt.

FABRIC REQUIREMENTS AND CUTTING GUIDE
45-inch (115cm) fabric pre-washed and with the selvedges cut off. NOTE: All yardage measurements include ¼-inch (7mm) seam allowances. We have allowed an extra 2 inches (5cm) on all border lengths for safety; you can trim to size later.

Blocks
If you look at the illustration of Yukiko's quilt (fig. 72), you will see that not only has she varied the coloring of her interlocking squares but she has also used several shades of pale blue for the background. In our directions, we only specify three fabrics—a dark solid and a medium print for the squares, and a light solid for the background. If you wish to vary the color scheme, place a piece of tracing paper over diagram 1 and experiment with some crayons.

NOTE: To avoid having bias edges on the outside of the quilt top when you cut out triangles #4 and #5, make sure that the longest edge lies on the straight grain of the fabric (diag. 2). And don't forget to lay your templates *face down* on the wrong side of the fabric when drawing around them because some of the templates are not symmetrical.

Diagram 1

From 1½ yards (1.40cm) of dark solid cut 48 #1 and 24 #2.

From 1¾ yards (1.60m) of medium print cut 42 #1, 18 #2, 6 #5, and 6 #5r.

From 1¾ yards (1.60cm) of light solid cut 42 #2, 16 #3, 12 #4, and 16 #5.

Borders

Fabric requirements for borders are based on cutting across the *width* of the fabric and seaming the pieces together. (NOTE: No allowance is made for matching patterns.) Yukiko has turned the edges of her outer borders over to the back of the quilt to avoid binding, so we have added an extra 1 inch (2.5cm) to allow for this.

From 2¼ yards (2.10m) cut:
2 81½ x 9½ inch (207.6 x 24.2cm) side borders.
1 79½ x 9½ inch (200.7 x 24.2cm) top and bottom borders.

DIRECTIONS

1. Following diagram 3, piece together:
12 blocks #A
6 blocks #B
4 blocks #C
6 blocks #D
2 blocks #E (top left and bottom right corners)
2 blocks #F (top right and bottom left corners)

2. Seam blocks together following diagrams 4 and 5.

3. Add side borders first, then top and bottom ones.

4. For her quilting design, Yukiko created a lovely texture by using two different sizes of Sashiko Pattern 3, Buddhist Symbol. The large squares #3 and triangles #6 were worked with the full-size version, and then she reduced the pattern by half on a photocopier to get a size small enough to fill the small squares #2 and triangles #4.

The interlocking squares were quilted with parallel lines (see Tips and Techniques 16 for marking methods).

5. Turn the edges of the borders over to the back of the quilt and hem.

Diagram 2

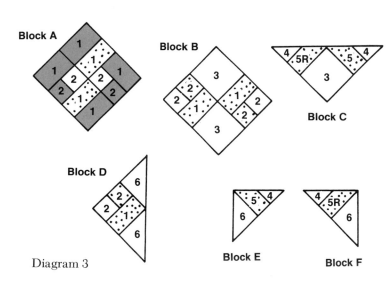

Block A

Block B

Block C

Block D

Block E

Block F

Diagram 3

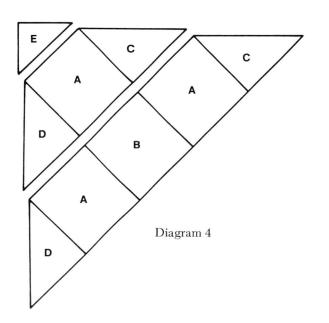

Diagram 4

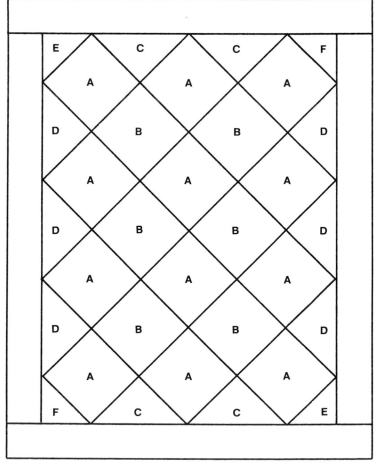

Diagram 5

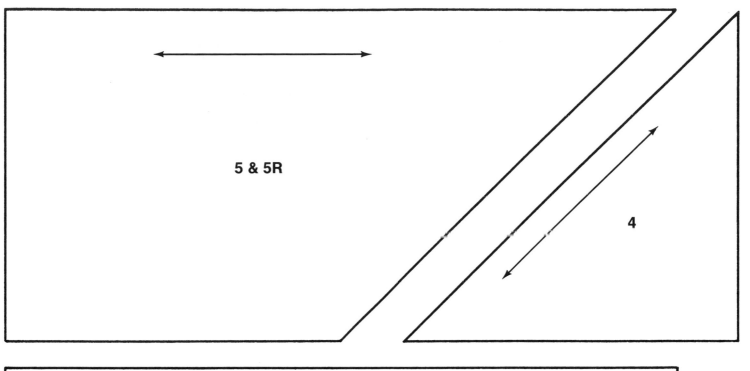

5 & 5R

4

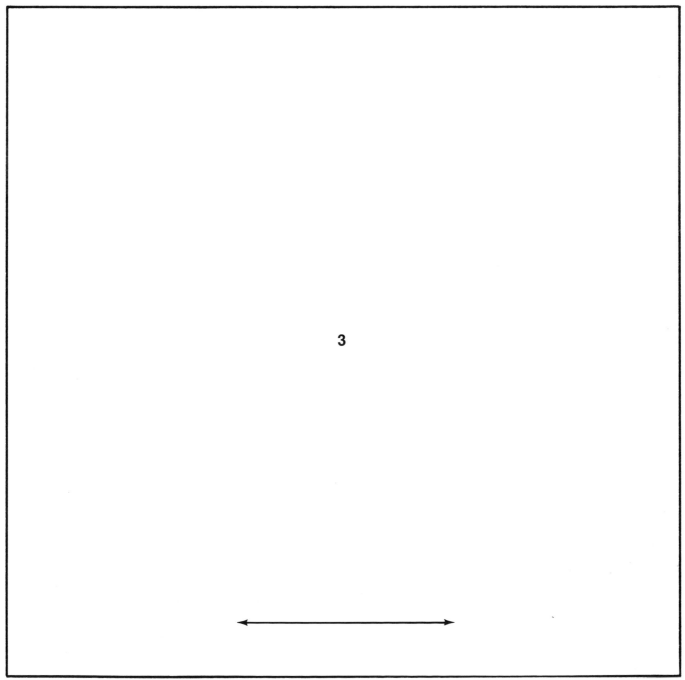

3

165

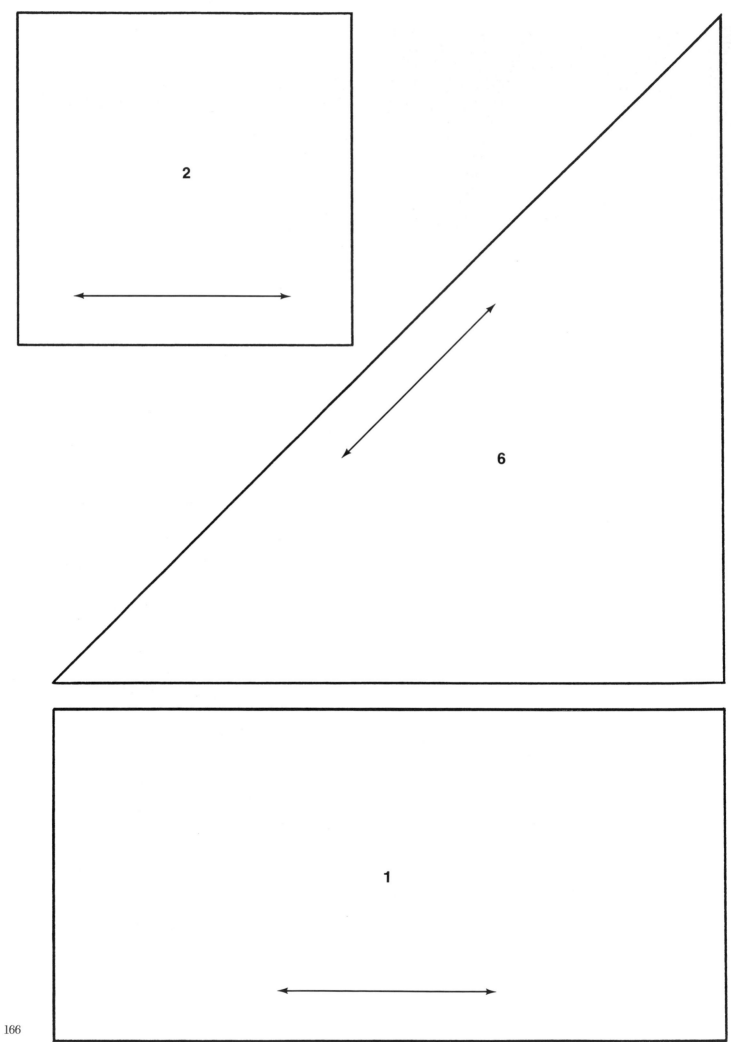

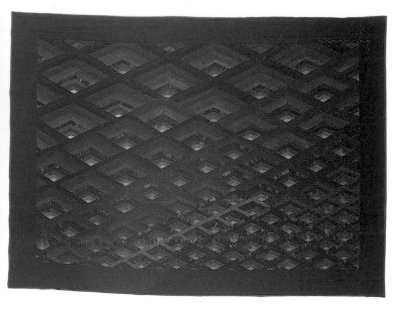

5.
Emiko Toda Loeb's
Sounds of the Sea

55 x 69½ inches (139.7 x 176.5cm)
Block sizes:
11¾ x 20½ inches (29.8 x 52.1cm)
5⅞ x 10¼ inches (15 x 26cm)
Add ¼-inch (7mm) seam allowances

Patterns
  2. Blue Wave
  New pattern for block A (templates below)
  New template for Sashiko Pattern 9, Linked Plovers.

The Blue Wave pattern is truly traditional, and Emiko Toda Loeb kindly agreed to let us feature a design based on her stunning patchwork quilt. She used four different-sized blocks, but we have simplified our version and only used two (diag. 1.) You will find the templates for all the blocks, including those for Pattern 2, given below.

Emiko created a wonderful sense of movement by sashiko-stitching the Linked Plover pattern all over the surface of her quilt, but it would be difficult stitching through all those seams so we suggest that you only use it on the borders.

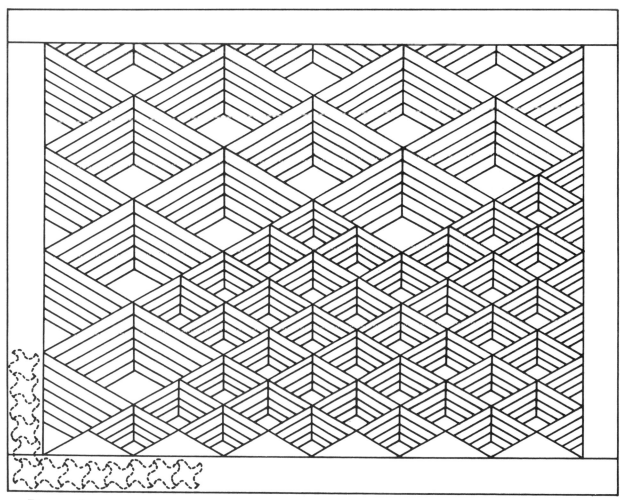

Diagram 1

FABRIC REQUIREMENTS AND CUTTING GUIDE

45-inch (115cm) fabric pre-washed and with the selvedges cut off. NOTE: All yardage measurements include ¼-inch (7mm) seam allowances. We have allowed an extra 2 inches (5cm) on all border lengths for safety; you can trim to size later.

Blocks

You will see from figure 73 that Emiko has used a variety of different blue fabrics, some patterned, some plain, which gives her quilt great visual interest. As it would be impossible to give specific directions, we suggest that you create a color scheme of your own based on her ideas. Therefore our measurements are for the *total amount of fabric* that will be needed for each pattern piece.

NOTE: Don't forget to lay your templates *face down* on the wrong side of the fabric because some of the templates are not symmetrical.

From ¾ yard (68.6cm) cut 82 #1
From ⅝ yard (57.2cm) cut 82 #2
From ½ yard (45.8cm) cut 82 #3
From ⅜ yard (34.3cm) cut 82 #4
From ⅝ yard (57.2cm) cut 38 #5
From a piece 3 x 18 inches (7.6 x 45.8cm) cut 6 #5b
From ⅝ yard (57.2cm) cut 23 #6a
From a piece 2 x 21 inches (5 x 53.3cm) cut 6 #6b
From ⅝ yard (57.2cm) cut 23 #7a
From a piece 2 x 27 inches (5 x 68.6cm) cut 6 #7b
From ½ yard (45.8cm) cut 23 #8a
From a piece 2 x 42 inches (5 x 106.7cm) cut 6 #8b
From ½ yard (45.8cm) cut 23 #9a
From a piece 2 x 42 inches (5 x 106.7cm) cut 6 #9b
From ⅝ yard (57.2cm) cut 23 #10a
From a piece 2 x 42 inches (5 x 106.7cm) cut 6 #10b
From ⅝ yard (57.2cm) cut 29 #11
From ½ yard (45.8cm) cut 12 #12a
From a piece 5 x 25 inches (12.7 x 63.5cm) cut 5 #12b
From ⅝ yard (57.2cm) cut 6 of block F. NOTE: We suggest that you make block F from solid-color fabric and quilt the divisions rather than trying to piece it.

Borders

Fabric requirements are based on cutting across the width of the fabric and seaming the pieces together. (NOTE: No allowance is made for matching patterns.)

From ⅞ yard (80cm) cut:
    2 side borders 49½ x 4½ inches (125.7 x 11.5cm)
    2 top and bottom borders 72½ x 4½ inches (184.2 x 11.5cm)

DIRECTIONS

1. Following diagram 2 make:
    9 block A
    5 block B
    3 block C
    38 block D
    6 block E
    Cut 6 block F

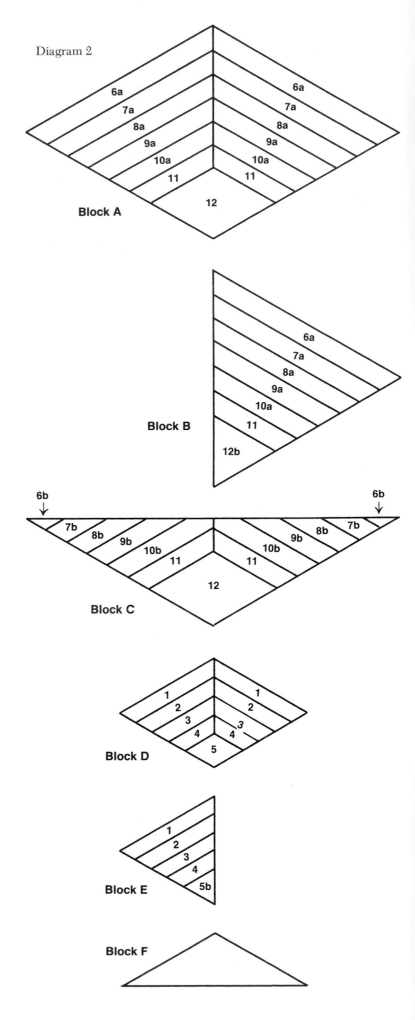

Diagram 2

Block A

Block B

Block C

Block D

Block E

Block F

168

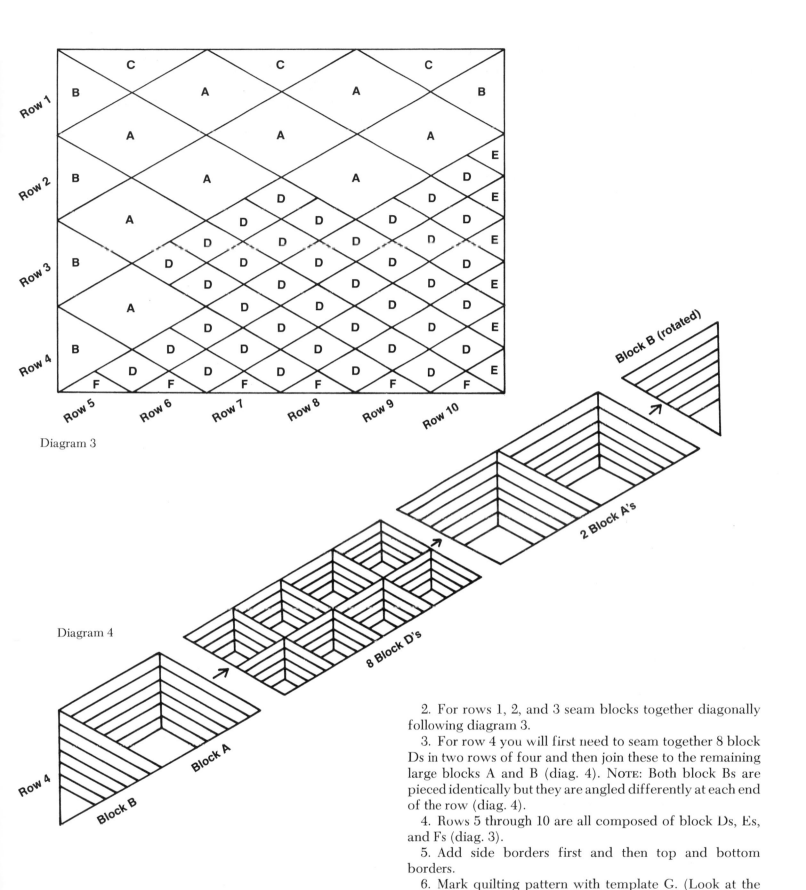

Diagram 3

Diagram 4

2. For rows 1, 2, and 3 seam blocks together diagonally following diagram 3.

3. For row 4 you will first need to seam together 8 block Ds in two rows of four and then join these to the remaining large blocks A and B (diag. 4). NOTE: Both block Bs are pieced identically but they are angled differently at each end of the row (diag. 4).

4. Rows 5 through 10 are all composed of block Ds, Es, and Fs (diag. 3).

5. Add side borders first and then top and bottom borders.

6. Mark quilting pattern with template G. (Look at the border in diagram 1 to see how the motif fits together.) Outline quilt round each block and, if you wish, quilt between each pattern piece. Mark and quilt the divisions in F blocks.

7. Bind to finish.

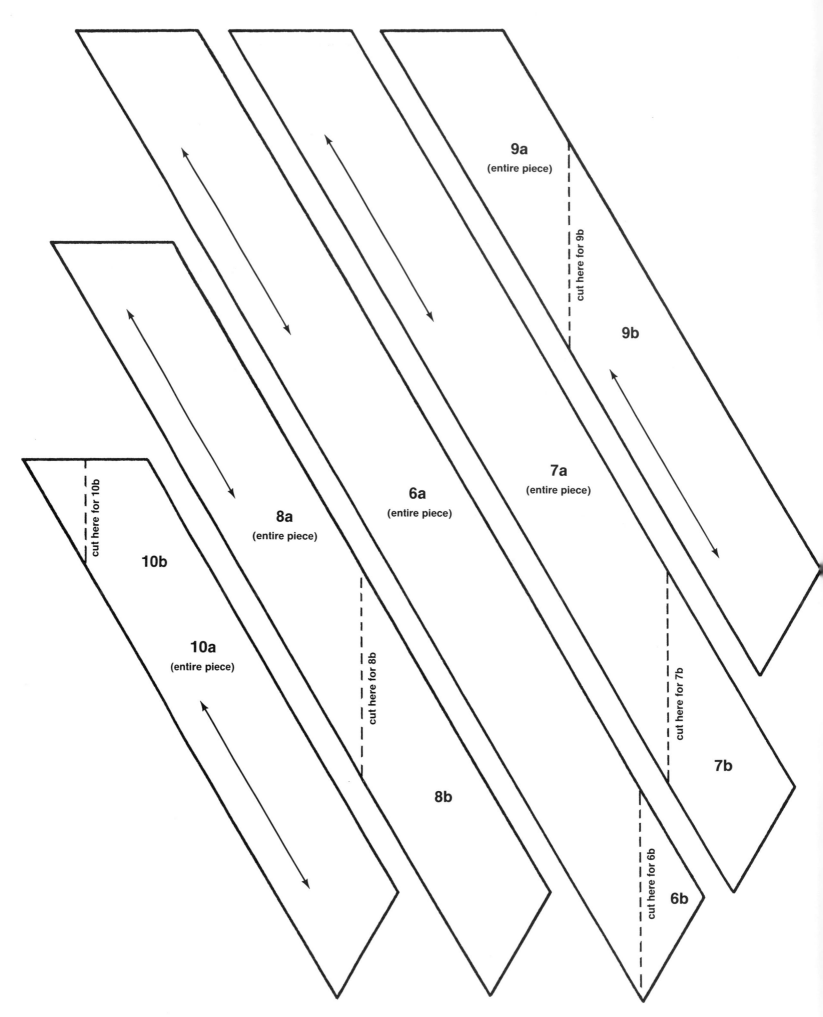

9a
(entire piece)

cut here for 9b

9b

7a
(entire piece)

8a
(entire piece)

6a
(entire piece)

cut here for 10b

10b

10a
(entire piece)

cut here for 8b

8b

cut here for 7b

7b

cut here for 6b

6b

170

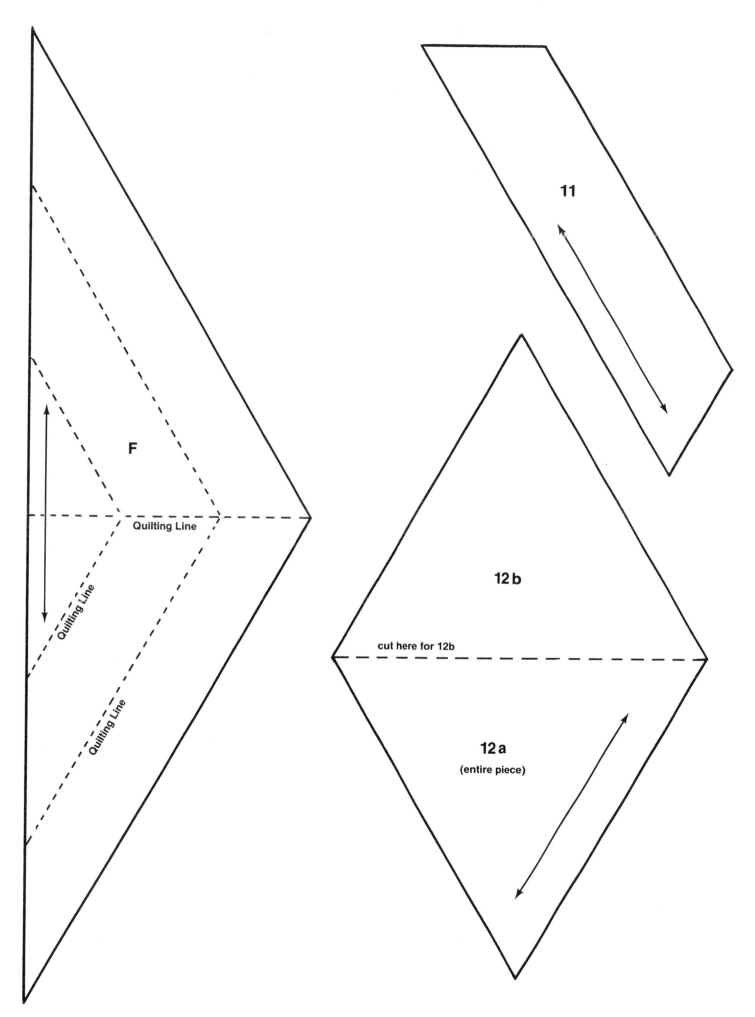

F

Quilting Line

Quilting Line

Quilting Line

11

12 b

cut here for 12b

12 a

(entire piece)

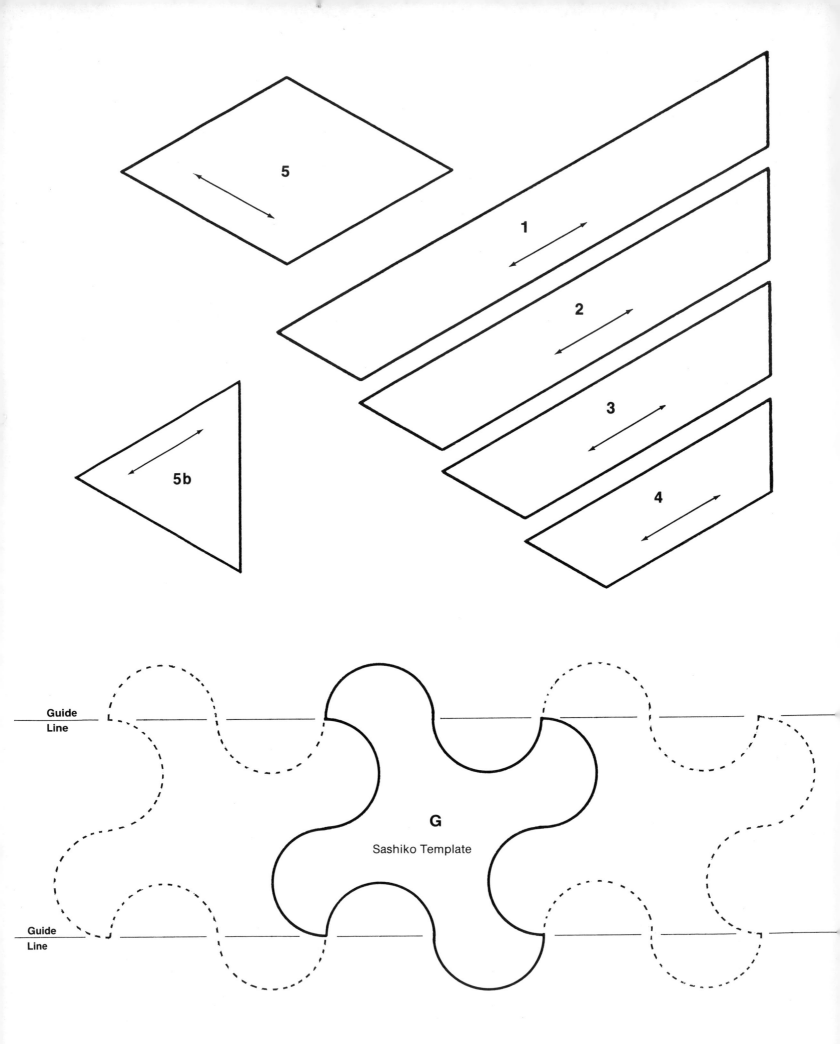

5

1

2

3

4

5b

Guide
Line

Guide
Line

G

Sashiko Template